PANNIERS, PEDALS AND PUBS

CYCLING TOURS IN BRITAIN

By
Robert Adams

Cover graphics and design by Adecia Adams

Copyright © 2005 Robert Adams

All rights reserved.

ISBN 1-4196-1595-5

To order additional copies, please contact us.
BookSurge, LLC
www.booksurge.com
1-866-308-6235
orders@booksurge.com

Dedication

This book is dedicated to my family. Each one has, in their own way, encouraged these tours, shown interest or pride in their completion and supported/tolerated the time dedicated to recording them in this book.

PANNIERS, PEDALS AND PUBS
Cycling Tours in Britain

A personal love story between man, bike and Britain spanning over forty-five years with lively accounts of five long-distance solo tours in Britain, including amusing anecdotes and eccentric characters The text is enriched with historical and scenic information, routes, maps, and helpful suggestions for improving the cycling experience.

Chapter	Title	Page

1.   IT'S IN THE BLOOD 3
   Brief history of author's early cycling experience

2.   COUNTRYSIDE 15
   Broad descriptions of the geography, geology,
   history and cultural aspects of the regions covered
   by the tours...

3.   END TO END TOUR 41
   –25 DAYS–1800 KM
   A saga stretching from John O' Groats in
   NE Scotland to Land's End at the SW extremity
   of England.

4.   PEAKS, LAKES AND DALES TOUR....................73
   –23 DAYS–1360 KM
   A rugged country tour of the Derbyshire Peaks, the
   Cumbrian Lake District and the Dales of Yorkshire.

5.   CIRCLE TOUR..115
   –21 DAYS–1550 KM
   A circuit through southern England, along Wales'
   eastern border, into Cumbria and through Yorkshire,
   Lincolnshire, Cambridgeshire and Essex. Includes
   visits to Bath, Cheshire, York, Lincoln and Cambridge.

6. **NORTH. ENGLAND/SCOTLAND TOUR** 171
   33 DAYS – 2060 KM
   A rail-supported combination of tours in lovely, lonely Northumberland, the Lake District, Edinburgh, the Scottish border country, and the isles of Arran, Mull and Skye.

7. **CELTIC TOUR** 217
   –30 DAYS – 1570 KM
   A six county tour of SW England, concentrating on Devon and Cornwall followed by two weeks of group and solo cycling in Brittany.

8. **GETTING UNDERWAY** 289
   Hints for cycle selection, set up, cycle loading and thoughts about the hostelling experience for those who may be inspired to plan similar cycling tours.

9. **APPENDIX** 301
   England and Tea – A brief history
   Teacake Recipe
   Recommended Teashops
   Cycle Calorie Counter
   Energy Consumption – Cycles vs the Rest
   Tour Costs
   Glossary

10. **END NOTES** 317

IT'S IN THE BLOOD

It all began with a blood-red bicycle at age nine. Fifty-five years and three cycle transfusions later, cycle touring still quickens my pulse. Cycling touring is in my blood but it had to be a mutant gene. There is no apparent normal genetic connection as neither my parents nor siblings have any interest whatsoever. With me, the interest started early, pulsed steadily, sometimes strong, sometimes weak over the years but continues to beat at an above average level for a man of 60 plus.

When I was about 9, my father surprisingly suggested that I go buy a bike. This was unusual because family funds were generally not wasted on such frivolity. I was not inclined to challenge this imprudence and set off immediately by myself to make the selection. Perhaps more surprising was that even though Dad had established no price limit, I was my father's son and 'chose' the least expensive cycle the shop had. It was a red, basic, full-size coaster brake version with no extra features. Now over 50 years later, I still remember the $39.95 price.

This was a grand day but my pleasure became somewhat muted later that evening during dinner when my father announced, "of course, you will share the bike with Byron". Byron was my brother, younger by 20 months. Fortunately he had some growing to do before riding 'my bike' was feasible. My youngest brother, Dan, at age three, was not a contender. This age gap put the two of us in different orbits for most of our formative period and gave Dan, a post-war baby, a more positive environment with a more consumer oriented economy. A couple of years later, Byron was allowed to select his own cycle, and less governed by the family penchant for frugality, chose one that had a built in horn and 'in' cosmetic features that cost forty percent more.

That red bike was my servant and companion for the three years I delivered newspapers and later was my trusty steed for an 1100+ km camping tour between New York's Finger Lakes district and Northern Virginia with a friend at age 15. Once there we stayed with Aunt Wina, my mother's sister, outside Washington and were written up in a local newspaper. I fell in love with my aunt's neighbour's daughter, Carita, a blond export from Texas. At the time, the song *Yellow Rose of Texas* was popular and immediately became my favourite.

On the return journey, my paternal uncle, returning from a visit to a lady friend in North Carolina, coincidentally saw us along the highway and stopped. He offered to ease the balance of our trip by driving us to some point just outside our home when we could get out and no one would be the wiser! My friend, Norman, was tempted but my innate stoicism won out and we declined his offer.

At age 16, cars and driving are strong competition for most alternatives but that year, my brother Byron and I, having carefully saved our paper route earnings, had enough to take a summer trip on our own to Britain and Europe. We sailed from Montreal on the Canadian Pacific Line's *Empress of France*. Almost our first action on arrival in Liverpool was to buy cycles. They were to provide our transport everywhere, an idea that soon lost its appeal on the steep climbs and desolate moors of northern England. I cannot recall at this distance of time how many days we struggled but when we reached Edinburgh the bikes were sold.

That trip began to shake my US-centric views, introducing different ways of life and exposing me to other perspectives. I returned home more receptive to criticism of US views and attitudes. This educational process was re-started by being accepted, on a non-matriculated basis, by the University at Edinburgh. I was the odd man out in digs that housed ten British students and a businessman. This environment, the classroom, the newspapers and television all challenged the views that I had absorbed, as if by osmosis, in my formative years and forced me to try to defend them. Often, I found that I could not.

My cycling activity had been dormant for almost two years following that initial struggle through northern England with Byron. Fittingly, this also resumed at Edinburgh during the Easter recess. My roommate and I borrowed cycles and headed for Paris, planning to camp along the way. Outdoor comfort in early April was minimal and we were not properly equipped for touring so by the time we reached Dover, we were definitely disenchanted with the cycling part of the holiday and probably with each other. The cycles were left behind, stored in the railway left luggage, when we caught the ferry to France. Our attitude toward cycle camping had not improved when we returned to Dover so the cycles went in the goods van and we went back to Edinburgh by train, limiting our cycling distance to perhaps 650 km.

That was the end of my cycling for over ten years. University back in the US, summer jobs, marriage, graduate school, a move to England, a responsible post in business and three children blunted both interest and opportunity.

In 1970, midway through our sojourn in England, my wife and I became certain that our family was large enough and that we needed some outdoor activity as a couple that we could both enjoy. I suggested cycling and was pleased that she was enthusiastic. That decision led to fun trips to cycle shops and the selection of two re-conditioned cycles. Mine (my second cycle) was a Carleton racer. Hers, unlike today, was a woman's style frame. Both had dropped handlebars, multiple gears and handlebar mounted brake levers.

Later on, I bought her a new cycle for Christmas. From that point on, one of our favourite activities was a Sunday afternoon ride in the Hertfordshire countryside near our home and finishing off with a pint in the garden of a pub.

One Saturday, the morning sunshine was just so inviting that I took an early morning ride on my own, leaving before the rest of the family was up. Country lanes were almost immediately accessible from our home so I was soon enjoying country air and landscape. I became so absorbed with the distant scenery that I missed a turn and flew off the road into a ravine. When I recovered consciousness, I had no sense of injury or of having lost any time and simply got back on the bike and continued. It was only several minutes later that I looked at my watch and discovered that only the crystal and watchband were still there. All the works had been ripped out by the fall! Well, perhaps it was late enough that I should go home.

My late morning arrival was greeted with 'Well, where have you been?' Given my fairly consistent shortfalls in the domestic responsibility department, there would have been more in this vein but then Mari saw that my face was covered with blood—I had not been aware of any injury other than the watch. She immediately took me to the emergency room of our local hospital. I was released shortly after treatment and consider myself lucky that this has been the most serious of any cycling mishaps.

We moved from England to New Zealand in 1973 and bought a home in Dunedin on a hill overlooking the Otago Harbour. I became a university lecturer, complete with beard, and was often seen flying down the hill to my office on my faithful Carleton. It was symbolic but coincidental that we wound up in Dunedin, a Scottish-settled city with the ancient name for Edinburgh. But cycling was not nearly as pleasant as in England because the country lanes and minor road system developed over hundreds of years in England did not exist in New Zealand. So cycling was a more utilitarian activity during our years there.

Robert Adams

Even when we returned to North America and re-settled in 1977 in the Pittsburgh area, the infrastructure and environment for cycling was not as inviting as our English experiences. Consequently, cycling slid further into the background until we moved to Oakville, Ontario in 1980 as a result of a job transfer. There, the nearby Niagara Escarpment, a United Nations World Biosphere site, beckoned with its rugged, rural atmosphere and cider serving orchards.

Nevertheless, England was still the epitome of cycling for us, so in 1986 when we felt that our last child Cameron was mature enough to be left with Allison, his 20 year-old sister, we planned to return. (Years later, our neighbours indicated that our confidence was not entirely justified—in either child!)

This trip started at Horley, Sussex, near Gatwick Airport where we had arranged to hire touring cycles for three weeks. We also planned to visit old friends from our years in England after the cycling tour and so left better clothes and our cases with the cycle hire firm. Then, liberally using the extensive British railway system, we visited Winchester, Exeter, and the Devon Moors, staying a few days in each at bed and breakfasts so that we did not have to carry our gear while cycling.

At that time, the train was an ideal way to get between areas quickly and reasonably. It was simply a matter of buying your ticket and then loading the cycle in the goods van just before departure. There was no extra charge and the only difficulty was determining what section of the train the goods van would be in so we knew where to stand on the platform. There was no consistency of location (nor is there yet) so we often had to run to the other end of the train to load up before the train's departure. Today, space for cycles is limited, sometimes to only two or three per train, often has to be booked ahead which involves a charge. Also, the privatisation of the railways that took place in Margaret Thatcher's period resulted in a variety of practices between the resulting new railway companies. Now, cycles are often carried in the same car as the passengers in a general luggage area. Sometimes, they must be hung up by the wheel from the ceiling, other times they are strapped along the inside wall of the car, near the doors. The difficulty remains in pre-determining which car will have these facilities and where it will be on the train.

Our next cycling explorations led us to discover the joys of van-supported tours in New England, with overnight stops in lovely country inns and fabulous food. Four of these trips followed before their popularity and the falling Canadian dollar made them unaffordable. But at the time, these trips were highlights of our year, combining lovely, English-like scenery and quiet country roads with interesting, fun companions.

My English Carleton racer become my son's about the time he turned 15 and I acquired a Japanese made Sakai tourer, manufactured 'exclusively' for the then large, now defunct, Bloor Cycle of Toronto. Friends at the office marvelled at its $500 price. The seeds were now and truly planted for a trip I had long thought about as almost an impossibility---the famous 'End to End'—from Land's End, Cornwall, England's southwest extreme to John O' Groats at the northeast corner of Scotland.

This cycle purchase happened mid-way through our New England excursions but the desire to do something bolder and longer grew until, six years later in 1990 I committed definitely to a solo run at the End to End. A scheduled job change and a considerate employer provided the opportunity to use my entire year's holiday entitlement between giving up one job and taking the other. I joined the Cycle Touring Club of Britain (CTC) in part because members were entitled to the Club's official tour route. At the time, I did not realise that the south to north orientation of the tour was designed to minimise the effect of wind. Although, I joked that my north to south plan was to take advantage of natural gravity, I really have no idea why I chose to do it that way; perhaps just my inherent perversity. Doing so certainly complicated the planning as the CTC route had to be completely re-written going the opposite direction. Changing left-hand turns to right-hand turns was the easy part. Finding out what road I was meant to be on involved working backwards through the CTC route to find the first indication of the road or lane description and made the task like negotiating a difficult maze. Organising the route was the most time-consuming task (now it is definitely one of the pleasures of the sport) but as a first time long-distance tourer I also needed to become knowledgeable about panniers, folding spare tyres and many other aspects. I've included a separate chapter to cover these important factors.

Later, in part to compensate my wife for her loss of a holiday in 1990 and because I now definitely had the bug, we rationalised the affordability factor sufficiently to move on to touring together in Europe. Our first trip, in 1992, was based at a goose farm lodge in the Perigord district of France. The tour company arranged the accommodation and provided us with suggested routes and maps. We took our own cycles.

Taking our own cycles was a big mistake for this first trip. Most tour companies offer cycles for their clients and provide repairs and replacements if problems occur during the tour. We thought we preferred our own familiar cycles and suffered dearly as a result. Packing a cycle for air transport involves a lot of effort at both ends of the journey to avoid damage and to restore the cycle to riding condition on arrival. I made after hours' visits to the rear of cycle shops to rescue their thrown away cardboard packing cases, then removed the pedals and front wheels, loosened and turned the handlebars to make the cycle fit the box. I now use a special crush resistant travelling case and with practice can reassemble my bike in less than two hours but this first excursion abroad was very difficult.

On arrival at Charles de Gaulle airport outside Paris we had to wait for a suitably empty coach for the trip to the train station for the journey into Paris. At the station we faced a turnstile that permitted one body at a time, but not a body holding a large cardboard carton. We solved this by having Mari go the through the turnstile first and unladen to grab or steady the cartons and cases as I lifted them over the turnstile. Once in Paris, we had to negotiate the underground Metro, up and down its escalators, stairs and through its labyrinth of tunnels to get to the railway station from which our train to the Perigord departed. The total volume and weight of our gear was such that we could not move together. I would move forward with as much as I could carry to deposit it, perhaps 30 metres ahead, and rush back to Mari who was watching the remaining. Simultaneously she would run forward to guard my deposit as I brought the rest to her. Understandably, this was time-consuming and tiring. At one point, a floor to ceiling turnstile blocked our passage through the tunnel. Although my almost non-existent French wasn't effective, hand signals and facial contortions persuaded the ticket seller to open a side entrance.

When we finally arrived at the Metro platform, we were quite exhausted and feeling blue. The train arrived and we quickly loaded everything but one cycle in one move but just as I picked up the second bike, the train doors closed! Mari was inside, at the door, peering through the windows yelling frantically ' where do I get off?' I had neglected to provide that detail, thinking we would be together. I shouted the station name but could not be sure that she heard it correctly. Waiting by myself fifteen minutes for the next train did not increase my optimism but we were re-united finally at the right station. Mari had used her better French with a Vietnamese passenger to get help unloading.

Different adventures awaited us at the train station. Mari watched our gear while I went to buy the tickets and learn which platform the train would leave from. Thinking it would save time and effort, I chose to first scout out the platform before going back for our gear. Platform 30 simply did not exist and I wandered unsuccessfully all over trying to find it before learning that it was the freight warehouse. In the UK, passengers load their own cycle on the train but this wasn't the practice in France.

At least 45 minutes had elapsed since I left Mari and after our earlier adventures she was worried; it hadn't helped that her waiting spot was immediately outside the gents toilet and she was receiving looks appropriate for a prostitute. I relieved her guard duty while she rushed off for a long overdue relief stop. Afterwards, we had to take the cycles to the freight area, pay a healthy extra charge and leave them there for the freight personnel to load on the right train. Unfortunately, they did not, so when we arrived at our destination for collection by the goose farm staff, the cycles were not there.

It was now after 9 pm French time, or 3 am by the clocks we had woken up to and there was another 45 minutes ride to the goose farm. We finally dined at the fashionable hour of 10.30 pm on soup and foie gras. Thus ended our first day.

Our farm hosts kindly returned to the railway and collected our cycles early in the morning. I spent several hours re-assembling them after breakfast so that our cycling was quite limited that day. Nevertheless, it was enough to whet our appetites for the balance of our stay. The narrow country lanes, gorgeous golden stone of the buildings and the warm sunshine dramatically lifted our spirits. We enjoyed our first French café au lait and a croque monsieur on the patio of a village square café. The scene was made complete with elderly farmers, clad in their famous blue overalls and drinking Pastis, as neighbours. Their ruddy faces and animated chatter provided good entertainment.

The good weather and lovely cycling continued for the rest of our week. This allowed us time and opportunity for the famous caves at Lascaux and the medieval city of Sarlat as well as a day's touring further a field by car. A work colleague who always spent his entire holiday in France knew that we were there and chose to be our tour guide for the day. Dave loved driving at speed and not slowing until absolutely necessary for stops. Mari was eager to return to the bike after a day's battering in the rear seat of his baby Renault.

The return trip to Paris and on to Calais was slightly less harrowing. The turnstiles and labyrinths of Metro were traded for cycling between railway stations during the morning rush hour. We thoroughly enjoyed our trip but overall the experience convinced us that using the tour company's cycles, at least in France, would improve things immensely. Subsequent trips to Burgundy, the Cruise and Provence have proved us right.

After another hair-raising experience in busy traffic and rain at Calais to move from the railway station to the Hovercraft port, we enjoyed the 45-minute voyage to Dover and 'home'. England was indeed welcome and familiar after our experiences with French transport. We had totally enjoyed cycling in the French countryside but the beginning and end of the tour had been nerve-racking.

From Dover we went north by train to York to explore this marvellous city and cycle the Yorkshire Dales. We spent our nights in some delightful bed and breakfasts and our days glorying in the rustic beauty and history of the landscape and were frustrated only by the IRA. Not the IRA directly, but the security measures adopted by British rail to avoid the risk of bombs. These measures included closing the left luggage facilities at Darlington railway station where we were to start our tour of the Dales. This meant finding an alternative for storing our cases and non-cycling gear. Our solution was both novel and naïve. A small taxi office on the station kindly agreed to let us leave our cases in the office for a few days. It was all on trust, theirs (but we did not sound much like IRA terrorists) and ours, as there was no payment and no receipt. How much faith we had placed in their honesty we did not realise until much later when I discovered that our passports, the return air tickets and Mari's gold watch were in the unlocked cases! The countryside was so inviting that we suppressed our worries and extended our planned few days to a week. Our faith and foolhardiness were rewarded with the intact return of our cases at the end of the week. Apart from the sheer relief, it was a good reminder that trusting your fellow man is justified more often than not.

Early in the 90's, we joined a cross-country skiing club, many of whose members were also avid cyclists. The club regularly organises mid-week training runs and Sunday rides of 50 + kilometres. In addition, they run a few motel-based weekend or longer trips during the year. We participated in a number of these in earlier years but now rarely go because their inherent competitiveness produces an early start, maximum distance, and minimal 'smell the roses' approach. Put another way, we are getting older.

At this point, our experiences pretty well covered the scope of cycle touring from weekend to multi-week trips, domestic and foreign, independently planned and undertaken, non-profit club organised and led, through commercial but basic, minimally organised excursions to the full-scale, luxury sort.

There are many commercial tour providers and all operate somewhat differently. Some stay at four-star hotels/inns or chateaux, have tour guides and support vans that accompany the cyclists daily. We prefer (and can afford) the operators that provide the cycles and routes, book two-star inns and move luggage from inn to inn but otherwise leave you alone unless you call for help. These operators tend to be much more flexible about starting dates and length of stay because each client is on their own except by coincidence of others booking for the same dates. This avoids the enforced togetherness that can blight other operators' offerings when your companions aren't compatible. Going as a group can be fun but it also tends to reduce the opportunities and desire to meet local people and learn something from them about local life.

In the years since 1992, Mari and I have taken three tours in France with Headwater, a British firm based in Cheshire. Headwater specialises in British clients and so makes flight or ferry arrangements from Britain to France, provides the railway tickets (with reserved seats) to the starting point. Their local representative meets you, gets you settled in the first inn and fits you to a good quality, well-maintained cycle. From that point on, you are free to spend your time as you wish, constrained only by the need to get to the next inn which is typically about 30-40 kilometres away along quiet country roads. You stay two nights at each inn and Headwater moves the luggage for you. This makes cycling easier and allows time for exploring on foot or simply whiling away a sunny day with café au lait or pastis on the patio with a good book.

My days of solo cycling in Britain, which are the principal focus of the rest of this book, provided good outdoor exercise, soul stirring and soothing scenery and memorable people and experiences. They were liberally laced with short stops to savour toasted teacakes, blackcurrant jam, tea and my latest novel about international spies or high finance. The passing years and a certain amount of introspection have led me to realise that much of the pleasure of these trips is dependent on these interludes. In fact, during the writing process, my provisional title for the book was *Touring on Teacakes*, but my family felt that while this had meaning for me it would not attract potential readers.

Each of the five trips described in the book relied on hostel or bed and breakfast accommodation. Although I now try to pre-book accommodation, nothing was pre-arranged for the first tour. There are advantages to both approaches. Camping would retain the independence and freedom of non-booking and avoid the possibility of there being "no room at the inn". I, however, need a certain amount of creature comfort and generally take middle ground planning my trips around hostel locations and pre-booking them. When these aren't available, I find that the British "Book–a-Bed ahead" (or BABA) service offered by the Tourist Information Offices in larger British towns is an efficient way to find a bed for the night. They make the calls to determine vacancies at your specified price and make the bookings.

A separate chapter follows on each of my five tours in the past fourteen years. A map, at the beginning of each of the tour chapters, shows the general area of the tour. A list of each overnight stop and the daily distances is also provided. Outstanding scenic spots or items of historical interest are incorporated in the tour chapters but for the most part; such material is covered in the chapter titled 'Countryside'. This relies heavily on the *AA Illustrated Guide to Britain*.

It won't have gone unnoticed that most of my adult life has been spent in various parts of the British Commonwealth. This has strongly influenced my views, attitudes and interests making me more critical, particularly of, but in no way limited, to the US. I have become a Canadian citizen, because Canada is home; but also partly because of a faint hope that being Canadian might ease future access to Britain, should I want to return.

So, in keeping with my own preferences and with the focus of this book, I have endeavoured to use British terminology, punctuation and spelling throughout. A glossary is provided for those terms that may be unfamiliar to North American readers.

The bulk of each chapter is devoted to the memorable people and experiences that I enjoyed on that tour. I hope these will please you as much as they still do me.

Britain

All my solo tours but one have been wholly within Britain's shores. Only the most recent tour ventured away and then I could only bring myself to go as far as Brittany! There is no doubt that I am a committed anglophile yet not an entirely blinkered one---my love is for the British countryside, its ample green space, its rural villages that appear all of a sudden without preliminary kilometres of hoardings, fast food stops and automotive dealerships to announce them. Britain's contributions to literature and science, far in excess of her proportion of the world's population, justify admiration for the erudition of its educated classes. Britain's influence, though now diminished, remains considerable.

After a year in a British university, six years living in Britain with my young family and these tours, Britain is familiar; in many ways, a second home. I am fortunate to live in Canada where British books are most often available in their original versions, not edited for spelling and terminology as they are in the US. TV Ontario and the Buffalo PBS channel offer a steady diet of the British drama so superior to most North American programs. We live within easy driving distance of the Shaw drama festival in Niagara on the Lake, Ontario and the Stratford, Ontario Shakespeare festival. So, my love for things British gets lots of nurturing and it is the reason for this book being written, to the extent that I am able, in British English.

Despite steeping myself in things British, I am not blind to the country's problems. The class structure continues to shape attitudes and behaviour often with destructive effect. Britain has one of the worst records among the industrialised world for keeping its children in school beyond normal leaving age. Property crime is rife. The gutter press rants about corruption and sexual misconduct of celebrities but often features topless women on its front pages and plays on the anti-rich, anti-establishment sentiments of the working class. Over the past few decades, the colour of Britain has changed through immigration from former colonies. As in most countries, these immigrants primarily choose to settle in areas where they will feel most comfortable, creating significant concentrations that breed resentment. In part, this has contributed to an increasing amount of violence in a country whose violence has always seemed to me to be particularly vicious. The infamous football (soccer) louts typify the behaviour and sentiments that most distress me about Britain.

But out in the countryside, along a leafy lane with a fresh breeze redolent of farm fragrances and the prospect of a village teashop around the next bend -- it's the only place to be!

COUNTRYSIDE

The British rural landscape brings me back time after time. It offers beauty, majesty and tranquillity populated with delightful villages housing appealing teahouses. Some remote spots are so elevated that bathed in the weak rays of an early evening western sun you can believe yourself the only human on earth. In these places, only birdsong and the occasional bleating of sheep break the silent, clean, clear air.

It is no secret that Britain offers a wealth of varied landscape and centuries of historic interest. My difficulty is describing this cornucopia accurately. So, I have relied on the AA's Illustrated Guide to Britain. The following extracts are taken from the AA's summaries of the several British regions that my tours involved. These are organised from north to south.

Scottish Highlands

Scotland means many things to the Scot, but to the non-Scottish holiday visitor it often means primarily the Highlands and Islands. Scotland's mountains would be lost in the foothills of the Andes or the Himalayas, but they yield nothing to the highest peaks in the world in terms of beauty, and their capacity to inspire awe. This is because they do not stand-alone. They share the landscape with wild sea lochs that gouge deeply into the land; with icy streams that rumble through green and wooded glens; with the calm waters of great inland lochs; and, above all, with an ever-changing sky that gives rise to a variety of colour.

It is a lonely land. The Highlands and Islands cover about a quarter of Britain's land surface—but fewer than 1 in 50 of the population live there. Vast tracts of land have no roads. Only the walker and the camper have any chance of penetrating these solitudes.

Unlike the world's other great wildernesses, some which have never known the hand of man, the Scottish Highlands, for all their loneliness, show many traces of human habitation. Every corner is a reminder of the past. There are crumbling crofts, recalling the enforced depopulation of the 18th and 19th centuries when the land was cleared of inhabitants to make room for large-scale sheep farming. Ruined castles are reminders of the turbulent Middle Ages, while Iron Age forts and even Stone Age cave-dwellings survive man's remoter past.

If man is largely absent today, wildlife is not. The Highlands are the last refuge of many mammals and birds found nowhere else in Britain. Golden eagles soar above the moors and crags, gannets plunge into the sea, and turkey-like capercaillies croak through the woodlands. The mammals of the Highlands include the wildcat, the pine marten, red deer and roe deer. Lochs and rivers teem with salmon and trout.

The Highlands and Islands are not all mountainous. Even on the rugged west coast there are many sheltered glens, where the land, warmed by the Gulf Stream, is green. At Poolewe in Ross and Cromarty, for instance, a large collection of sub-tropical plants thrive in the gardens of Inverewe, on latitude further north than Moscow. Caithness, Scotland's northeast extremity, is largely flat and treeless—a rocky lunar landscape which forms an appropriate background to the Space Age outline of the Dounreay nuclear reactor. The monotony of inland Caithness contrasts with the wild and breathtaking seascapes found along its shores. Further south, Easter Ross and the Black Isle are softer, greener areas, with many fertile farms. The lands bordering the Moray Firth and the lowlands of eastern Aberdeenshire are rich farming areas. Picturesque fishing villages huddle along the coast in sheltered bays or on precipitous hillsides. Inland stand the Grampians—the highest and largest mountain mass in Britain. Perthshire, south of the Grampians, offers a Highland landscape in miniature—heavily wooded, very green and prosperous. Perthshire's pride is the area known as The Trossachs that contain unparalleled views of mountain, loch, river and woodland and are dominated to the south by 2393 foot Ben Venue which overlooks the eastern end of Loch Katrine and the Pass of Achray.

Then there are the islands. The scenic beauty of Skye is enhanced by the romance that surrounds every inch of its ground. In the Outer Hebrides, the old Gaelic way of life survives with its language, its music and its crafts. The Orkneys and Shetlands were for centuries Viking strongholds, and their people and buildings are still more Norse than Scottish. There are hundreds of other islands, from tiny, deserted St. Kilda -- a bird watchers' paradise—to the great hump of Mull, where red deer roam the hills. (1)

Scottish Lowlands

Traditionally, the southern half of Scotland is known as the Lowlands – a description which suggest flatness and a certain lack of variety. But the Lowlands, though not challenging the grandeur of the

Cairngorms, are more hilly than most parts of England, and the climate, particularly in the central areas, can be as harsh in mid-winter as that endured by any lonely hamlet in the Highland mountains. The dour and determined people of the Lowlands are typical of the Scots as the world tends to think of them, and the history of the Borderland between England and Scotland has been even more turbulent than that of the remote Highlands.

The change from Lowlands to Highlands, along a diagonal line from Dumbarton in the west of Stonehaven in the northeast, is a fairly abrupt one. Below the line, the land is often gentle and pretty ---a rolling tableland of grassy hills and green dales. It is a countryside that is rich in farming and busy with sheep rearing, yet it manages to support nearly all Scotland's industry and two-thirds of her population.

The western Lowland seaboard, mainly agricultural and unspoilt, also has the popular seaside and golf resorts of Ayrshire. These include Ardrossan, from which boats sail to the Island of Arran, 15 miles across the Firth of Clyde; Troon and its offshore bird sanctuary of Lady Isle; and Girvan, with lonely and rocky Ailsa Craig, a breeding place for birds, 10 miles out to sea. To the east, on the southern shore of the Firth of Forth, the fertile soils of East Lothian favour highly developed horticulture and agriculture. Just south of East Linton is one of the three Forestry Commission tree gardens in Scotland, where collections of rare specimen trees can be seen by the public; the other two are in Argyll. The two major cities of the Lowlands are Glasgow and Edinburgh—less than 50 miles apart in terms of travel, but a world apart in terms of their industry and architecture. Edinburgh is one of Europe's most beautiful capitals. It is built upon hills in a superb natural setting, overlooked by a mountain-in- miniature, Arthur's Seat, and with a 1000- year old castle at its centre. In the 18th century, Edinburgh was the home of philosophers and wits, poets and scientists. They helped to bring a cosmopolitan atmosphere to the city that is still sustained each year by the Edinburgh International Festival of music and drama. Superb wild countryside is within easy reach of the capital—southwest, the 16 mile long Pentland Hills which Robert Louis Stevenson loved; southeast the lonelier Moorfoot Hills.

From country town to shipyard city

Glasgow, with its satellite towns, forms the huge industrial heart of the Lowlands. It grew from being a pleasant burgh in pretty countryside into a great city –starting first in the 17th century as a major seaport to which sugar and tobacco were imported from America, then completing its development in the last 150 years with the establishment of steel works and large docks and shipyards along the River Clyde. Today, Glasgow is Scotland's largest city and is the third largest in population in the British Isles, after London and Birmingham.

Widespread redevelopment and reconstruction are transforming the quality of life in a city whose people have always been fortunate in one respect—there are few places in the western world where the grime and clamour of shipyard and steel mill can so quickly and easily be left behind for the delights of an inspiring and romantic countryside. To the northwest, only 15 miles away is Loch Lomond; to the west, the Kintyre peninsula and the beginning of true Highland scenery.

The central Lowlands, which include Dunbarton, Kinross-shire, Stirlingshire and Clackmannanshire, Scotland's smallest county, also offer a promise of the Highlands. Around ancient and busy market burghs, the countryside begins to lengthen between towns, the hills get higher, and pretty lochs and wooded rivers add their rippling beauty to the countryside. Despite the modern road bridges over the Forth and the Tay, Fifeshire remains strangely independent of the rest of Scotland. The coalfields are being worked out, and the seaside villages are busier today with pleasure craft than with fishing boats. Only the ancient university town of St. Andrews –world famous as the headquarters of golf, which was played there as long ago as the 15th century—and the rich farmland of northern Fifeshire, retain their traditional character.

Land that inspired Sir Walter Scott

The great tourist attraction of the Lowlands outside Edinburgh is the Border country, consisting mainly of the Lowland counties of Roxburghshire, Peeblesshire and Selkirkshire, but also including parts of Berwickshire and Dumfriesshire. This is a land, separated from England by the Cheviot Hills, of magnificent ruined abbeys –at Melrose, Jedburgh, Dryburgh and Kelso—of the mighty River Tweed, famous for its salmon fishing, and of beautiful hill scenery rich in the romantic stories of Border warfare that inspired many of the novels of Sir Walter Scott. His last and most famous home, Abbotsford House, is in the heart of the Border country.

Equally beautiful scenery is contained within the less visited area of Galloway, in the west of the Lowlands. Galloway consist of the counties of Kirkcudbrightshire and Wigtownshire, where the wild and lovely slopes of the mountain ranges—dominated by Southern Scotland's highest peak, the 2770 ft Merrick –have earned themselves the name 'The Galloway Highlands'. This is the land of the red deer, of the thickly coated and hornless Galloway cattle, of the golden eagle, and of wild goats with long, curly horns. Remote and tiny lochs dot the foot of the Merrick slopes where, around Loch Trool, spreads the 200 –square mile Glen Trool Forest Park, formed by the Forestry Commission in 1945.

The Galloway landscape has been a source of inspiration for many famous names in popular literature. S. R. Crockett based the 'Rathan Isle' of his novel *The Raiders* on Hestan Island at the entrance to Auchencairn Bay; Dorothy L. Sayers wove the countryside into *Five Red Herrings*; and much of the action of John Buchan's *The Thirty-Nine Steps* takes place around the Cairnsmore of Fleet, a towering 2331 ft peak to the northeast of Creetown.

The Lowlands' historical links with the past are strongest in the cities and towns north of the central industrial belt. Dunfermline is an ancient capital with a beautiful old abbey in which Robert Burns is buried; and the town was the birthplace of James I in 1394 and of Charles I in 1600. James II was born at Stirling Castle in 1430 and James VI (James I of England) was christened and crowned there. The Scottish patriot William Wallace is commemorated by the 220 ft. high Wallace Monument on Abbey Craig, north of Stirling Bridge. Perth, Scott's fair city, is all of that, and more—a prosperous market town, rich in the character of its streets and buildings.

Artistic talent from the Lowlands

In matters of the arts, the Lowlands have the edge over the Highlands. An intellectual maturity was reached in the 18th and early 19th centuries –Robert Burns, a Lowland farmer's son, and Sir Walter Scott, born in Edinburgh, are world-famous figures. The Scottish poet Allan Ramsay, a mining manager's son whose verse was to influence Burns, was born at Leadhills, Lanarkshire. David Hume, the mid 18th century philosopher, and James Boswell, friend and biographer of Samuel Johnson, were both born in Edinburgh.

The Lowlands have a splendid heritage in the visual arts, too— from the paintings of Sir Henry Raeburn, whose was born at Stockbridge, Edinburgh, to the more domestic skills of textile-making, which have produced the linens of Dumfriesshire, Ayrshire's white needlework—a form of embroidery used in making table mats—and a wide array of woollen checks that are sold throughout the world. (2)

Northeast England

Northumberland, Durham and Yorkshire were once part of the great Saxon kingdom of Northumbria, and they have shared a history as turbulent as that of any region in Britain. Many ties between the counties have endured through the centuries. Their combined resources of iron ore, coal and engineering skill played a key role in Britain's Industrial Revolution. But despite this, their wild hills remain unscarred and form one of the largest tracts of unspoilt countryside in England.

The heart of the Northeast is the broad, lowland corridor that carries the main rail and road routes from London and the midlands to the Scottish border. York is the great city of this lowland country. It stands on a site between two rivers and was chosen first by the Romans as a place that could be easily defended, then by the Norman conquerors as the capital of the North. It became a walled city – a city dominated by its great Minster, a market centre and a hub of commerce and the arts.

The Pennines, stretching from Derbyshire to the northern parts of Northumberland, form the western ramparts of the lowland corridor. Among them is some of England's finest walking country. Pen-y-ghent and Ingleborough Hill are characteristic of the flat-topped limestone hills which stand out as familiar hikers' landmarks above miles of open moorland. In Northumberland, the Pennines merge with the Cheviots where the remote summits command inspiring views of Scotland. Roads threading their way through valleys do no more than skirt the hillside edges, and the best way to savour the attractions of the Pennines is to walk. The huge moorland expanses of grass, heather and peat—looking much as they have done since the beginning of history—are the haunt of grouse, curlew and the splendid, swift-flying Emperor moth. It is possible to walk for a morning, a day, even a whole weekend, and meet only a lone shepherd. His speech is likely to have a Scandinavian lilt, for many Pennine hill-folk are descended from Norwegians.

The beauty of waterfalls and abbey ruins

There is also a softer natural beauty among the rugged landscapes, in the treasury of Alpine flowers left behind by the Ice Age around Teesdalehead in Durham. In the valleys below are the splendours of waterfalls such as Cauldron Snout and High Force on the River Tees, a host of smaller falls at Keld on the River Swale, and the cataracts at Aysgarth in Wensleydale in the beautiful Yorkshire Dales. There is historic beauty, too, in the remains of monastic buildings that are scattered all over the Northeast. Yorkshire's Fountains Abbey, founded in 1132, is the best known; Bolton Abbey, in a wooded gorge beside the River Wharfe, has the most romantic setting.

An added richness of the Northeast lies in its castles and great houses, which show an increasing emphasis on fortification the nearer they are to the Scottish border. For Northumbria is frontier country, and the wild wastes of the Northumberland moorland were once a no-man's land between England and Scotland. Hills which now echo only to the cry of the curlew were once alive with the clash of swords in the fierce, hand-to-hand fighting of the Border wars; and the mist-laden dawns were a cover for the wild tribes who crossed the Border to raid, pillage and murder among the landowners of the south. In Roman times, straight, paved roads led through the North-East to the furthest outposts of the Roman Empire, and to the great wall built by Emperor Hadrian from the Tyne to the Solway to keep out the unsubdued northern tribes. The finest surviving section of the wall is at Housesteads, near Hexham; two well-preserved Roman roads are on the Wheeldale Moor, near Goathland, and at Blackstone Edge, on the Lancashire border west of Ripponden.

In the Dark Ages that followed the Roman withdrawal, Anglo-Saxon people from across the North Sea settled thickly all over Northumbria, naming their farms and villages in a distinctive way with words ending in --*ton* (an enclosure), --*ing* (place of), *worth* (homestead), and –*field*. Then, in the 9th and 10th centuries, Northumbria was raided by the Danes, who brought names ending in –*by* (a settlement), --*toft* (a house site) and –*thorpe* (a farm). There were also invaders from Norway, who brought with them the word *dale* (a valley). Following the Norman conquest, William the Conqueror's merciless harrying of a rebellious North laid most of the land waste from the Humber to the Tweed.

The revolution that transformed the Northeast
The rebirth of the Northeast followed the union of the Crowns of Scotland and England in 1707. The land was successfully farmed and became the scene of many innovations—shorthorn cattle were first bred there, and experiments were carried out with new crops, rotations and machinery. Later came the Industrial Revolution, which transformed those areas which had coal into vast mining and industrial complexes.

Shipbuilding, glass-making, chemical and iron works sprang up along the banks of the River Tyne. Ships for the first modern Japanese Navy were built on Tyneside between 1880 and 1905, and an iron and steel town grew at Middlesbrough, which at the beginning of the 19th century consisted of two farmhouses. Woollen mills were built in the West Riding valleys, and Sheffield became a great city of steel.

The variety of history is nowhere more clearly reflected than in the people of the Northeast. Though welded together in an unmistakable northernness of speech and manner, the people of the cities, towns and dales each have their own distinctive dialects and ways of life. But they all have a genuine interest in a visitor's welfare, coupled with an informality of manner; for this is the least class-conscious part of England.

Many men and women from the Northeast have contributed to the Arts. In literature, the Venerable Bede, John Wyclif, the Brontës, J. B. Priestly and the Sitwells; in music, Frederick Delius, who was Northumbria's most original composer; in painting, Lord Leighton, the mid-Victorian artist who specialised in Classical themes. The Northeast has given the country Border ballads, and many folk songs such as 'Bobby Shafto', 'The Lass of Richmond Hill' and 'Blaydon Races'.

Where Captain Cook learnt to sail

People of the Northeast also played an important early role in the world of communications. In the late 1500's, Christopher Saxton, of Tingley, near Leeds, became the first English mapmaker; the pioneers of the railway, George Stephenson and Timothy Hackworth, came from Northumberland; and Captain James Cook, who completed the map of the modern world by charting Australia and New Zealand, learnt his seafaring on Whitby boats.

Superb beaches stretch for mile after mile along the Northumberland coast and around Bridlington Bay. Inland, a visitor may walk the Norman walls of York or the Elizabethan walls of Berwick-upon-Tweed, visit a Georgian town at Richmond, and admire the medieval stained glass in York Minster—or simply relax at a variety of resorts that range from tiny fishing villages, such as Craster, to Scarborough, one of the most visually striking east-coast towns.

Sports flourish in the Northeast. Almost every town and village in Yorkshire has at least one cricket field and every other person seems to be an expert on the game. Football has a large following, while throughout County Durham the lure of pigeon racing has added a new feature to the landscape in the pigeon lofts that can be seen almost everywhere. (3)

Northwest England

The four counties that make up the northwest of England—Cheshire, Lancashire, Westmorland and Cumberland (the latter two are now known as Cumbria)—have always been different in character, even before the arrival of the Industrial Revolution which was to scar parts of Lancashire and Cheshire, yet leave untouched vast areas of the other two counties. Differences in accent, too, will strike the visitor, for Cumberland and Westmorland, protected by their mountains, remained predominantly a Celtic domain long after the Anglo-Saxon invasion had colonised much of Cheshire and Lancashire.

The area's greatest scenic distinction lies in the Lake District, set like a jewel among the Cumbrian mountains. There are 16 major lakes, ranging in size from Windermere, 10 ½ miles long, to tiny Brothers Water, less than half a mile long. Towering above them are four mountains topping 3000 ft, including Scafell Pike, England's highest peak at 3210 ft. The mountains are separated by England's highest mountain passes, on three of which (Esk Hause, Sticks Pass and Nan Bield Pass) footpaths climb to 2000 ft. To add to Lakeland's superlatives, Seathwaite in Borrowdale is the country's wettest inhabited place.

The Lake District is a part of Cumberland to be relished slowly. The most popular centre for touring the lakes is Keswick, where in summer the roads are crowded with traffic streaming into Borrowdale. The roads to Buttermere over Newlands Pass, and to Lorton over Whinlatter Pass, avoid this bottleneck at the height of the tourist season and lead towards the quiet and majestic valleys of Ennerdale and Wasdale.

The remaining parts of Cumberland convey the impression of a forgotten country. West Cumberland's coast has industrial outposts that appear at Maryport, Workington, Whitehaven and Seascale like breakaway fragments of the south Lancashire scene. Around these towns, however, is the best coastline north of Blackpool. There are superb sands from Silloth to Millom and, inland, roads that cut across the hills offer glorious views. From Hartside Pass over the Pennine fells northeast of Penrith a third of northwest England, stretching beyond the Lake District to the Solway Firth, can be seen at a glance.

Damson blossom and dairy farming

Lakeland is surrounded by fertile country. There is dairy and stock beef farming on the Solway plain and in the Vale of Eden, and orchards flourish in sheltered valleys –the Lyth Valley, west of Kendal, is a mass of damson blossom each spring. Further south, much of the agricultural landscape of Lancashire, and to some extent of Cheshire, is as man-made as the mills, factories and mines of the counties' industrial centres. To keep pace with the demands for produce, brought about by the Industrial Revolution of 100 years ago, peat bogs had to be drained in south and west Lancashire, and pastures were improved in Cheshire. Today there is large-scale dairy farming on the Cheshire Plain and a variety of crops is grown in Lancashire. Potatoes grow around Ormskirk; tomatoes on the Fylde plain around Blackpool; asparagus at Formby; and market gardening flourishes at Southport.

Lancashire is the most varied of the northwestern counties. It has a windy moorland at its heart, and a great industrial tradition which grew first on cotton, 200 years ago, then on coal-mining, chemicals and engineering. In contrast, the fertile Lancashire plain has rural, wooded country, with sheltered hamlets and tiny villages around Pendle Hill. Further north is the rugged Bowland Forest and, beyond this, the green valley of the River Lune. Limestone hills rise north of Morecambe Bay, and the peninsula of Furness is rich in iron ore.

The white cliffs of Westmorland

Westmorland at once conveys an impression of great beauty. Most of the land is limestone, seen at its most striking south of Kendal, where cliffs flash white from Farleton Knott, a high and isolated grass-topped ridge flanking the M6 motorway. Similar ridges line the valley of the River Winster to the west, where hamlets stand on knolls above flat peatland, thick with foliage and flowers.

The more exposed limestone outcrops of Orton Scar, north of Kendal, have been plundered by the lorry-load to provide stones for rock gardens all over England. A rarer form of limestone, Coniston limestone, runs through Westmorland from Shap, cutting across Kentmere, Ambleside and The Tarns. It can be best seen at Boo Tarn, near Coniston.

Throughout the Northwest there is a profusion of architectural styles, with stonework in a variety of colours. Stately homes include Lyme Park, at Disley in Cheshire, one of the noblest English mansions, with an Elizabethan drawing room which is hardly bettered anywhere in

Britain. Equally attractive are the gracious houses such as Brantwood on the shores of Coniston. Black is the dominant colour in many a row of terraced cottages in the Lancashire valleys; a blackness not of industrial grime, but simply of years of weathering of yellow-gritstone walls. Blackened timbers and whitened plasterwork are the ingredients of the so-called 'magpie' houses that are a familiar sight throughout the Cheshire Plain. Blue and green slates cover the roofs of many Lakeland homes, contrasting with their whitewashed walls, while the sandstone areas of north Westmorland have villages of red-walled houses.

The main holiday centres of the Northwest are Southport, Blackpool and Morecambe on the coast, and Keswick and Windermere in the Lake District. Blackpool is by far the largest, drawing huge numbers of day-trippers—especially for the autumn illuminations. Morecambe, with the M6 motorway coming almost into the town, is also crowded for the illuminations. By contrast, the Trough of Bowland, the fellsides above Tebay Gorge and the Westmorland countryside north of Appleby are large and unspoilt tracts of lonely and lovely land which can all be reached easily from side turnings off the M6.

Lancashire's scars begin to disappear

Much of industrial Lancashire's legacy of decaying buildings, described by George Orwell as 'festering in planless chaos', has disappeared. Even the 300 ft high slag heaps, which were unkindly named 'the Wigan Alps', have been broken down and churned into the foundations of the M6 motorway; and there are plans to make ski-runs out of the slag heaps that remain above the disused coal-fields. The town centres themselves are also beginning to change. Wigan, Bolton, Blackburn and Burnley are all redeveloping their shopping areas as attractive pedestrian precincts; but at the same time they are retaining among the modern buildings the best of the old architecture, which is mainly Victorian.

The one unchanging facet of the Northwest is the Lake District. Its protection as an area of unspoilt countryside has been assured by its designation in 1951 as a National Park—the country's largest, with 866 square miles of mountainous countryside. Its superb scenery is much the same today as it was more than 150 years ago when Wordsworth lived there and found inspirations among its hills and lakes. (4)

North Midlands

An enormous diversity of scenery is contained within the five counties that stretch across England from Shropshire, on the Welsh border, to Lincolnshire on the North Sea coast. The designation 'north Midlands' may suggest to many in the South a picture of red-brick houses huddled together in rows of identical streets, stained with the grime of the Industrial Revolution. This impression is far from the truth, for the North Midlands have broad expanses of rural landscape.

Shropshire, the westernmost of the five counties, is a land of stock rearing and dairy farming, scattered with orchards. Neighbouring Staffordshire has the heath and woodland of Cannock Chase and acres of lush farmland, while Derbyshire has the Peak District –a landscape of moorland, deep green valleys and rough stone crags.

In Nottinghamshire, the contrast ranges from coalfield slag heaps to pasturelands and acres devoted to mixed farming. The county has an area of intensive rose cultivation southeast of Nottingham, and the green woodlands of Sherwood Forest, home of the legendary Robin Hood. The rich, dark fenland soils to the east make Lincolnshire Britain's largest agricultural county, with huge acreages of wheat, potatoes and barley, and a concentrated market-gardening industry.

Two major rivers divide the North Midlands—the long River Severn that drains to the Bristol Channel from its source in the Welsh hills and, on the east, the River Trent, carrying much of the pollution of the industrial heartland to the Humber Estuary.

Inspiration for novelists and poets

Two hundred years of industrial growth have obviously left their mark—especially in Nottinghamshire and Derbyshire, where colliery winding gear and slag heaps frequently line the horizon. But the importance of the industrial North Midlands is not only economic. The area has made its contribution to the cultural heritage of the nation, too, for the mining town of Eastwood in Nottinghamshire was the home and inspiration of D. H. Lawrence; and Arnold Bennett, whose novels portray life in the Potteries, lived at Stoke-on-Trent in Staffordshire. The Midland counties have other literary links: Somersby in the Lincolnshire Wolds, was the birthplace of Tennyson; and another poet, A. E. Housman, drew inspiration from the views across Shropshire. The history of England is reflected everywhere: Danish place-names are common in Lincolnshire—an aftermath of Viking raids—and Shropshire, where the Welsh influence is strong, has many people of Celtic stock.

A village that braved the plague

Eyam is the Derbyshire village where, in 1665, the Rev. William

Mompesson persuaded people not to flee from the plague, brought to the village in an infected box of clothes. Five out of every six inhabitants died, including Mompesson's wife, but the plague was prevented from spreading. The Civil War raged across the North Midlands and Slash Hollow, at Winceby, was the scene of a major battle in 1643, which ended in defeat for the Royalist forces.

The cathedral at Lincoln, dominating the skyline for 20 miles around, and the 'village cathedral' at Southwell, Nottinghamshire, are among the best ecclesiastical architecture in the North Midlands. Derbyshire's stately homes at Chatsworth, Haddon and Kedleston owe much to the mellow beauty of the yellow and grey building stones of the county. This use of local raw materials by masons of centuries past has left a rich variety of ordinary domestic buildings throughout the counties—stone-and-slate farmhouse along the Welsh border, honey-coloured limestone villages in Lincolnshire, and the Tudor 'magpie' style of darkened timber over whitened plaster walls seen in villages to the west.

Sea walls that shelter holiday sites

The holiday locations of the North Midlands, though fewer than in some other areas of Britain, are becoming increasingly popular. Thousands are attracted each year to the vast caravan and chalet sites that dot the Lincolnshire coastline, protected from the bracing east winds by dunes and sea walls, and to the booming resorts of Skegness, Mablethorpe and Cleethorpes. But for scenery and natural beauty, the Derbyshire Peak District must take pride of place. Here, among bracken clinging to rock outcrops, are opportunities for the energetic to enjoy rock-climbing, or for ordinary travellers to enjoy the mental relaxation of hill walking. (5)

Eastern Counties

The eastern counties present a green, brown and yellow vista of farmlands, more extensive than anywhere else in the British Isles, some rolling over low, whalebacked hills, others fading into infinity across the dark, flat land of the East Anglian Fens. The land is a rumpled counterpane—a patchwork that is flattened along its seaward rim and in its fenland heart, and rises in other places into colourful ridges, never gaudy but full of subtle shadows and changes of hue.

There are gentle, undulating hills; little, domesticated valleys; rolling heathlands; dominant church towers that often appear too large for their villages; and towns which perch on hummocks, or nestle by rivers and streams. This is a breezy part of Britain, too, especially in the area of the Norfolk Broads. Even on the hottest day, the sunbather may need to shelter from the wind. But there is consolation –long hours of sunshine and the lowest annual rainfall in Britain.

The roads, too, are generally easy to travel. Away from the busy A1, Huntingdonshire is secluded and full of leisurely lanes; away from the A12, Suffolk is expansive and unspoilt. Even the large towns such as Peterborough, Chelmsford, Cambridge and Norwich are reasonably accessible out of rush hours for visiting motorists.

By every roadside there are flowers, fruit and vegetables for sale. Around Wisbech, root crops grow alongside orchards. Beyond, bulb fields run on into Lincolnshire. The twisting Norfolk and Suffolk lanes open out suddenly above spacious levels of pastureland and glide into warm-hued villages. The very flatness of the Fens emphasises a variety of skylines, and the sparseness of trees gives prominence to the most insignificant wind-hunched clump. The skies everywhere seem to take on an importance of their own. On a summer's day they can offer a dizziness of untainted blue or, in a single afternoon, a dozen variations in the weather—dazzling sun in one quarter, the rainbow-arc of a shower in another, a mounting storm on the far horizon. There are no dawns like those over Winterton, Southwold and The Naze; no sunsets like those across the shimmering Fens.

The light in the eastern counties is incomparable, too. There is hardly a trace of industrial pollution in the air, apart from the brick haze outside Peterborough. To make up for that, Peterborough has one of the great Norman cathedrals, companion to Norwich and Ely cathedrals.

Land of the North and South Folk

The kingdom of East Anglia was originally made up of the North Folk (Norfolk) and the South Folk (Suffolk). Its boundaries were once almost as impregnable as nature could make them—the sea to the north and east; the swamps of the undrained Fens to the west; a barrier of oak forest cutting off Saxon Essex to the south. Over the years the forest were thinned from the banks of the Stour, and the Fens were drained. When main roads were cut through the defensive earthworks across the Newmarket causeway, the boundaries of the counties began to blur—so much so that, today, the tortuous inlets of the Essex coast and much of its urban countryside, together with the Fens and the upland fringes of Cambridgeshire and Huntingdonshire, are all loosely classified as being parts of East Anglia.

Successive waves of invaders, including the Angles themselves and the marauding Vikings, swept in from the sea and left their mark on the countryside. Everywhere are Roman remains, Saxon burial grounds and names and word-endings such as the Danish by (meaning a town or settlement) and the Old English *ea* and *ey* (signifying an island). Later came more peaceful infiltrations. Icelanders from the cod-fishing trade settled in the coastal towns. Flemish weavers brought their skills to the wool towns and also set up as brewers—notably in Woodbridge and Ipswich from where they exported beer to their former homeland.

The Dutchman who turned a dream into reality

The Dutch contributed to the architecture and agriculture of the land. Until the coming of the Dutchman, Cornelius Vermuyden, in the 17th century, the drainage of the Fens remained an improbable dream. Other Dutchmen, for a brief span in the mid-17th century, posed the first serious threat of invasion since William the Conqueror. Today, there is a brisk holiday and commercial trade with the Danes, Dutch and Germans in and out of Harwich, Felixstowe, Great Yarmouth and King's Lynn—ports whose trading significance in the past can be assessed by the richness of their merchants' houses, customs house and exchanges. Later contributors to the welfare of the counties were the Scottish tenant farmers who came there during the depression years between the two World Wars and, shocked by the impoverishment and neglect of the land, set to work and revitalised derelict holdings.

Much of England's history was influenced by the people of the eastern counties. The names of great men and women—soldiers, sailors, noblemen and reformers—are remembered not just on tombstones but in historic buildings.

Hereward the Wake, Nelson and Wolsey belong to East Anglia; Boadicea ruled there, Mary Tudor lived there before she was Queen, and Catherine of Aragon died there. Oliver Cromwell came from Huntingdon. Among the powerful Dukes of Norfolk was Thomas Howard, who was the uncle of Henry VIII's second wife Anne Boleyn and grandfather of his fifth wife, Catherine Howard. He helped to destroy both Wolsey and Thomas Cromwell. Elizabeth Fry, the prison reformer, and Thomas Clarkson, who in the early 1800's strove for the abolition of slavery, were both born in East Anglia.

Tranquillity that inspired Constable

The eastern counties also have a proud association with the arts. Many writers have passed through the halls of Cambridge, learning or teaching—men as different in time and style as Hakluyt and Rupert Brooke, Rider Haggard and Cowper, Borrow and Pepys. Among the painters inspired by the tranquillity of the countryside were Constable and Gainsborough. The area's links with music range from the sardonic folk-song 'The Foggy, Foggy Dew' to the compositions of Benjamin Britten, and to the music festivals which are held at Aldeburgh, King's Lynn and Norwich.

For the naturalist, the eastern counties are a delight. The multitude of creeks are a vast sanctuary for birdlife. The Fens, the Broads and the coastal marshes provide the finest opportunities for bird watching in the British Isles. Though some of the wildlife and nature reserves had had to be protected from careless intruders, there are still numerous conservancy areas to which visitors are welcomed.

With the exception of booming Southend, Clacton and Yarmouth, the seaside resorts are small, intimate places, rarely harassed by streams of traffic, and ideal for the family. There are no sumptuous cliffs, and only a few sheltered coves. But there are magnificent skies, unbroken highways of sands and lovely, unspoilt tracts of heathland.

Flower festivals and county shows

The River Great Ouse is navigable for cruisers between Denver Sluice in Norfolk and Tempsford in Bedfordshire, and also along its offshoots to Cambridge, Mildenhall and Stoke Ferry. Huntingdon and St Neots have sailing regattas during the summer and there are also races and regattas on the Broads and Broadland rivers. Coarse fishing is excellent. Everywhere are agricultural shows, county shows, flower festivals, fairs and traction-engine rallies. Many of these events sound parochial. It is remarkable, though, how many are worth a detour and a visit—and in this, they are very much like the villages and towns that foster them. (6)

Home Counties

The five counties to the north and west of London have a landscape that is as varied as any in England. There are windswept heights and dense, silent beechwoods; one river where holiday craft jostle through busy locks, and another that drifts in seclusion along willow-lined banks; historic houses that share the past with grassy tracks and hill-carvings of even older times. The towns are equally varied—

ancient Oxford is famous for its scholars, Witney for its blankets, Luton for its cars. But within this patchwork are some unifying themes.

The pattern of the landscape is set by the three hill regions of the Chilterns, the Berkshire Downs and the Cotswolds, and by the rivers that wind through them—especially the Thames and the Great Ouse. Beechwood forests, so dense that they only rarely allow views across the countryside, cover most of the Chilterns, especially in Buckinghamshire. The Berkshire Downs, on the other hand, are bare and open. At Inkpen Beacon, in the southernmost corner of Berkshire, they reach almost 1000 ft, the highest point of any chalk downs in England, giving a sweeping vista across the River Kennet to the Lambourn Downs. The Cotswolds, which cut across the extreme northwest corner of Oxfordshire, are different again, presenting a landscape of green fields and grey limestone. Walls, cottages, manor houses and churches are all built of this local stone that, around Banbury where the Cotswolds meet ironstone hills, takes on a honey-coloured tint.

The Thames from its source in the Cotswolds retains much of the atmosphere of Jerome K. Jerome's *Three Men in a Boat*. The locks may be easier to navigate today and the pleasure craft using them may have sleeker lines, but the riverside inns are as welcoming as ever, and fields lining the river banks are still a popular spot for weekend picnic parties. The River Ouse has an entirely different character. It rises east of Banbury, and on its winding journey through Buckinghamshire and Bedfordshire to The Wash it has no need for the elaborate system of locks necessary on the Thames. Instead, the Ouse runs at its own natural level, setting an idyllic pace under willow trees lining the banks.

Throughout the Home Counties are many prehistoric and Roman remains. One of the oldest links is the Ridge Way, a track across the Berkshire Downs that was in use as a main trading route during the Bronze Age. St Albans is the site of Verulamium, one of the finest Roman towns in Britain; and the Great White Horse of Uffington, possibly carved in Iron Age times, is the oldest of Britain's hill figures.

The Home Counties are rich in other byways into history. At Wantage market place a statue of King Alfred records his birth in the town in AD 849. Near Kinston Lisle there is the 'Blowing Stone', which Alfred is said to have used to summon his subjects to battle against the Vikings. In the 18th century, Thomas Gray composed his 'Elegy Written in a Country Churchyard' at Stoke Poges, and the notorious Hell Fire

Club held its meetings at Medmenham Abbey, near High Wycombe.

Oxford's architectural treasure-house

There is a scarcity of medieval castles—probably because this part of the country, set so far inland, was considered safe in the Middle Ages. But the Home Counties have Vanbrugh's masterpiece, Blenheim Palace, and the royal residence of Windsor Castle, rich in work of every period since the Middle Ages. The greatest treasure houses of medieval architecture are the colleges and other buildings of Oxford University. Outstanding examples of earlier architecture include the cathedral of St Albans and many fine parish churches such as St Mary's, Iffley, one of England's most famous Norman churches. The best examples of later architecture are the splendid Jacobean Hatfield House, in Hertfordshire; the 18th –century Luton Hoo, in Bedfordshire; and many smaller houses such as Hughenden Manor, in Buckinghamshire, which was the home of Benjamin Disraeli from 1847 until his death in 1881.

Londoners' demands for recreation are met in the Home Counties in many varied ways. The steep slopes north of Luton are used for gliding; Whipsnade Zoo attracts visitors in their thousands; Ascot and Newbury racecourses are among the best in the land. There is pony-trekking among hills, and polo at Smith's Lawn, Windsor, patronised by royalty. There is coarse fishing from riverbanks, and trips along the Thames in pleasure boats, hired cabin cruisers and punts. As this is part of the vast commuter country surrounding the capital, there are golf courses in plenty. By contrast, off the main highways there are numerous secluded villages that still preserve an unspoilt rural remoteness within the confines of their own green boundaries. (7)

Southeast England

The southeast corner of England juts boldly into the quick run of glittering tides. Its marshes, wide beaches and high chalk cliffs fronting the English Channel are backed by the rolling Sussex downs, the orchards of the Weald and the heaths of Surrey.

The shores of Kent and Sussex have been the 'Gateway to England' through the centuries, and still bear the signs of successive waves of invaders. The Romans under Aulus Plautius landed there in AD 43 and left behind them the closest concentration of Roman shore-castles in Britain; their runs survive today, sometimes incorporated in medieval castles. The Anglo-Saxons under Hengist and Horsa landed on this coast and later the Cinque Ports were created to stave off Danish intruders. The Normans landed there too, and set up a girdle of mighty fortresses such as those at Rochester, Dover and Canterbury.

Against this historic tapestry of war, the coast today has the longest stretch of holiday resorts in Britain. By contrast, the shoreline has also the lonely north Kent marshes, the windswept Isle of Sheppey, and the great empty levels of Pevensey Marshes and Romney Marsh, where sheep graze among lonely churches. Along the shore of Romney Marsh were the secret landing-places of 18th-century smugglers, who took cargoes of brandy, tobacco, silk and lace far inland by secret forest tracks.

The Sussex coast is backed by the South Downs. These grassy slopes are the land of skylarks and sheep—Southdown sheep are exported all over the world. The South Downs Way is 80 miles of Britain's finest riding and walking country, along ancient paths where primitive Stone Age man grazed his sheep 5000 years ago. Valleys cut through the chalk and are followed by rivers beloved of anglers—the Arun, the Adur, the Cuckmere and the Ouse—where there are reeds and water lilies, wild duck and snipe. These valleys flood in winter into long lakes alive with widgeon and teal. Amberley Wild Brooks is a sweep of 12 miles of cattle pastures and reedy dikes by the Arun, between Arundel and Pulborough. The steep escarpments of the North and South Downs face each other inwards across the Weald—once deep forests, today a countryside of enchanting villages, splendid mansions, rich farms, orchards and hop gardens with conical oast-houses. Here grew the oaks that built the British Navy. Charcoal burners also felled them to smelt the Sussex iron; and gunpowder mills were set up in lonely wooded valleys, giving rise to the many hammer ponds, surviving today, which drove the water-wheels of forges and powder mills. Some of the ancient forest magic still lingers in the Wealden forests of St. Leonards and Ashdown, where herds of deer roam wild. To the northwest, woods of pine and spruce and stag-headed oaks surge to the slopes of Black Down and Leith Hill, the two highest points in south-east England, which have views rivalling those from many a mountain peak.

Beyond, on the western fringe, poking their fingers in here and there among woods and downs are the moorlands, wooded valleys and heather covered hills of Surrey. These lands---Bagshot Heath, Chobham Common, Pirbright Common and Bisley Common—are so poor and acid in soil that it was never worthwhile, over the centuries, to enclose them for farming. A century ago, the sandy Surrey pine-and-heather country was as wild as parts of Scotland. Today, the mock-Tudor dwellings of the stockbroker belt are widespread; but there are still many commons and heaths—thousands of acres open to the walker and the picnicker.

The Weald that Kipling Loved
The Weald that Kipling loved The popularity of Kent as a place of residence near to London for great families in medieval times has left a legacy of stately homes—Penshurst Place, the semi-fortified 600-year old birthplace of Sir Philip Sidney; Ightham Mote, half-timbered and moated, secretive in its Kent valley; and Knole, with its priceless treasures of furniture, Notable buildings in Sussex include the restored 13th-century Michelham Priory, near Hailsham, which has one of the largest moats in the country; Petworth and Goodwood, classic 17th and 18th-century buildings; and the Royal Pavilion at Brighton, the Oriental extravaganza which was rebuilt for the Prince Regent by John Nash in 1822.

This rolling countryside has inspired some heroic English literature. Dickens lived and wrote in Kent. Defoe wrote Robinson Crusoe at Cranbrook. Kipling wrote of 'the wooded, dim blue goodness of the Weald'; G. K. Chesterton and Hilaire Belloc sang the praises of Sussex. The people match the land. They have rich, soft dialect, a ruddy English look and a character that is as tenacious as Wealden clay. They, like their lovable land, are English to the backbone. (8)

Southern England
The south of England, dominated by the chalk-lands of Salisbury Plain, is the country of white horses and other hill figures. Until the early years of this century the counties of Wiltshire, Dorset and Hampshire were closely alike in character and the accents of their people sounded similar to the ear of the stranger, for they all once spoke Saxon. This was the core of King Alfred's Wessex, a small, closely knit kingdom with its capital at Winchester, from which was to grow a vast empire.

Though mainly chalk-land, southern England has areas that are vastly different from the huge expanses of its plains and downs. The corner nearest to London shares the heathland and scrub of Surrey. The centre is dotted with water meadows, and in the south the New Forest is a mixture of heathland, wooded country and pasture. The whole area is cut by the valleys of numerous rivers and streams, whose clear waters form a twisting network stretching down to the sea. The coast, flat in the east, rise gradually to Hengistbury Head in western Hampshire, then runs in spectacular cliffs through Dorset to the edge of Devon.

Saxon Wessex was predominantly farming country and, outside the towns, so it remains today. There are sheep and wheat on the hills; some fine diary land in central Dorset and along the Hampshire river valleys; beef cattle in all the counties; hops in the east, round Alton; and strawberries in the Southampton-Portsmouth coastal belt. Apple orchards, though, are a rarity except for some in Dorset. Left to themselves the soils of southern England produce scrub and down grass, beech groves and yews (the yew is called the 'Hampshire weed'), birches and oaks.

The holiday activities of the south are centred on Bournemouth. Behind its 6 miles of sea front is a broad swathe of hotels and boarding houses, and in the summer season its normal population of 150,000 is doubled by visitors. By contrast, the New Forest is a vast and virtually unspoilt tract of virgin land. It attracts thousands of summer visitors, even if surprisingly few of them venture far from the main roads. Southern England has its share of stately homes, but perhaps its greatest architectural wealth lies in the manor houses—some of them little more than prosperous farmhouses. There is one in almost every village. To this day most villages maintain their medieval structure, with a manor house, a church, a farm, often a village green and pond, and then the cottages—thatched and limewashed, looking as smart as ever.

Hampshire is the most diverse of southern England's counties, with sharp town and country divisions. Like all the south it is largely chalk country, but the county is rich also in trees, and in the south the spur of the South Downs running into Sussex is clad with 'hangers'—the hillside copses characteristic of the village of Selborne, which was immortalised by the writings of the 18th-century naturalist Gilbert White.

The Isle of Wight's resorts are charmingly set on a coastline of chalk downlands; but its inland villages such as Godshill, Bonchurch and Mottistone hold the essence of an island which visitors—'overners', as the islanders call them---do not always have time to appreciate.

Stonehenge and Woodhenge in Wiltshire, along with grave-mounds throughout the area, and Avebury on the Marlborough Downs, are the most important survivals of prehistoric Britain; it is hard to believe that these great bare uplands were once the main inhabited region of southern England and a place of European importance. By contrast, the county town of Salisbury lies among fertile water meadows, and the sight of its cathedral spire rising above the trees was a compelling subject for John Constable and for hundreds of lesser painters.

The Wessex of Thomas Hardy's novels

Dorset averages almost 2 acres of land for each of its inhabitants. It has remained a private and rural county largely because it has not suffered the intrusion of a major road, except where the A30 cuts across its northern boundaries. Even its seaside resorts, Weymouth, Swanage and Lyme Regis, have kept their Dorset character. Inland, Dorset remains a county of quiet villages tucked away in remote lanes, and of county towns like Dorchester, which have kept their traditions without conscious preservation because they are true to the character of place and people. The quality of Dorset has never been caught more effectively than in the Wessex novels and poetry of Thomas Hardy. Readers of his works will recognise here the country of Tess, Jude, the Mellstock Choir and whole gallery of not-so-fictitious people. For Hardy's characters were drawn from real life and their descendants live in Dorset today. (9)

Southwest England

The principal attractions that make the southwest of England Britain's most popular holiday region are its warm climate and its magnificent coastline. But inland, too, there are great riches; scenery grand or gentle, wild or pastoral; a switchback landscape of upland moors, rolling hills and steep river valleys; and the tangible remains of some 5000 years of history.

The Mendip Hills, riddled with many spectacular caves and gorges, have provide the limestone used in building Wells Cathedral and many other great Somerset churches. Southwest of the Mendips, central Somerset dips like a basin to fenlands, drained in the Middle Ages, which are now rich pastures. Further west the land rises again, first to the heathery line of the Quantocks, then to the Brendon Hills, and finally to Exmoor where 1705-ft Dunkery Beacon is Somerset's highest point.

From brooding Dartmoor to a sub-tropical coast

Brooding over much of Devon are the great granite uplands

of Dartmoor; but around these relics of volcanic upheaval 400 million years ago lies a great variety of scenery. The northern coast offers sandy beaches, stark cliffs and bracing winds. Inland there is a feeling of remoteness, among high, open roads and sunken lanes. Palm trees and sub-tropical flowers grow along the famous south coast, not far from the boggy, rock –strewn heights of Dartmoor. Cornwall is almost an island, for the River Tamar flows along all but 5 miles of its border with Devon. It is a marine county, with the sea never more than 20 miles away. Its coves, bays, creeks and drowned valleys, interspersed with fishing villages and dramatic cliff scenery, are offset by the gentler landscape inland.

The earliest remains of man in the Southwest date from the Neolithic Age, while the Bronze and Iron Ages have left barrows, cairns, standing stones and hut circles. The Romans left numerous remains in east Devon and Somerset, where their empire ended. Among them are the Foss Way that linked Exeter with Lincoln; the Mendip lead mines; villas at Ilchester, East Coker and Camerton; and the baths of the Roman city of Aquae Sulis, now known as Bath. As the Britons were driven west by the invading Saxon tribes, Cornwall became, with Wales, a bastion of the old Celtic ways, and kept a separate Celtic language until the Middle Ages (it has recently been revived by students of Cornish history and traditions). The county remained virtually isolated from the rest of the country until modern times. By contrast, Devon people took the 'stage of history' in the reign of Elizabeth I, when Drake, Raleigh, Grenville and Hawkins, all sons of Devon, helped to fight off the might of Spain.

After the Civil War and the Monmouth Rebellion, peace and a new prosperity came to the region. The tin and copper mines of Devon and Cornwall flourished, while the fishing and shipbuilding trades were carried on in seaports that were among the finest in Britain. Quarries were opened in the Somerset hills, the cloth trade prospered, and local industries grew up—such as leather tanning and shoe-making at Street, printing at Frome, and lace-making at Honiton. Much of this industrial prosperity has now died away, and the tourist trade has become a most important element in the region's economy. But the Southwest remains predominantly a region of farmers and fishermen, free from the blight of modern industrialisation.

Great buildings and famous people
Notable buildings are not lacking in this essentially rural

setting. Bath, with its superb Georgian terraces and crescents, is justly renowned. Medieval building can also be seen at its finest in the cathedrals of Wells and Exeter; in Well's unique moated Bishop's Palace; in spectacular St Michael's Mount off the Cornish coast; and in the great towers of Somerset's late-medieval churches. Outstanding domestic architecture includes Pendennis Castle, Montacute House and Cotehele House –one of the finest Tudor manor houses in England.

Writers such as Herrick, Blackmore, Wordsworth, Coleridge and Kingsley brought renown to the South-West; and among its other famous residents were Beau Nash, uncrowned king of Bath, and Sir John Millais, the Victorian artist, who used the beach at Budleigh Salterton as the setting for his *Boyhood of Raleigh*.(10)

Brittany

To many people, Brittany conjures images of the sea and the coast. That is valid but there is much more. The coastline is so jagged and indented that its twelve hundred kilometres would be less than half that length without its multitude of bays and coves. And the most vivid memories of Brittany are of reefs and islands; of scarred cliffs of red, grey or mauve and huge piles of rocks; of high head lands with wide seascapes which show why the west is called 'Finisterre'—the end of the world; of secretive inlets and long beaches of fine sand. There is Armor, 'the land next to the sea', as the Romans called it. But there is Argoat too; the interior of Brittany, which was called 'the land of the woods', for it was forested until the trees were felled for heating, building, and especially for building ships.

The forests have vanished, though there are still wooded hillsides amid fields bounded by wooded banks, heaths covered in gorse and brush which look mysterious and melancholy in mists or rain, rocky slopes and little rivers which somehow open up into big estuaries. Inland Brittany is not only a land of granite but of sandstone.

It is here, in the hamlets, the villages and the little farms, that the old Celtic mystery and myths still thrive. It is here that legends of the old Breton saints survive—stories of dragon slaying, of fighting sorcery and casting out devils and of instant miracles. Brittany is said to have seven thousand, seven hundred, seven score and seven saints—7847. Most of them seem to have been Cornish or Welsh monks who came over as the head of their people in the great emigration from Britain when the Celts were driven out by the Anglo-Saxon, from 460 AD for about two centuries.

     To say that Brittany is the Wales of France is a cliché and like so many clichés, largely true. The Bretons came from Wales and England from the fifth century, absorbing the old tribes and brought their Celtic language with them. They called their new land *Cornouaille* after Cornwall, or 'Little Britain' and gradually dropped the 'little'. (11)

END TO END TOUR

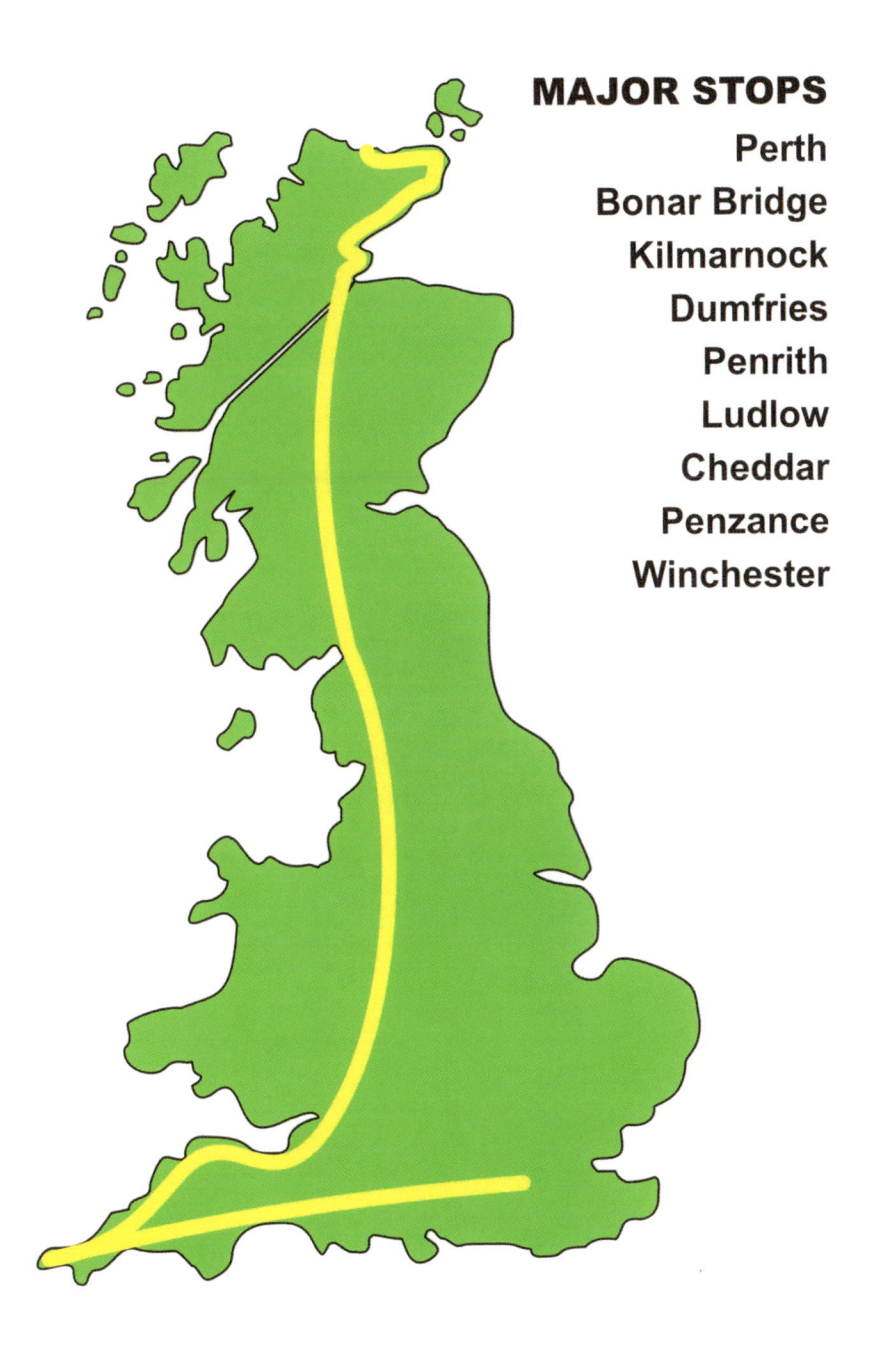

MAJOR STOPS
Perth
Bonar Bridge
Kilmarnock
Dumfries
Penrith
Ludlow
Cheddar
Penzance
Winchester

END TO END TOUR – 1800 KM

Overnight at	Day's Distance in Km
Perth, Perthshire	By Train
Thurso, Caithness	By Train
Latheron, Caithness	87
Bonar Bridge, Cromarty	95
Lewiston/Inverfargaig, Inverness	87
Onich (Loch Linnhe), Inverness	95
Inverarnan, Perthshire	90
Kilmarnock, Ayrshire	89
Dumfries, Dumfriesshire	101
Castle Carrock, Cumbria	72
Penrith, Cumbria	35
Broughton in Furness, Lancashire	68
Kirkby Lonsdale, Cumbria	66
Bolton, Lancashire	108
Hinstock, Staffordshire	111
Ludlow, Shropshire	82
Coleford, Herefordshire	87
Cheddar, Somerset	68
South Molton, Devon	116
St Gennys, Devon	90
Truro, Cornwall	85
Penzance/Land's End, Cornwall	81
Winchester, Hampshire	By Train
Coolham, Sussex	70
Welwyn Garden City, Hertfordshire	Perhaps 40 + Train
Gatwick Airport	

END-TO-END TOUR

The Route
As shown on the map at the beginning of this chapter, my route was roughly diagonal. It ran from John o' Groats in northeast Scotland to Land's End, the most southwesterly point in England. These are the Cycle Touring Club (CTC) official end points of the End-to-End. My personal route deviated somewhat from the official one, totalling some 180 km more than the distance the CTC was willing to acknowledge on my completion certificate. After finishing the End-to-End, I added more distance travelling east through southern England to Gatwick Airport for the flight home.

But first, I had to get to John o' Groats. After arrival in Scotland, British Rail took me from Glasgow through Perth for an overnight, to Thurso and pelting rain. Despite being early June, Gulf Stream benefits were in short supply so that my first day of cycling was damp and decidedly cool.

Arrival
The evening flight from Toronto was uneventful with sleep a virtual impossibility due to constant interruptions for beverages, the food service and the film. First stop was Edinburgh whose early morning ten degree Celsius temperature suggested reasonably comfortable riding conditions later in the week. My flight continued to Prestwick, a former military airport about an hour outside Glasgow.

I needed to go into Glasgow to get a train to the north coast for the start of my top to bottom version of the End to End. So, after collecting my cycle and gear, I approached a waiting taxi and asked the fare into Glasgow. It was the mind-numbing equivalent of C$50, over half of my daily budget! Then the bus driver refused to take me, saying 'you cannae take a bike in a bus—it's against the law.' This reception, added to the lack of sleep, robbed the day of its sunny warmth.

Back inside the terminal at the information desk, I sought the assistance of the very pleasant and efficient schoolmarmish attendant. Within thirty minutes, she had booked B&B's for me tonight in Perth and tomorrow in Thurso as well as arranging and paying for a taxi to take me to the nearby Prestwick railway station for a train to Glasgow. Her kind help quickly erased the blues and very soon I was on the railway platform basking in the sun and marvelling at the scenery with five minutes to spare before the train arrived.

Lost in a jet-lagged but warm and contented reverie, I failed to notice a train arriving on the other platform or to hear the announcement that it was the Glasgow train. Somehow, I came to my senses at the last moment and made a mad dash up the steep steps to the platform bridge over the tracks. My demented dash lugging a boxed cycle, duffel bag and a rucksack up and down those steps had to be comical to any observer. Thank goodness, the train driver was one of them and held up the train for a minute or two until I got on.

Glasgow Central Station was in a festive mood filled with travellers in good spirits. It appeared to be a very well managed station with nice shops and in good condition. I later learned that Glasgow was chosen the 1990 cultural centre of Europe and the city has been freshened up for celebrations later in the year. My train to Perth departed from nearby Queen Street station. This transfer was eased by different legislation in Glasgow that allows buses to carry cycles! (Perhaps it was bloody mindedness in Prestwick rather than legislation).

On that brief journey to Queen Street, I was impressed by Glasgow's human-scaled and architecturally consistent cityscape. With its fresh paint and newly scrubbed facades, it looked friendly and impressive—well worth a return visit.

At Queen Street, the ticket agent informed me that reservations were necessary for cycles at the particular time I wished to travel and reservations were now closed! I was quickly learning that this type of trip requires resourcefulness, a willingness to act independently and perhaps a bit of personal bloody-mindedness. I rushed into a lunch shop, bought a cheddar cheese salad sandwich and a coffee and grabbed an earlier train for Perth, ignoring the possible need for a reservation.

As the train exited from Glasgow, I began to feel that the trip had really started, although much of the close-in residential areas were uniformly bleak, grey and without relief. The countryside became lovely with rolling hills and lots of green dotted with sheep and cattle.

By 2.30, the train arrived at Perth. A porter helped to put my still boxed cycle in left luggage. As tomorrow was Sunday when the left luggage service would not be available, he made special arrangements for me to collect the cycle in the morning for the trip to Thurso. I bought my ticket, made the necessary cycle reservation and set off for the B&B. This proved to be a convenient three minutes walk away but no one was at home.

The B&B faced a massive park with lovely gardens set off with an impressive honeysuckle with coral and yellow flowers immediately opposite. It was a very British park with lots of space, borders of grand old trees, a pond for canoeing, a trampoline centre, miniature golf and a bowling green. I parked myself on a nearby bench to watch a wedding party emerging from the church across the road. The aged Bentley limousines, kilted males and picture taking provided entertainment until my landlady arrived.

My room had three beds, a strong smoke smell, colour television and tea making facilities. So, my first cuppa on the 'old sod' I made myself. The cup was Pyrex, made in Corning, New York –just 29 km from my birthplace! Thus fortified, I went out to walk the town and find something for dinner. This was acquired in the food department of Marks and Spencer (then Britain's largest department store chain)—two ham, cheese and pickle sandwiches and some Greek honey yoghurt.

Although it was now just about six, my body and mind were telling me 'get to bed'. It had been 39 hours since I left my bed at home. Back at the B&B, the sandwiches and yoghurt were washed down with another cuppa and I was soon fast asleep.

The final leg of the rail journey to Thurso involved a change at Inverness with over an hour's wait. I took advantage of the time between trains to unpack and re-assemble my bike. The chain gave me a bit of bother but everything was in working order a good half an hour before departure. All that was left to do was remove the cycle grease collected in the process.

My activity attracted considerable interest. A couple of men came over to talk. They had just returned from a month in Florida and really loved it. There were a number of other cyclists: three British Air Force men had just completed a training run on the west coast in preparation for an attack on the Pyrenees in August and some female cyclists that I did not meet.

A few stops after the train got underway a cycling couple joined the train and my car. They were University of Edinburgh students; he was a doctoral candidate in Geography and she was a third year student of Economic History. He was an Oxford graduate, clearly displaying a sense of superiority that was betrayed somewhat by their overt displays of affection.

Overcast skies and cold showers greeted my 7 pm arrival in

Thurso that evening. The B&B was some distance from the station and I got soaked in transit. The weather was so off putting that I did not bother with a proper dinner subsisting instead on my host's complimentary supper of tea and sandwiches about nine. We sat and talked together, discussing the limited economic opportunities in this part of the country. I remember being impressed with the quality of their television images and with the availability of useful information on certain channels. My hostess tried to persuade me to alter my trip so that I could visit the Orkneys where her uncle lived.

The journey began in earnest the next morning in a light mist, with the temperature about seven degrees Celsius. I should not have been surprised. The latitude at Thurso is about 58.5°, slightly north of Moscow. As I recall, this chilling baptism lasted nearly two hours before I was able to take temporary refuge in the tourist shops at John O' Groats.

The balance of this chapter relates experiences that I found amusing or interesting or both along the way. These are told in approximately chronological order.

Old Cyclist

The Glen Albyn A82 road ran in a narrow valley between two mountain ranges along the south shore of Loch Lochy. The wind was strong and draughts created by lorries passing on the other side of the road had a frighteningly magnetic effect sweeping me towards them. Cycling was difficult and the horizon went on seemingly forever. I was in a minor funk, feeling sorry for myself, when I heard a voice behind me. Drawing along side was another cyclist—a man, perhaps in his 70's, dressed more appropriately for a mountain hike than cycling. His gear was stowed in a wooden box strapped to the luggage rack, his feet, clad in heavy boots, were not in toe clips let alone on clip less pedals! I learned that he, too, was doing the End-to-End but to benefit the blind. We talked for a while, but after less than ten minutes, he said 'I can't keep on at this pace, I'll have to say goodbye now'. He sped on ahead. Talk about a demoralising experience!

Loch Linnhe

One of the things I learned on this trip is that arranging accommodation in advance definitely enhances the experience. Doing so doesn't guarantee comfort or interesting places but it saves a lot of time and frustration. Today, after strolling the town, I left Fort William about half past five planning to do another 8 km before stopping for the night. All the B&B's disappeared after 5 km. At 11 km, there was a hotel but the budget would not stretch to the twenty-two pounds they were asking. Another 2 km produced a most interesting tiny village with five different B&B's each displaying a vacancy sign and every one of them telling a fib! By the time I had hopefully knocked on all their doors and left rejected, it was half past six and it was raining again. The map indicated that the next village was some twenty km further on. But all of a sudden, there, gracing the sea-fed Loch Linnhe shore was a white, small red roofed bungalow sporting a B&B sign.

This time there really was a vacancy. The couple running the B&B was about 70 and looked as if they had to squeeze every penny until the Queen protested. I knew that there was no chance of an evening meal with them but counted on supper, that just before bed Scottish tradition that might just keep me going until breakfast. In this household, however, supper was limited to tea and digestive biscuits, with no sandwiches or chocolate bars. It was fortunate that I had a late lunch.

My room was very cold and could be tolerated only when under the goose down duvet. Next morning at breakfast, the husband wore a wool shirt over heavy underwear and topped it off with a quilted jacket. His wife was as ecstatic as an aged and polite Scot can be when I asked for a low cholesterol breakfast. She left out the eggs, made no substitute, serving me two wee tomatoes on toast. Hoot Mon, there would be an extra ten pence of profit on this client!

The husband talked of his youth when he would regularly cycle 80 km after tea during the week and as much as 200 on a Sunday —all of this on a fixed-speed cycle. As you may have noted at the beginning of this chapter, my daily distances averaged considerably less than 100 km. Cycling clearly was much more a part of people's lives here in mid-century than in North America both for regular transportation and for recreation.

Daughter's Room

Depressed by the weather and a visit to the Loch Ness tourist-focused tearoom and gift shop at Drumnadrochit, I carried on in drizzling rain along the northern shore of Loch Ness. It was only shortly after teatime but given the conditions, I easily persuaded myself to take the first B&B that appeared. It was a cottage set high up on the slope opposite the lakeshore, operated by Valerie with Pam, her 16-year-old daughter. I agreed to pay the double room price of the only room they had and since the prospect of going out again in that rain for a meal was totally unattractive, I persuaded Valerie to allow me to share their evening meal.

While she prepared the meal, we chatted about her interest in naturopathy and her ability to read people's allergies and other afflictions from simply having them hold different types of food. Dinah, her black and white cat, deposited herself in my lap and completed the domestic scene. Later, as we were concluding the meal and Pam was serving the sweet, a couple arrived looking for accommodation. After a few minutes of hushed conversation in the front hall, Valerie returned to the kitchen to ask if I would mind sleeping in Pam's room. Perhaps because males are subject to occasional fantasies, I initially misunderstood. The salesman and farmer's daughter stories of my youth flooded to mind. I should have known better.

The meal together, Dinah's acceptance and sleeping in Pam's bed made me almost one of the family, but one without background. Next morning, at breakfast, Valerie filled me in on her life as an abused child, contracting multiple sclerosis and recovering through homeopathic medicine. She also suffered from the class divide as her husband's family rejected her because her attendance at a grammar school and subsequent employment by a bank made her a snob intellectual!

Glen Falloch Farm

Heading east from Loch Linnhe, I made a pleasant stop at the Glencoe Centre for lunch and to see the short film on the Glencoe Massacre. Afterwards I faced the wind and seemingly endless upgrade of the route at this point. My ankles and backside were in agony. The wind was so fierce that it felt as if I was sitting still, going nowhere. At my current pace of about 10 km per hour, it would take until 6 pm just to reach Crianlarich.

Given the conditions, I decided to be satisfied with a 60 km day and stop there. Just as this decision was reached, my odometer quit, adding to the sense of making no progress. But then I noticed the historical small tombstone-like, white stone road markers placed a mile apart and began using them to measure my pace. Suddenly, Bridge of Orchy arrived on the horizon at 2.30 leaving only 18 more kms to

Panniers, Pedals, and Pubs

Crainlarich—obviously I had been speeding!

Unfortunately, this gave me an excuse to stop for a beer and sandwich at the nearest pub. I should have anticipated the effect of the beer on my cycling efficiency. Without any sunshine, the scenery became oppressive, remote, dark and deserted. Perhaps hoping to escape this quickly, I made surprising speed for the way I felt, reaching Crianlarich in an hour. Finding that all the single rooms were taken dashed my joy at this accomplishment. This discovery took a fair amount of time as, once again, very few B&B's bothered to indicate no vacancy outside, thus requiring several minutes at each B&B to wind up rejected. At Crianlarich's final possibility, the landlady had no vacancy but suggested a 10 km distant farm by the name of Glen Falloch. At this hour, I thought it might be wise to first check by telephone whether Glen Falloch had a vacancy. Her response was. 'Ach no, I couldna do that. It's a different exchange and I wouldna ken the number'. I suspect the real reason was the cost of the call.

As it turned out, Glen Falloch did have a vacancy and the ride there was at that beautiful time of evening in Britain when the sun makes perhaps its first appearance of the day, producing a soft angled golden glow on the landscape. The road ran gently downhill crossing many gurgling streams rushing over rocky beds. The pace and setting were serenely uplifting, just what was needed to overcome what had otherwise been a dismal day.

Glen Falloch was very much a working farm. My arrival was greeted with loud, in my face, barking from three of the twenty dogs diligently guarding their territory. The farmer in the yard was busy moving buckets of some vile liquid down to the barn so he passed me on to his wife who was responsible for the B&B part of their enterprise.

Yes, they had a single room. She led me to a narrow staircase that provided access to my room and its orange coverlet draped bed. The single window had a loose pane held in place with a bent nail but leaving a significant gap that ensured totally unnecessary air conditioning. My hostess said nothing about any supper, but I assumed there would be something—it was too late to go back to Crianlarich to find another place to eat. Finally, at 8.30 she called up to say that there was a cup of tea ready. Another guest, a gardener for the National Trust on a walking holiday, had arrived in the meantime.

She took us into the lounge where an open coal fire was generating a warm, cosy atmosphere. The heat also intensified the odour of wet dog that permeated the room. Unlike my experience at Loch Linnhe, this supper included a multi-tiered plate stacked with sandwiches and cakes. Our landlady joined her guests for tea and conversation and we soon discovered a couple of connections. Her niece had lived in my town of Oakville, Ontario and a New Zealand girl that had worked on the farm was now back living in Dunedin where my family lived in the mid seventies.

The farmer came in about 9, his day's work on this 17,000 acre, 5,000 sheep farm finally done. After a full day's work he badly needed a shower. Nevertheless, he joined us immediately for the meal. The room's wet dog odour slowly acquired additional natural nuances. When his wife asked what her guests wanted for tomorrow's breakfast, I said 'no eggs, please; my wife doesn't want me to have more than one a week to reduce my cholesterol.' The farmer immediately exploded. 'There'd be hell to pay in this place if that happened to me.'

My egg-free breakfast was served in the front parlour that thankfully was devoid of wet dog odour. The breakfast was more substantial than my hostess at Loch Linnhe had provided, with an addition of baked beans to the tomatoes on toast. Another guest, Bill, told me about his business and how he avoided income tax by forming a company and charging virtually all of his expenses to it. Apparently there is a special low rate for new companies so he plans to form a new company every year.

Gretna Green

Gretna Green nestles near the eastern edge of Solway Firth, conveniently close to the English border and enjoys a good tourist trade for its history as a place where clandestine marriages could be performed. England made marriage for young people illegal without parental consent in the middle of the 18th century but for over 100 years neither such consent or even residency was necessary in Scotland. Scotland later established a minimum three-week residency for one of the parties prior to the marriage. Until 1940, the local blacksmith could perform the ceremony. Today, the blacksmith shop is a popular location for wedding photos and weddings with benefit of clergy.

As I arrived, a freshly minted couple was having its picture taken next to the town sign and the shop itself was full of German tourists. It is a lovely setting with more of an English than Scottish ambiance. The streets here are winding, there are stonewalls and generally a bit more affluence and optimism than I have seen in Scotland so far.

Site of Many a Hasty Elopement Wedding

Further south and now in England just west of Carlisle, I stopped at the Brampton tourist office on the first floor of the clock tower in the village centre. My arrival coincided with the daily winding of the clock. My ankles were still playing up making the climb up to first floor quite painful, so I decided to take the first available B&B. This turned out to be an ancient working dairy farm called Gilt Hill in the nearby village of Castle Carrock.

The Gilt Hill B&B sign was attached to a dairy storage building that abutted the road just at a bend and I almost missed seeing it. As I rode up, I could just hear the wife giving instructions to her pre-teen daughter as she was setting off to make village milk deliveries on foot. 'That's for the vicar and …that's for', I did not hear the rest.

Their white stone house was attached to the farm buildings. Real log beams supported the upper floor and there were many lovely antique pieces amidst the awful overstuffed sofa and chairs of the guest lounge. My attic-like room was quite large with a single and double bed. Annie diplomatically instructed me to use the single as that what was I was paying for.

After a shower, I hobbled across the road for a pub meal. There were two choices but *The Weary Sportsman* seemed more appropriate. It was small and cosy with low ceilings, beams and window seats. I chose one of these next to a retired Welsh couple who had just finished a damp holiday in Scotland. Their conversation seemed mechanical and desultory. It was mainly about the weather or if she should have the raspberry pavlova. She seemed particularly eager to expand the scope of conversation and bravely spoke to a strange man (me) while hers went to the washroom. It probably wasn't much of an improvement for her after he returned as he chose to tell me about the pebbledash finish for houses that he had used as a builder.

Back at the farm, I strategically positioned myself in the guest lounge to read, hoping that I might be offered a cup of tea before bed. Whether this was her custom or not, I do not know but about 9, Annie asked if I would like a 'cuppa'. When this arrived, a cheese and tomato sandwich and a small chocolate bar accompanied it. Success! Later she joined me and embarked on a sad and complicated tale about her extended family and an awkward division of an estate that created resentment. A visitor wishing to borrow a hat for a wedding interrupted our conversation. This appeared to be a lengthy process so I took the opportunity to escape to my room.

Whitehaven

A English friend of Mari's in Oakville lost her husband in a terrible construction accident earlier this year and she subsequently moved to Cumbria to be closer to family. Mari asked me to take a detour from my route to see what her friend's new town looked like. At the time, we found it hard to imagine a better place to live than Oakville.

Whitehaven, in the northwestern corner of Cumbria, was considerably off route so I decided to go by train. The most convenient station to my route was at Foxfield. This proved to be a new experience, as the Foxfield railway station had no ticket sales or available snacks. No train stopped at Foxfield on a regular basis. You had to stand on the platform and flag the train down as it passed. So, after a preliminary pleasant tea and teacakes at a café on the nearby Broughton-in-Furness town square, I did just that and boarded the train. At this distance, I can't remember how the cycle was accommodated but I obviously put it somewhere!

Most of the other passengers were young people dressed in their party clothes for a Friday night out among the bright lights of Whitehaven. The northward journey hugged the coast, passing ramshackle little huts on the beach that I was told were 'holiday houses' that people hired in the summertime. To my eye they looked as if they should be condemned. The route also passed the famous school of the films—St Bee's-- as well as the ominous looking cooling towers of Calder Hall nuclear power station. Calder Hall's reactors were the first in the world to be used to generate electricity on a commercial scale. In general, the scenery and the mindless high-spiritedness of my fellow passengers were depressing.

Arrival in Whitehaven at about 7.30 did nothing to raise my spirits. It was too late to use the Book a Bed Ahead service or to get a pub meal so I rode round the town looking for B&B signs. When one finally appeared and the landlady offered me dinner, I felt temporarily fortunate. This feeling quickly evaporated when dinner was served. It had been intended for her husband and been sitting in the oven awaiting his return from the pub. Since he was at least an hour and a half overdue; she must have been trying to punish us both. Denying him his dinner and serving me the dried out roast beef, boiled potatoes and a desiccated mass of mushy peas that clung to my plate. The only partially redeeming feature was an ice cream and fruit sweet at the end that owed nothing to culinary skill. Next morning, contradicting my experience with dinner, I discovered her catering diploma proudly gracing the dining room wall. It was obvious that her catering school did not have a continuing education requirement. Perhaps understandably, the husband never showed up.

I took a few pictures in the town and checked property prices at the estate agents to be able to report something about Whitehaven to Mari but discovered more negatives. I found no pleasant residential areas although the *AA Illustrated Guide to Britain* claims that Whitehaven is 'a town of great character developed in Wren style in the 17th and 18th centuries...Lowther Street, in particular, has some elegant old houses....'

The harbour is also of interest to see ships that bring phosphate rocks from North Africa for the detergent chemical works on the hill and as the place where John Paul Jones set the boats on fire in 1788. At that time, Jones was a privateer, not the hero of wars between Britain and the US. I was told that the detergent works dumps their untreated crap right into the sea without restriction.

By mid morning, I was ready to leave and re-boarded the train back to Foxfield. The day continued in demoralising fashion as the cycle pedal jammed into the back of my leg cutting it badly while I was carrying the bike down steep steps to the platform. The bike was fully loaded and too heavy to control properly. Later that I day I collected a nasty stinging nettle rash on the other leg.

The day was very warm and humid so that my helmet quickly became unbearable once I was back on the bike. Dripping with sweat, I took off the helmet and tied it on the back rack. Soon after this the road plunged down and I was quickly travelling at over 50 km/h. This speed dislodged the helmet enough that it came off the rack and hung over, bouncing on the rear tyre. By the time I became aware of this, my once bright yellow helmet was covered with black marks and had a great groove down the centre! This was a fitting end to an almost totally unpleasant diversion.

Page Hall

The new day was cool but dry—perfect for cycling! It was to be an easy day with Penrith, my objective, little more than an hour away. The B6413/2 route ran almost due south from Castle Carrock. The roads were a good mix of up and down providing both exercise and thrills. One downhill produced a temporary 58 km an hour! There was very little traffic; I counted only 4 vehicles over 9 km. The country side was just right with stone or vegetation hedges, stone houses and rolling meadows with that particularly British semi-circular sweep of majestic deciduous trees which mark parks and country estates. Sheep and cattle abounded, streams ran under single lane hump back bridges, and villages appeared regularly. Kirksowald was one of these; stereotypically perfect with its winding main street running gently down hill with pubs at each bend. I stopped in the Crown Inn for an early tea and scones and extended the stop for an hour to write a few postcards.

Penrith was immediately interesting, lots of winding streets, narrow alleys and pubs. The first two places I inquired about a room were full, so I went directly to the Tourist Information Service and was quickly booked into Page Hall. This turned out to be an old farmhouse now completely surrounded by the town. Ken, my amiable host, was painting the outside windows as I arrived. He is an avid cyclist and an early retired forester who is now actively encouraging the growth of natural native British flora. He is currently cataloguing the several varieties in his garden and is up to 68 without counting any trees.

Since it was still early, Ken suggested a 15-minute excursion to the Beacon—a spot on the hill where fires were lit in Elizabethan times to warn of danger. His fifteen minutes were thirty for me—blame it on the ankles? The route to the top was a forest footpath on very rocky terrain amidst tall pines. The path offered a complete vista of the valley and town with the misty bunched clumps of mountains that are Lakeland in the distance. A small tower called the Pike that had been re-constructed in 1712 perched on the hilltop.

Penrith is an ancient city that originally was the capital of Cumbria and Strathclyde. It's name could mean Red Hill for the sandstone about. There are lots of little alleyways and interesting looking pubs. After dinner in one of them I walked back to Page Hall where Ken showed me some more of his garden. Although it was after 9 pm, there was still adequate light. We retired to the sun porch where his wife had set out tea and biscuits for supper. The temperature was cool but soon warmed with Ken's passionate conversation about a variety of topics that quickly established Ken as decidedly left of centre. He was obviously very intelligent and felt cheated by the lack of a university education. His family had been very poor and required him to leave school to help them. A government grant would have made university possible and he clearly resented that it had not been available.

Next morning, at breakfast, I met John, a mature photography student from South Wales who was staying at Page Hall while completing a project on the horse fair at nearby Appleby. This is an annual Gypsy (Traveller, Tinker) event that draws gypsies from all over. Horses are the focus of the several day event that features swapping, selling and buying. On a later trip I purposefully scheduled a visit to Appleby while the fair was on and saw men riding bare back galloping up and down narrow lanes to show off their horses. Money changed hands somewhat covertly from great wads of notes stuffed in shirt pockets. But I was disappointed at the lack of the stereotypical colourful clothing and shortage of gaily-painted wagons that we associate with Travellers (this is how they prefer to be known). I later learned that my timing was off, this was the final day of the fair not the first as I had thought.

The park opposite the Penrith railway station provided yet another example of military monuments that I see almost everywhere—

this time dedicated to the Boer War. I have noticed that war memories loom large in the British psyche. One man, noticeably under the influence, stopped me as I was about to enter a pub for lunch. He just had to tell me his war history of burying the dead in 1945 in Belgium. At one point, he even pulled off his cap to show me the shrapnel scar on his scalp! In 1990, the idea of German re-unification was so new that there was concern about the power and intentions of the new united Germany. This war 'top of mind' aspect of life here may also be true on the continent but it seems strange to a North American with no experience of war on his own soil. I am surprised though that there isn't more evidence here on the edge of Lakeland of honour for Wordsworth or its other famous poets.

Oakvillians

A few days later following learning about the Oakville connection at Glen Falloch, I booked into a lovely B&B in Kirkby Lonsdale, Cumbria, managed by a gracious lady that had worked for nine months in Oakville as a physiotherapist. In a later trip I returned to Kirkby Lonsdale and stayed with her again. Sadly in the few years between, she had become a widow and was wondering what her life would have been like had she accepted an offer of marriage from a Canadian doctor while she was in Oakville.

After my first night in Kirkby Lonsdale, some distance further south, I had great difficulty in finding a place to stay. By 8.30 pm, still bed less, my Presbyterian upbringing made me feel sure that I had somehow transgressed and did not deserve to find any accommodation. The offending action had to be glancing through an issue of the nudist magazine, Health and Efficiency, that I found the previous day.

I might also have gone without dinner if I waited much later, so I stopped in the Three Horseshoes pub for a late meal at about nine pm. The publican heard of my problem and phoned ahead to book me a spot at Sambrook Farm. Darkness had fallen by the time I finished my meal and I was concerned that finding the farm would be difficult and dangerous. Another gentleman, who was also booked at the farm, happened to overhear me. Intrigued by my voice, he asked me to 'talk some more'. As was usually the case, he initially mistook me for an American. He had to know where in Canada I was from. When I replied Oakville, he said, 'Oh, do you know Mary Clark? She lives on Trafalgar Road and was here just two weeks ago.'

Near the end of this tour I had another Oakville experience in a laundrette in Penzance, Cornwall. I was settled down with my book waiting for the machine to complete its cycle when I noticed a woman adjacent to me staring at the tag on my laundry bag. Finally, she introduced herself as a former resident of Oakville. She and her husband had spent the last several years in Saudi Arabia where he was an insurance consultant to the government. He was to retire in December but next on their agenda was a three to four month cycle tour of New Zealand. So we had plenty to talk about. Her husband arrived later and we had a good chat about cycles and touring. These coincidences add so much interest to these tours and they never seem to happen at home!

Church Stretton, Cheddar and Beyond

The morning at Sambrook Farm broke beautifully with fleecy clouds and bright sunshine. I took photos of the lovely garden through my attic bedroom window because the window would have fallen off had I opened it.

After breakfast, at the invitation of my hosts, I cycled a short distance to the Sambrook Mill—a lovely house with ponds, streams, hump bridges and a very nice garden. The building is a restored mill with the grinding blocks and lots of the machinery right in the lounge. A small window in the lounge wall looked onto the turning millstone.

My hostess gave me a complete tour, explaining that the water that turns the wheel comes from a pond that belongs to another family but these people have perpetual control rights over the water.

Back on the bike, I struggled with the route finding discrepancies between my map and the infrequent signposts. At Acton Burnell, I stopped to collect one of the required post office stamps that will prove to the CTC that I actually completed this ride. While there, I saw a sign for Church Stretton, only 13 kilometres away and decided on a side trip.

Church Stretton was the home of my one and only pen pal, Andrew Hensman. My younger brother, Byron and I stayed with his family briefly in 1957 during our summer European tour. I clearly remember this first stay in an English home---my pal Andrew's fun with the conversational confusion caused by his dog also being called Bob and being told to sit down because I looked untidy standing up. Andrew's father was a clergyman and their financial situation must have been very tight as his mother asked if we would mind re-using the same sheets when we returned for another brief visit a few weeks later. She wanted to avoid the cost of laundering them in the interim. I had never been aware of anyone that had to be quite so careful with money before. Now, I reflect back on that visit with some guilt. Feeding two extra people for a couple of days must have been difficult and we did not have the common courtesy to take a gift of any kind. But we did not have any relevant experience to drawn on. Virtually all our social experiences to date had been with relatives; reciprocal visits took the place of gifts, not that I even thought about these aspects.

Shopping District, Hereford

The road to Church Stretton started off normally but became dirt (and other brown material) from the contributions of daily cattle crossings. I was held up, along with other traffic, while cattle were put back to pasture after milking. A number of them had sterling silver plates with spikes attached to their noses. The farmer told me the plate was to stop them sucking the other cows' udders!

The road quickly narrowed to barely a track and was so

completely overgrown that I felt immersed in a tunnel of vegetation. At the side of the road, the ground rose sharply and steeply and the road was littered with fallen rocks. I hit one of these, snapping it up to strike my leg. Fortunately it hit just at the top of my sock and caused no damage.

The countryside provided very pleasant valley scenery with rolling green hills in the distance. It was very good cycling country but not particularly memorable. Church Stretton was more pleasant than my dim memories recalled. I searched for the church that Andrew's father was the pastor for and where we attended a harvest festival but I could not find it. Another church, St. Laurence's, was very peaceful and inviting. The United Reform Church seemed familiar inside but the exterior setting was wrong so I could not be sure.

After a brief lunch enjoyed on a bench in the High Street, I pressed on south towards Ludlow where I had booked a B&B tonight. After my experience yesterday, I wanted to be certain of accommodation tonight. Of course, after arriving in Ludlow, I found the place stuffed with B&B's most of which had vacancies.

Ludlow has a few very ancient hotel buildings. Most notable of these is the Feathers with a renowned elaborate Elizabethan driftwood like timbered front, where a single room was £60. Needless to say, I did not stay there.

I had a pleasant quiche and salad at the Church Inn while reading the Times about new ranks for the police, controlled council spending on council houses and increasing rents. The chairman of Marks and Spencer got a 46% rise in annual salary to £600,000.

I returned to the B&B and watched a 1981 version of *To the Manor Born* but was then effectively run out by the landlord wanting to watch football and smoke.

Pretty Woman

The next day began badly and continued much the same but ended most pleasantly. Most of the day was wet with rain. This and the terrain slowed my progress. I took refuge from the morning mist in a laundrette at Leominster for a couple of hours to take care of my accumulated dirty clothes. Of course, the heavens opened when I left soaking my fresh laundry and me.

As soon as I had dried out from this rain shower, the rain came again. I kept promising myself tea and cakes and finally found a likely spot at Ross on Wye at a park built into the sweep of a granite hill. It would have been lovely if dry. The not very swift English waitress could not help with directions and had to enlist the help of an Italian!

The next part of the route went through the Forest of Dean and offered all sorts of side-trip attractions such as Goodrich Castle and Symonds Yat but I did not have the energy for a diversion. I was headed to Coleford, some 18 km beyond Ross on Wye but encountered many inviting looking B&B's along the way. Stoically, I ignored them to achieve my self-inflicted goal. Once there, the first B&B had no single room, the next showed a vacancy sign but was full. After that, I found a superb looking place but it was also full. These people directed me to the Forest Hill Hotel at the far end of the village, just past the cinema.

Pretty Woman was showing at the cinema, a film that was just the sort of tonic I needed at that point. The hotel was an expensive £14 but I wasn't about to argue. I had just enough time to clean up quickly, cross the road to a supermarket for a few snack items for my supper and get back to the cinema in time for the first showing.

It was only about 60% full, populated by middle-aged couples and young people. There was about twenty minutes of ads, some of which were cleverly inventive while others were very amateurish. This interval before the film prolonged the experience and was strangely relaxing. The audience talked all the way through these ads but immediately became silent as soon as the film started. I enjoyed the film very much and felt that I had experienced true luxury. It is all relative isn't it? After today's ride, a dry soft seat in a warm room was indeed luxurious. Back at the Forest Hill, I enjoyed my snack items with a cup of tea and read, concluding my day perfectly.

The following day was again wet. I followed the CTC route as far as the Severn Bridge but once across the bridge could not find the route again. There were no route signs or place names that matched. The wind and wet made it impossible to check my map, so I crawled under some bushes to do so. But given the mist on my glasses, general low visibility and possibly blurred images on the map, headed for Olveston instead of Alveston.

At lunch I got some directions for Bristol at the pub. The rain continued and both the bike and the passing traffic were splashing me. It was cold. I could barely see for the rain on my glasses. My initial views of Bristol were not impressive and the road signs were ambiguous. My route was posted and then it wasn't.

A van driver that I stopped to ask directions took pity on me and gave me a lift through the city. It would have been impossible for me to duplicate the route he took. The rain appeared to let up but then started again just as hard. It was very demoralizing. I decided to cut the day short and stop at Cheddar.

But as has happened so many times on this trip, something happens to put things right. Despite the weather, I had two interesting stops today both before crossing the Bristol Channel. The first was a station on the old Tintern Railway that has been converted to a tourist destination. Old railcars were shops and the station was a tearoom. The scene was energised by lots of children doing exploratory searches to complete a school treasure style quiz. Then I stopped at Tintern Abbey where Mari and I had taken her mother over twenty years ago. I did not repeat the visit because so much of the Abbey ruins are visible from the outside.

I wound up in a very pleasant B&B called the Laurels, a Victorian house with an extensive, pleasant garden and most surprising interior. It was decorated in a 1950's cottage style—pine and stone. Green, the dominant colour, was featured in the walls, the carpet and bath fixtures.

The new day turned beautifully bright with lots of sunshine and strong winds. After breakfast, I rode into Cheddar Gorge but did not visit the caves on the principle of avoiding tourist attractions. This one is heavily developed. The entrance to the gorge was choc-o-block with cafes and gift shops but also had a pleasant garden and small cycle path alongside some small falls. The gorge itself was a lot smaller than expected and thus a bit of a disappointment.

In the early afternoon, I stopped for an expensive but excellent cream tea at a farm operation that offered dairy, trout, pig and sheep products. Their range included sheep's milk and ice cream, bakery goods and spreads and an intriguing runner bean chutney. A dairy exhibit showed how everything was used from milk to cheese to butter with the whey going to the pigs and a methane unit.

I also stopped at Dunster, near Minehead, Somerset, at the entrance to the Exmoor National Park. Dunster is an old market town that had been a centre for the yarn industry and looked worth a longer visit next time.

The sunshine and dry conditions made the day glorious enhancing the tremendous mixture of desolate high moorland above

North Molton, Devon with distant finely sculpted fields in shades of gold and green. The road was just a narrow ribbon of asphalt and even though it was so steep that I had to walk---the isolation and peace at this top of the world were well worth the effort.

Grazing sheep and babbling brooks bathed in the weak, watery evening sunshine improved the visual experience creating an almost spiritual atmosphere. Nevertheless, it was just a little scary for being so remote. If anything went wrong, I could be up there a long time before any help arrived. The remoteness also meant that there were no places to stay. It was after eight pm before I found a place and could stop--- completing what would prove to be my longest daily distance of the entire trip –116 kilometres.

The Scillies

This morning, I was awakened at 4.30 to the cacophony of seagulls immediately above me. The Cornish B&B room was in the attic and my window was in the ceiling. The gulls' squawking continued without abatement so I finally gave up the fight for sleep at seven.

Breakfast was not available until eight. This landlady was totally organised. She even had me complete a form selecting my breakfast and time in advance. Each table in the dining area was numbered to correspond with the bedrooms. Fortunately I chose the correct table without realising the system. Her portions were just adequate –a two cup pot of tea, two pats of butter, etc. The room showed similar loving care. There was one teabag, two packets of sugar and a single tiny container of milk. Everything possible was labelled with some instruction about its use, energy conservation or times. She talked incessantly about trivia and called everyone 'love' or 'pet' but I don't think she really liked people.

Today I'm booked to see the Scillies, islands to the southwest of Land's End that were former Prime Minister Harold Wilson's favourite holiday spot in the Sixties. Departure was from the lighthouse pier but was twenty minutes late due to the fog that also nearly obscured St Michael's Mount off to the east. The ship's horn sounded a constant warning and seagulls coasted alongside at upper deck level. I sat outside, ostensibly reading, but really observing my fellow passengers. One of them was particularly intriguing. He was an old man in a dilapidated yellow plastic hat, red tartan tie, non-coordinating wide tartan jacket, and contrasting waistcoat, eating Mars bars!

The ship called at St. Mary's, one of the several islands in the Scillies, for long enough to have a meal, take a brief hike and acquire souvenirs. Typically, the shops are most popular and the immediate first stop for most of the passengers. I was part of this herd until I took hold of myself mentally and set out to see as much of the island as possible in the time allowed. The sun made an appearance and stayed in sight long enough to grace my visit to a lovely old church in Hughtown with an overflowing cemetery populated with gnarled trees and other vegetation amongst the gravestones. The church building was very small and quite basic. There was no stained glass and the seating was on hard primitive benches. But the baptismal font was adorned with fragrant carnations. I also visited a pottery, the 16th century ruins of a fort, and took a Cornish pasty for lunch on the terrace of an exhibition centre where the birds hopped brazenly around on the tables seeking crumbs.

It was an interesting trip but I saw nothing different enough from the mainland to justify the fare. The most interesting sight was my sartorially challenged fellow passenger. He removed his hat for the return voyage, revealing patches of wispy, white hair. His brown trousers were well wrinkled and their zip has been crudely re-stitched. His shirt collar was frayed, dirty and undone. He did not interact with anyone, so I assumed that he was no one's guest. The £24 fare would have been a lot for him.

Experiences like this are a big part of the attraction of solo cycling. They may not all be pleasant or desirable but they are memorable!

Lost Railway Ticket

Having completed my End to End objective, I was ready for a change of pace and planned to visit Ann, a friend from Oakville who had moved back to England a couple of years ago to look after an aged relative. She lived near Winchester, a considerable and expensive train journey from Land's End. Nevertheless, I bought a ticket for the following day and went off to visit St. Michael's Mount.

This is one of those spots in England, like Holy Island, that is accessible by land only when the tide is out. Here the cobbled path led to a castle-like building set on a hill. The sea provided a huge moat except at low tide. Originally, St Michael's had been a monastery but had been taken over during Cromwell's time and given to one of his aides. That family still lives here with the financial assistance of the

National Trust. Once at the hill, access was up a very steep, cobble stone path through lovely varied, almost jungle-like, vegetation emitting a faintly sweet odour. There were also very tall, wind swept evergreens that were bare apart from the needles and cones that clung tightly to the very tops. Battlements and small cannons hugged the base of the castle whose entrance was at least thirty metres above sea level.

Much of the building had been refurbished in the late nineteenth century but there was an interesting mix of styles. Most impressive for me was the Monk's refectory with a long, oak table with a shimmering patina, the arched, timbered ceilings and the tiny mullioned windows overlooking the sea.

An interesting exhibition in the former kitchen called "Trail of the Dons" described the history of the late 16th century war between Spain and England. This is the war that many of us know primarily (if at all) as the one in which Sir Francis Drake defeated the Spanish Armada in 1588. It began well before that and continued for years afterward. Parts of the southwest English coast were invaded and burned by the Spanish. The *causa di bella*, as best I recall, was an attack by the Spanish against a renegade English trader off the coast of Mexico. The trader was transporting African slaves to the Spanish West Indies against Spanish regulations.

One of the villages burned by the Spanish in 1592 was Mousehole (pronounced Mouzel), where I headed next to find a B&B and some nourishment. In just over an hour, I had settled in an inexpensive B&B and was relaxing in the garden of a nearby coffee house with a cream tea and the Times. The coffee house courtyard overlooked a small semi-circular harbour that was dotted with sailboats and colourful fishing boats bobbing on their ropes. Squawking seagulls stood guard on the surrounding chimney pots. The entire scene was bathed in warm but watery sunshine.

Later, after a dinner of smoked mackerel and salad at the Ship Inn, I watched the Queen Mother's 90th birthday celebrations on television with my landlady, Mrs. Reynolds. We stayed up until midnight talking about all sorts of things but primarily the injustice of the EC. Her son was skipper of a fishing vessel that typically was out for a week at a time. She said that every trip required a visit to the authorities for rules and there could still be countermanding orders on radio bulletins that forbid them to take fish from certain areas. 'The other countries don't obey the rules.' According to Mrs. Reynolds, the Cornish dairy farmers had been ruined by a EC quota system that forced them to produce below capacity, thus lowering farm values and there had been no compensation.

Next morning, about an hour before I was to board the train for Winchester, I discovered that my previously purchased ticket was missing. The railway people were sympathetic but even my charge card receipt did not convince them to issue a replacement as I could have sold the ticket or anyone finding it could use it.

Frantically, I tried to remember what I had done after buying the ticket. Suddenly, I realised that it could have been left on the counter of the bank where I negotiated some traveller's cheques. I rushed back there and explained my problem—this time getting a very sympathetic and helpful teller. Yes, they remembered finding the ticket and setting it aside—but where? The young man, Julian, went through drawers, checked all the nooks and crannies of the counter, and went upstairs to Accounts but all to no avail. It was now just 25 minutes to train time and Julian was about as frantic as I was. Fortunately, it was early enough in the day that yesterday's rubbish was still waiting collection and after about eight minutes he emerged from the cellar proudly brandishing the badly rumpled ticket.

Britain isn't known for customer service. When my family lived in Hertfordshire, it was often a case of 'the customer is always wrong'. It took us years after returning to North America to overcome the automatic thought that returning anything or making any kind of a complaint to a retail store or a service provider would be an unpleasant experience. Today, Julian proved that service is definitely improving but as the next part of my story clearly shows, the improvement is spotty.

I got back to the station with about 10 minutes to spare and asked if it was necessary to have a cycle reservation. 'Donnow—please see enquiries.' With time evaporating, I joined another queue only to be told that they did not know either. At least this clerk provided a useful suggestion, 'why don't you take the following train –that definitely doesn't need a reservation so you can save the three pound reservation fee.' At this point there was really no alternative, so I went back into town and used my newfound time to book a B&B ahead for Winchester. On the way back to the station I saw three cycles set up for touring and camping. They belonged to a Swedish father, son and daughter. We talked for a while and he told me that he had completed the End to End in 9 ½ days after his wife threw him out! I did not press for details.

Winchester

As indicated earlier, the primary reason for my visit to Winchester was to see Ann, a friend that had moved from Oakville. But nostalgia was also a component as Mari and I had a very pleasant time here in 1986 on our first UK cycle excursion.

My pre-booked B&B was very close to the station in an elite residential area as the last house on a dead-end street. The proprietors were definitely up-scale from my experiences to date. They provided a welcoming pot of tea.

The next morning, a Friday, breakfast had to be early so that Mrs. Simms could get her daughters off to school. They are a very active family with four girls—all blondes—involved in tennis, swimming, horses, music and ballet. The mother was run ragged.

She left with the girls before I was ready to go. I needed some time to organise myself and sort out my 'best clothes' for meeting with Ann later. Mrs Simms lent me her iron for my trousers and a key to the house. Amazing trust. She knew virtually nothing about me, had left a camera and other valuables lying about and had not yet asked for any payment from me!

My objective for the first part of the day was to find the lovely villages where Mari and I had cycled four years ago. As ever, my directional memory was faulty and those specific villages proved elusive but beauty in this part of England is so prolific it did not matter. I had a great day anyway. At Alresford's Globe pub, I had a Pate Ploughman in a garden that sloped down to a lake and marsh studded with ducks and swans. The sun was shining and it was warm—probably the best weather of the trip so far. The ducks were very bold—begging like dogs at your feet. A large sign advised that if Duncan the swan took your food, please complain to Phil and Betty at Buck House. (All swans in England are the property of the Queen).

Later, Ann collected me from my B&B for dinner at her caravan home in Alresford and then took me to an old time music hall performance by a group of which she is a member. It was a new experience that I enjoyed very much. The compere provided articulate, skilful commentary and abuse for a variety of singers, actors and other performers engaging the enthusiastic audience at every turn. The costumes, acts and smoky atmosphere seemed authentic historically.

Panniers, Pedals, and Pubs

On Saturday morning, I was feeling pretty rough. Friday's pint of ale, two gin and tonics at dinner and smoke inhalation had combined to create a stuffy nose and throbbing sinus headache. Nevertheless, I came down for breakfast at 7.45 since no different time for Saturday had been set. Mrs Simms was all ready for me despite having been at a dinner party until 2 am! The girls are off to tennis lessons this morning.

My old faithful, Sinutab, came to the rescue and restored me to near normality. So, I roamed Winchester, revisiting the lovely riverbank walk, Winchester College and Cathedral. An Evensong service was scheduled tonight and I thought Ann might enjoy going. So I rang her at the home of a man, Bert, that she 'did for' on Saturdays to see if she could join me. She could and in return I was invited to share lunch with them at his home.

Bert proved to be a very likeable chap, a professional architect, and currently single but with obvious intentions to install Ann in his home more permanently. (I am pleased to report that Ann resisted his blandishments and returned to Oakville where she remains a close friend). Bert's home, at least 300 years old, sat on a slope down to the river. When he had moved into the property last October the gardens were badly overgrown. Ann encouraged him to improve them. This was still a work in progress. At the time of my visit it was all elderberry and black current bushes but there were plans for a summerhouse.

Bert took me on a tour of the house and property, pointing out the restored and added bits while Ann finished the lunch preparations. This proved to be a stew, potatoes and peas with a chocolate pie for the sweet. Conversation was easy, interesting and fun. We carried on until 3.30!

Later, Ann and I attended Evensong at Winchester Cathedral. This is an Anglican service that I enjoy very much and try to attend whenever I am in England, although I am not particularly religious. It is rare to find Evensong in North America. The service consists primarily of hymns sung by the choir, interspersed with a few readings from scripture. It is an opportunity to close your eyes and simply absorb the soul enriching sounds in an atmosphere of peace and inspiring architecture. English choirs are generally very good and those at the main cathedrals are superb.

Afterwards, a short walk from the Cathedral took us to the pedestrian precinct and the Tudor façade restaurant God Bagot where we made a light meal of superb Welsh rarebit washed down with a celebratory Scotch and ginger. We then hurried to the nearby but nearly hidden tiny St. Lawrence Church in the Square. It lies between the statue and arch on the precinct that continues to be the gathering place for dissidents, sort of a Speakers' Corner in Winchester. Earlier in the day as I passed by, people were collecting signatures against the poll tax. This tax was an interesting but ultimately unsuccessful Margaret Thatcher idea. It taxed every citizen over 18 equally for the local services provided by the municipality on the premise that everyone had equal access and benefit. This tax replaced property rates (taxes) and had to be paid to retain the right to vote. I thought the plan made a lot of sense but It was wildly unpopular and did not last long.

But I digress; we were headed for a piano recital at the St. Lawrence Church. The 17 year-old pianist, thin as a rake with wiry, long and totally undisciplined hair, played very well despite having only taken up piano two years ago! Unfortunately he had not yet developed any stage presence and showed no sign of enjoying the playing or the audience's appreciation. Ann and I finished our evening at "Waffle On", a newish bright café on the pedestrian precinct that specialised in waffles.

Blue Idol

The trip to Gatwick, after Winchester, for the homeward journey, involved an overnight at a Quaker B&B, the Blue Idol, which I found purely by good luck. I had stopped just outside of Billingshurst at a very unappealing B&B—no one was home. Several kilometres further on, down a country lane, was a B&B set in lovely grounds with an aroma of pig manure. This would have been very acceptable but for the fact that they only had a double room that I could not afford. Nevertheless, the landlady rang round and found me a room at the Blue Idol, so named because the late 16th century building had been idle for many years and was painted blue. It too was set well back from the road down a lane.

I was accepted somewhat reluctantly as the proprietors had hoped for a quiet night without guests, to the point of putting out their "no vacancy" sign. Falling through one of their lounge chairs did not endear me to them either. As I recall, my room was called the George Fox after a Quaker pioneer. A wing of the building housed a small Quaker meeting room where William Penn had worshipped. His home, where he drafted the constitution for Pennsylvania, was only about seven kilometres away.

Like the other Quaker B&B I had experienced, breakfast included my favourite grapefruit segments. I had a healthy helping of them and of the muesli followed by egg, perhaps a quarter pound of bacon together with brown toast and four cups of tea. Total cost of the overnight was £12!

The new day was beautifully sunny and after capturing the Blue Idol on film, I set off towards Haywards Heath. This is a much older and more prosperous part of England. There are lots of Elizabethan homes and some fantastic gardens. At Worthy there were several new homes under construction in small estates. These were all detached but probably less than 2000 square feet in size with gardens of perhaps an eighth of an acre. Based on similar homes in estate agents' listings, I would estimate their prices at about £160,000.

About five kilometres from Horley, I began thinking that it was a shame that I had so far not had an opportunity to test the cycle repair skills that one of my son's friends had patiently imparted before my departure. I wished I had a puncture just to complete this adventure. It was definitely a case of mind over matter! Almost immediately, the back wheel felt a little funny but the road surface was pocked so I assumed that was the cause.

Not so. I got my wish! Eagerly pulling off the road and onto a convenient open bit of parkland, I unloaded everything and rested the bike on its saddle and handlebars, removed the rear wheel and replaced the tube quite competently only to discover that my pump was broken!

Fortunately there were some handy bushes to conceal the remains of my bike and other gear when I set off, rear wheel in hand, in search of a petrol station with an air pump. Half an hour later, I found one and inflated the tyre to the proper pressure. The station's washroom was equipped with a supply of grease removing compound that worked very well and somehow made me feel even more a real mechanic.

This sense was eroded a bit by some difficulty in re-fitting the wheel and properly engaging the gears but I was still pleased that once back at the bike, the entire process took only fifteen minutes. This allowed me to reach the Parson's Pig Pub with two minutes to spare before they stopped taking lunch orders at two pm.

I enjoyed a beef and horseradish sandwich and a lager in their garden. This was a very nice pub with an airy, big room off the bar that would have been pleasant for a prolonged session of lager and book but I was eager to get to Horley where I could get a train to Welwyn Garden City and possibly see some friends there on my next to last night.

This side trip worked. My friends were in and were 'happy' to feed me and put me up for the night. I left my cycle at the left luggage at Horley and made my way to Welwyn Garden City via train, underground and train. We sat up until almost midnight, showing pictures and exchanging family stories. Next morning I returned to Horley, the closest village to Gatwick Airport.

A Long Night

The tour has drawn to a close. It was the afternoon before my flight home tomorrow morning. I contacted the airline regarding packing up my cycle for the flight. All that was required was to remove the pedals, deflate the tyres and turn the handlebars sideways—no carton necessary. That was good, as I had discarded my carton over three weeks ago in Inverness.

Having established that, I began the search for a B&B. The Yew Tree that Mari and I stayed at in 1986 had been booked since noon and the cheapest single I could find was twenty pounds—more than I had paid anywhere on the trip. To add insult to injury this price included only a continental breakfast not a full English! The south of Britain has many more facilities than the north and Midlands but the prices are significantly higher and the service often offhand and uninterested.

With such bleak prospects and an eye on the budget, I decided to sit up in the airport overnight. I stored my bags at the railway station left luggage and toured the village. The prospect of saving so much on accommodation clearly justified a stop at a tearoom run by a Hospice organisation. I read my book, prolonging my stay there as long as was decent then migrated outside to a bench to write the Cycle Touring Club (CTC) to claim my certificate for completing the End to End.

My proof was a page of postmarks collected at various post offices along the route. This was the CTC's suggested approach but had proved a bit embarrassing to explain to each of the post offices. Many were suspicious and acquiesced only grudgingly.

After a walk through one of the residential areas, I returned to the railway station. Fortunately, I arrived just in time, as the left luggage attendant was sneaking away a full 25 minutes earlier than the advertising closing time. I unloaded my panniers and their contents into my rucksack, marvelling at how heavy it was, wrote in my journal for about an hour and then cycled over to the Curry Garden for a nostalgic meal. Mari and I had dined here twice in 1986. Just recently I read that many Indian restaurants in Britain use up to four times the healthy level of food colourings in their meals. This is because the British consumer considers that the brighter the colour the spicier the food. My Tandoori chicken was fiery red.

Later, at the airport, the wisdom of my decision to sit up all night paled. I had prepared the cycle for the journey, become bored with my book and could only nap briefly. The hours dragged on and on until I could join the queue for the flight. Then there was another long wait to actually board. Airline travel has certainly lost any glamour it ever had. This was a charter flight with cramped seating and indifferent service but I have had a memorable trip, achieved a long held dream, and become fitter. It was an experience well worth repeating.

PEAKS, LAKES & DALES TOUR

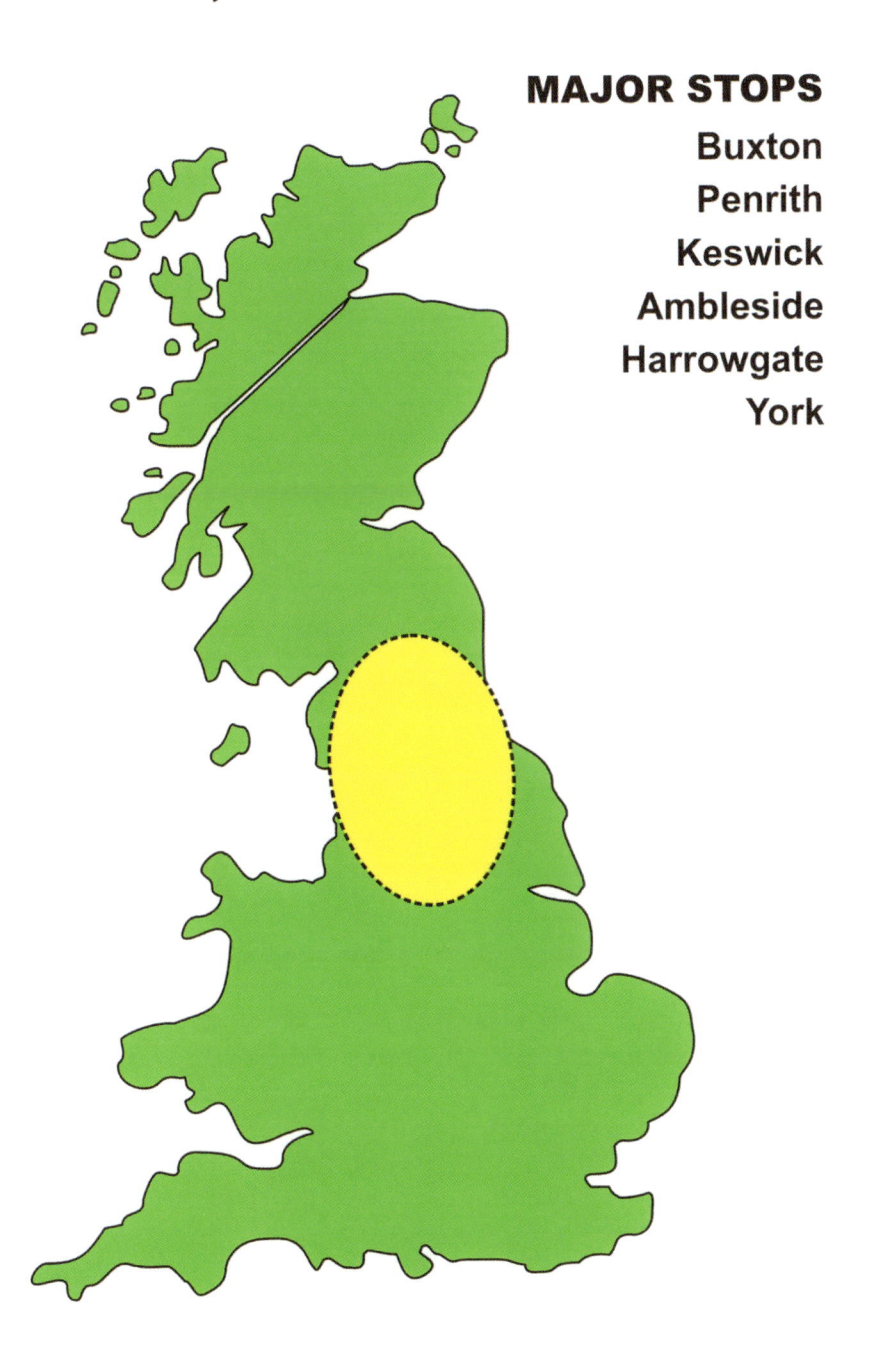

MAJOR STOPS
Buxton
Penrith
Keswick
Ambleside
Harrowgate
York

PEAKS, LAKES AND DALES TOUR – 1360 KM

Overnight at	Day's Distance in Km
Buxton, Derbyshire	40
Ilam, Derbyshire	74
Ashbourne, Derbyshire	66
Monsal Head, Derbyshire	62
Wigan, Lancashire	25 (more by train)
Penrith, Cumbria	42
Dufton, Cumbria	63
Keswick, Cumbria	64
Cockermouth, Cumbria	70
Boot, Cumbria	74
Ambleside, Cumbria	41
Kendal, Cumbria	53
Kirkby Lonsdale, Cumbria	59
Stainforth, Yorkshire	59
Asygarth, Yorkshire	75
Eshton Grange, Yorkshire	82
Harrogate, Yorkshire	55
Harrogate, Yorkshire	48
York, Yorkshire	75
Scarborough, Yorkshire	15 (more by train)
Great Broughton, Yorkshire	84
Carlton in Cleveland, Yorkshire	44
York, Yorkshire	93

PEAKS, LAKES AND DALES TOUR

Five years had passed since the End to End. In between, Mari and I had cycled in comparative leisure and luxury in both France and England. During our 1992 trip, we discovered the allure of York and fell in love with the dales of James Herriott fame. Ever since, I longed to explore them at greater length.

Thus the Dales became the foundation of my next solo journey. Years before, as a young family, we had spent part of an Easter holiday in the Peak District of Derbyshire and been introduced to Bakewell tarts, a local delicacy not enjoyed since. An aborted family trip to the Lake District in those early years and my reading since had embedded an interest in finally seeing that area. So, all three areas were incorporated in my planning for this trip –a combination of nostalgia and challenge.

The Route

The route started in Derbyshire, south of Manchester, moved west into Cumbria and followed a circular route through much of the rugged Lake District countryside entering Yorkshire at its southwest corner to explore the Dales, York and the North York Moors.

Arrival

For this second trip, I upgraded from a charter flight to British Airways, taking advantage of a special promotional fare. The flight service and accommodation were welcome improvements but choosing BA meant flying first to Heathrow and transferring to Manchester. On arrival in Manchester, I heard an announcement for me and learnt that my cycle didn't make the transfer from London. This delayed my start by two hours.

Another two hours were used to unpack and re-assemble the bike. This was a new bike, twice the cost of my ten-year old $500 Sakai but custom sized for me. I prepared it for the journey with sponge like pipe lagging protecting the top, down, and seat tubes as well as the forks and chain stays. This time I used an airline provided thick flexible vinyl sack for the cycle. The saddle, post and pedals were packed separately. But the handling apparently had been rough. The brakes were out of alignment and I had a puncture! (Six weeks later, back at home, the repair shop replacing a wheel bent on the return flight found that the frame itself was badly torqued. This cost C$200 to fix. Since then I have used a rigid vinyl bike box).

My plan was to store the packing material and my two cases at the airport left luggage office. The charge would have been a pound a day for each case or about $115 for my 24-day stay! My distress must have been very pronounced as the attendant suggested we stuff the two bags into one and that he give me a long stay discount. This reduced the total cost to C$36. Reflecting back on this incident, I can't be sure whether the attendant was being kind or had just initially assumed I was a rich and naïve North American that would not blink at such a charge.

Now, finally at 2.45 pm, I was ready to go. Airport and residential areas disappeared quickly; the countryside became fine, pastoral and reasonably flat. Then suddenly, I was in Cheshire on the western edge of the Peak District National Park. The now rugged countryside had climbs so steep that it was all I could do to continue pedalling. These were followed by steep descents that my brakes could not control. At the junction of Penny Lane and Bull Hill Lane, I stopped to inspect the situation and found that the front wheel was bent so that the brake pads could not grab the wheel rim properly.

The rugged countryside continued past the Cat and Fiddle pub and dropped into Buxton, Derbyshire, which was today's destination. Despite the downhill run, Buxton is one of the highest towns in England at 307 metres. It is a spa town that owes its fame to the 5th Duke of Devonshire who, at the end of the 18th century, built the town's beautiful Crescent as a rival to fashionable Bath.

On the way down, one pannier fell off and the computer stopped registering speed or distance. Despite all these problems, the 40 km run to Buxton had been accomplished in just over three hours. B&B's were plentiful and I was soon installed. It had been an eventful first day.

Ilam- My First Hostel

Next morning, I breakfasted alone at a separate table but could overhear a group of middle-aged British tourists travelling together. Their conversation was that hushed tone of trivia that one encounters so often in Britain. You struggle to overhear the secrets being discussed only to learn what the chiropodist said about Aunt Edith's big toe.

After breakfast, I set out to find a cycle shop that could repair the in-flight damage done to my bike. The Buxton cycle shop had me back on the road within half an hour. The repair turned out to be a simple matter of tightening and loosening some of the spokes so that the front wheel ran true again. I headed south on my way towards what I hoped would be my first hostel at Ilam. The B road ran through Peak Park with its rocky outcroppings, sheep, cattle and stone fences bordering lovely green pastures that were nibbled so evenly they looked mown.

I arrived at the hostel shortly after noon and due to a last minute cancellation was successful in getting the last male bed. The building had been a private home but was given by its flour magnate owner to the National Trust on the condition that it be maintained as a Youth Hostel. At the time of his gift in 1934, Ilam was the largest hostel in Britain. My room was elegant with wainscoting, a fireplace and paintings in gilded frames.

After depositing my panniers in the room, I set off unladen for lunch and some leisurely riding. The Dog and Pheasant, a moor-top pub, provided a tuna stuffed jacket potato and lager that produced severe lethargy about an hour later. I just had no energy and had to walk a bit to recover. The balance of the afternoon involved the lovely village of Alton and a super 5 km stretch of downhill back to the hostel. Some brave or foolhardy sheep wandering across the road added excitement and colour to the thrill of the descent. Their cowardly, less energetic brethren watched my dodging manoeuvres from the overlooking hills. It was a rugged, rocky green country that perfectly matched my rural British stereotype.

Like other large hostels, Ilam offers prepared meals. Tonight's dinner was fish fingers, tomato soup, chips and peas. Today's even larger hostels such as Manchester often have two or more choices generally including a vegetarian option. The large hostels also regularly have coin-operated beverage machines that dispense just drinkable coffee, tea and hot chocolate. At meal times, the requirement for coins is turned off.

Young people were all over the place under the supervision of a few adult handlers. There was also a group of about 15 black women from a cosmetics firm on a treasure hunt and training course to build morale and firm loyalty. For someone accustomed to hearing the 'south' in North American black voices, their northern English accents sounded out of place. A hostel venue for such corporate bonding exercises was certainly downmarket compared to those I have attended.

The quiet room was now anything but with 14 young ones! I moved away from my seat to allow a new arrival to sit with his friends but he said, 'no, stay—I insist'. He was perhaps seven or eight!

California in Derby

Next morning I cycled to Dovedale, the acclaimed beauty spot, and walked along the river for about an hour. Craggy hills rose directly from the riverbed somewhat reminiscent of Switzerland. Later, my lethargy returned so perhaps yesterday's lager wasn't responsible. Fortunately, this malaise did not last long. I carried on into Ashbourne and on to Sudbury where some birds decorated my panniers while I was in the village post office. I chose to stop at Sudbury for postcards because my daughter Allison then lived in Sudbury, Ontario where she was newsreader for the local television station. I spent a pleasant weekend with her there and was proud to sit in the studio for her evening broadcast. Her jacketed professional appearance belied the jeans below the news desk. The job required her to select the news to be reported from the various wire service releases, to determine what and how much to say about each story and to establish the story order. The few minutes before broadcast were hectic, making last minute changes and loading the monitor that she would read from. I learned that the papers that sit on newsreaders' desks are primarily for show and in case of monitor failure.

The day's route was pretty ad hoc. I didn't have any accommodation booked and only needed to stay within a reasonable day's ride from Bakewell where I was booked tomorrow. This route freedom allowed a stop at a small cottage and teashop at Longford where a man and his son were chopping wood while the woman was tending her lovely flowerbeds. She served up a huge pot of tea on a redwood picnic bench on the lawn and I chatted with the men about the 1932 Morris Minor ash-frame convertible that they were restoring. After tea, they took me on a tour of their vegetable garden, chickens and collection of 25 reo lawn mowers with tools for making a good edge.

My route brought me back into Ashbourne (the third time today). It had started raining so I started looking for a place to stay. The B&B's were already full so I wound up at the Old Vault pub on the market square. It was a black and white Elizabethan building with an alley off the square on either side. There was no convenient or obvious place to store the bike so I took it up to my room.

The pub had a warmer ambience than many and wasn't smoky so I was encouraged to stay there for dinner. This proved to be an excellent choice and breakfast was equally pleasant---good quality and quantity. Later I learned that the proprietors had been in business only ten weeks. Their previous occupation was looking after an 18,000 square foot home in Irvine, California but they got homesick for their grandchildren. They told me how they had selected this particular pub and showed me pictures of the California property. Made for a most interesting breakfast. I was certain that their time in California had a positive effect on the quality of food and service.

Bakewell Tarts and Well Dressing

Today, I am booked in at a B&B in Bakewell and hope to re-acquaint myself with Bakewell tarts (the pastry variety). Bakewell is only 29 km from Ashbourne, so I took the advantage of the light cycling day to explore the town. My first find was a fabulous shop that specialised in tools for real craftsmen, such as elegant wooden planes. It was reassuring somehow that the old skills still survive and are being catered for.

I succumbed to a shop that advertised 'the original Bakewell pudding' and was disappointed—possibly because they focused on tourists rather than purists. According to the story (again, perhaps, modified for the benefit of tourists) the pudding (tart) was the result of an accident in the Rutland Arms at Bakewell when a junior cook poured the egg mixture over the strawberry jam instead of in the pastry batter—creating its unusual appearance and the distinctive short pastry.

Next stop was Ashford in the Water where they are well dressing today. This is now a Christian custom but is based on pagan well worship. The dressing is a design sculpted in clay into which flower petals are pressed to provide the colour for the picture. The first well I saw was set in the wall of a garden; others were spotted round the town. There were supposed to be six different dressed wells but I could only find four. Two of these had war remembrance themes, one was of working dogs; the biggest and most impressive was dedicated to women that managed the farms during wartime.

My booked B&B wasn't in Bakewell at all but at a nearby place called Monsal Head across the road from a magnificent river valley view. My landlady recommended a pub in Little Longstone for dinner so I cleaned up and ditched my panniers for an unladen ride to the pub. It looked a little worse for wear when I arrived and was still closed. So, I sat on a bench outside until opening time at seven. By that time there was a queue to get in! A group of six at the pub recognised me as the cyclist they had seen earlier in the day at one of the Ashford dressed wells. They invited me to join them for dinner. I had a very good duck and orange pie with vegetables and a pleasant conversation with the group.

Well Dressing Display, Ashford in the Water, Derbyshire
Ken Mills

My next objective was Wigan, west of Manchester, the home of friends that Mari and I met on a Headwater tour in France in

1994. Getting there involved returning to Buxton for a train to Wigan, changing at Manchester. I bought a Wayfarer ticket that allowed me to go anywhere within a particular area that day for the equivalent of about C$12. Wigan turned out to have two separate stations and of course, the one I wanted was just outside the designated area. A sympathetic conductor allowed me to go on to the more distant station anyway and did not make much fuss about my cycle that was stashed in the wheelchair storage area.

At Wigan, on my way to my friends' home, I stopped at a big Gallery—an indoor mall in the centre of town to find a bottle of wine to take them. I was impressed by how well lit and laid out it was but distressed to see teenagers simulating intercourse on a bench.

Next morning, after a pleasant evening and excellent restaurant meal with my friends, I headed for Penrith by train from Manchester. I hoped to be able to see Ken Mills at Page Hall where I had stayed on the End-to-End tour. However, the Tourist Information Centre people told me that he had retired. I booked with another B&B but decided to drop in and see if Ken was at home. He was and invited me to stay for dinner! Ken's politics and mine conflict so the dinner conversation was spirited but respectful. That is a rare experience for me; I generally find that when people disagree with you they also think less of you for your contrary opinions. Ken talked of his trip last year to Canada where his first stop was Oakville! He knew people there that knew the great Canadian author and naturalist, Farley Mowat. Ken had gone by freighter carrying only a rucksack and one of Mowat's books. His wife Jan is going out to Calgary next month for a three week hiking trip

Ken is overseeing a reforestation project for a Buddhist group on an island in the Clyde. He is trying to ensure real reforestation—replacing the types of trees that populated the forests 1000 years ago and selecting and growing the seeds himself. Ken believes that the world would be better with earlier retirement so people could lead more fulfilling lives. Ken thinks that it true for him—that all he learned in the past is now being brought to bear doing good things. He is a very strongly opinionated man but admirable for his achievements.

Appleby

The sequencing of this year's trip and my return to Penrith was in large part based on the timing of the Appleby Horse Fair in mid June. I had learned about this during my End-to-End tour stop at Page Hall in

1990 and wanted to see it ever since. Appleby is only an easy hour's ride away from Penrith on the A66.

What a mess! Litter was strewn all over the road as if it were an overflowing massive rubbish bin. This continued on the hill where the travellers' (gypsies) caravans were parked. In the town, even the river was littered. Nothing related to the fair was happening in the town so I headed back towards the caravan site. On the way out of town a man standing on the river bridge told me that a horse had drowned in the river earlier in the week. The horse had been driven into the river for the traditional buggy wash ceremony only to be dragged under when its buggy fell into deep water.

Back at the hill, I wandered round the stalls, many of which were typical of any other sort of fair catering to the mass tourist trade and with no particular connection to travellers. Mari and I have often wondered where British television drama finds people with the faces that are often used for their rural and period characters. This fair provided at least part of the answer. People like that were everywhere; ruddy-faced farm folk and some really villainous looking types. Others were trying to look the part of the wealthy horsey set. However, there was very little evoking any kind of a gypsy atmosphere. Traditional clothing and music were missing and only a few of the colourful horse drawn wagons were visible.

While watching a farrier shoeing a horse, I got into conversation with a traveller who claimed that the British government treated travellers much as North Americans had treated their indigenous peoples by forcing them on to reservations (caravan parks). He encouraged me to go see the vestiges of horse selling (today turned out to be the final day of the fair rather than the main day as I had thought).

The horse selling was conducted on a straight stretch of tarmac at the edge of the hill where the horses, drawing their buggies, were driven at top speed up and down, racing each other to impress potential buyers. A light rain had made the pavement wet and some the horses were having a tough time staying upright. Once or twice a horse slipped and nearly fell. I witnessed a sales transaction conducted by a complex slapping of hands to negotiate the price; the agreed price called for a special slap. The price was at least £1500 (C$3600) based on the wad of notes the buyer pulled out of his shirt pocket! I also overheard part of a conversation that sounded as if someone had been cheated of twice that amount.

Panniers, Pedals, and Pubs

**Annual Gypsy Horsefair, Appleby, Cumbria
Dufton Hostel**

Despite providing some interesting experiences, the fair failed to meet my expectations. Perhaps an earlier day would have been busier and better. I left at about four to book in at the nearby Dufton hostel along the Sea-to-Sea hiking track. It was a lovely ride—the perfectly pastoral scenery blended rugged rock outcroppings with lush, green, manicured-looking paddocks ringed by distant rising hills.

It was immediately obvious that Dufton hostel attracted a different clientele than Ilam. Here, all the members were male adults walking the Pennine Way but for a photographer/artist travelling by motorbike. He was the most interesting of the lot; a former sailor with tattoos over his entire upper body (the intimacy of hostel living offers aspects other accommodation rarely provides). We had a philosophical discussion much along the lines that I had with Ken at Page Hall. This man didn't believe that profit should be a component of any essential service such as water, gas or education (Margaret Thatcher had privatised the utilities). His recommendation of John Preeble's books on the Highland Clearances reinforced his general anti-establishment viewpoint. He was a gentle, big man whose intelligence, behaviour and interests totally contradicted my generally negative stereotype of tattooed motorbike riders.

The other hostel members were friendly enough but a bit rough round the edges. At this hostel, members are responsible for tidying up before departure. The dining area was assigned to one of the dimmer lights of the hiking group who displayed his general unfamiliarity with housekeeping by standing on the dining tables and using a broom and dustpan to clean them.

Next morning while packing up and lubricating the bike, I met two mountain cyclists who must have come in after dinner last night. They were doing the Sea-to-Sea route that cuts west to east across the country using bridle paths. One of them was concerned that my tyres were about to give out. He had never seen 'slicks' –a tyre that has a totally smooth centre surface bordered by a rugged tread. This design is intended to reduce friction on regular roads and still provide grip when needed.

Keswick and Beatrix Potter

Today, I was heading west from Dufton for the Lake District. Pooley Bridge, at the head of the beautiful Ullswater and just into the District, appeared in a little over two hours from Dufton. There, at a bend in the road, was a perfect-looking tearoom with outside tables by the river. The timing was perfect for lunch. Although the prices and food quality shouted tourist trap, I could not resist taking advantage of the setting and glorious sunshine to enjoy a leisurely lunch riverside with my book.

A few kilometres beyond Pooley Bridge, I came to Aira Force, a National Trust property. Force is the term used for waterfall in this part of the country. Seeing the Force required a hike up the hill. I did not feel comfortable leaving the cycle and panniers unattended in the car parking lot and so carried it with me—a very cumbersome task and an incongruous sight on the fairy-tale like forest trail. This went through ferns, moss-covered trees and jutting rocks in the rushing brook bed. At the end of the trek, Aira Force suddenly emerged pouring forth from beneath an arched stone bridge.

The rest of the day's ride west into Keswick was uneventful but through lovely country. There were huge rhododendrons everywhere making some stretches of road like a route through a flowered-forest. Other stretches featured sheep, stonewalls, and birdcalls that were overlaid with a pungent aroma of manure. This was virtual reality at its best! Keswick, ringed with soft green mountains, was immediately impressive. I stopped at a riverside park to soak up the ambience and read a bit. There I met a man who claimed to have just completed the End-to-End in fourteen days.

My pre-booked B&B, Skiddaw House, was in sight of and named after the mountain famous with hikers. It was located in Portinscale, a residential area adjacent to Keswick, with access across a park that was as much pasture as park. It was obviously multi-purpose as I encountered people, dogs and cows enroute!

The next day I wanted to explore Keswick on foot. My landlady, Marian Townsend, kindly allowed me to leave my gear with her during the day. Despite my general antipathy towards many tourist attractions, I chose to visit the Beatrix Potter exhibit. This included a 16-minute film about her life with Dame Judi Dench playing the part of Beatrix. In that short space of time we learned how she started writing, got published and then used the proceeds to buy and keep land from development. The man that eventually founded the National Trust introduced her to the concept of land conservation at age 16.

Beatrix ran Herdwick sheep on her property, a small but sturdy breed that have been in Cumbria for about 400 years. The rest of the exhibit was mainly devoted to storyboards that elaborated on various aspects of the film.

Keswick was so appealing that I was entertaining the idea of proposing it to Mari as our retirement home. Later that morning in one of my regular bookshop prowls, I learned that Keswick's summer time temperatures average 15 degrees Celsius and that rainfall averages 145 centimetres annually. This would never sell to a woman brought up in the dry heat of Oklahoma! The book that revealed this disappointing information was Hunter Davies' 'A Walk Around the Lakes', an otherwise delightful saga of a year he spent doing just that.

Cockermouth Hostel

My brief walking tour of Keswick completed, I was again on the road again by 12.45, on a clockwise route to Cockermouth via the Honister Pass between Borrowdale and Buttermere. The terrain was benign until the Honister Pass -- the most severe climb yet encountered.

Cycling was impossible; I was going so slow that the odometer did not even register!

Despite this, it was perfect with gurgling, rushing brooks, rocks, mountain sheep and a glorious, almost total, absence of man's presence. An occasional car pulled off the road, its occupants quietly soaking up nature's beauty, was the only example of human habitation.

The Pass finally reached its peak of 754 metres falling away to Buttermere where I stopped for a mug of tea (actually two) and a cheese sandwich at an outside picnic table. Soon the scene was like our bird feeder at home. Without invitation or fear, several birds hopped about on the table hoping for a titbit.

I reached Cockermouth too early to quit for the day. Since I had only covered 40 km so far today, I carried on in the area adding another 30 km delaying my arrival at the hostel until 6.45. This hostel is a 300-year-old former corn mill that sits right on the river at the bottom of a steep, rough track

It was almost too late for the evening meal but since only two people were staying tonight, the warden agreed to serve me as well. After a quick wash, I joined the other man for dinner and talked about politics and the comparative beauty of the Peaks, the Dales and Lakeland. My dinner companion had just completed a week of walking in those areas. Last month he had done the same in Crete and claimed that finishing off a day's walk with a swim in the Mediterranean was very pleasant. He felt that Margaret Thatcher had changed the country's ideas about work for the better and that this would have lasting benefit. And he also believed that she had greatly improved the professionalism of the police and the army. It is rare to hear anything positive about her so this was refreshing.

Experiences like this dinner and the peaceful isolation are the real joys of solitary travel. I believe that conversational opportunities are greater for a person on their own and the choices made about route, when and where to stop for meals, accommodation and activities can be totally your own, not a compromise with others' wishes. The downside is that solitary travel can also be lonely and limiting if you aren't naturally adventurous or curious.

As I was the only person at breakfast, I used the opportunity to talk to Martin, the warden, about his job. He gets his afternoons and two full days off plus his board and room and a net £100 per week. During the four months of winter that the hostel is closed he has no home or pay but is free to do as he wishes. Last year, he and his girl friend spent three months in Nepal financed by his savings.

Joss Naylor

Later that day and further south at Cleator Moor, I stopped for pictures of a beautiful little river with some ducks being fed by children out with their father. The ducks were making a lot of noise, mainly directed at one duck. Another duck attacked it and repeatedly pushed its head under the water holding it there. Another one rushed into the water from the bank. Oh, good, I thought, a rescue attempt. But no, this new duck entered the fray to help the attacker! The poor victim, the only white duck among them, had all the down pecked off his neck and was bleeding. To complete the scene, the father allowed his daughter to throw an empty tin into the river. Both sights saddened me about our world, its cruelty and stupidity. I carried on in the hopes of a peaceful, fortifying morning coffee. This wasn't available until Gosforth, where I stopped for lunch at an upstairs café. My attire apparently wasn't common there as all the heads turned to stare as I entered. My shame was soon assuaged somewhat by the arrival of some even scruffier looking cyclists; so I thoroughly enjoyed my cheese and onion quiche, salad and tea.

On Martin's recommendation, I headed next for Wast Water, one the least visited lakes because there is only one-way in. This made it isolated and thus dramatic, mysterious, and a bit unsettling. The road ran along the west side of the lake and eventually to a hotel. Standing guard were two of the higher peaks in Lakeland, Seatallan at 688 metres and Scafell Pike at 977 metres. Wast Water is perhaps best known for Joss Naylor, a sheep farmer who holds many world records as a fell runner. Hunter Davies, whose book on Lakeland was mentioned earlier, has this to say about Naylor: 'Joss Naylor is known for doing something which requires that much admired quality, hard graft. He runs hard and he works even harder, combining a tough life as a sheep farmer on the high fells where it's surprising anything can live, with running up and down peaks or combinations of peaks, sometimes all day and all night, depending on the particular madness of the race he is running.

Fell running is a sport so easy to admire. You can see the peaks. You know how hard it is to walk up them. So imagine tearing up—and down—seventy-two of them in twenty-four hours, just for the fun of it. World-class marathon runners have failed to beat Joss, not aware of the variety of terrain which has to be covered, the complexity of pacing yourself, of knowing how to run over swamp and rocks, how to avoid hidden peaty holes and leap over bracken, what sorts of grass and moss to trust. It's not just long-distance running—it's long-distance, obstacle running.' (1)

The Minis

My hostel for the night was at Boot, east of Eskdale and close to the famous Hard Knott and Wrynose Passes. Hard Knott appeared quickly the next morning and proved to be even tougher than Honister. Climbs like this with grades of 1 in 4 are not uncommon in this country. They would have been difficult enough unladen but with four full panniers, it felt like pulling a heavy anchor. When my speed dropped below 6 km an hour, I gave up and walked. Today, the odometer failed to register any speed at all whether walking or riding. Pushing the cycle up such slopes forces a leaning forward posture to cope with the slope and counter the significant weight pushing back. I tried unsuccessfully to work out whether it would be safer to walk with the bike between the traffic and me or vice versa.

The strain of this uphill climb was endurable because it had been anticipated and there was the prospect of an exhilarating downhill to come. The weather was cool and breezy but the exertion quickly had me sweating. Every so often I paused to cool off, look back down the valley, and soak up the hills, rocks, wind and sheer magnificence of this scenery.

This particular Sunday afternoon, the hills roared with a rally of colourful darting Minis buzzing up and down and round the hairpin bends like angry hornets. Then, at the peak, one of the Minis went off the road. No one was hurt but I was suddenly alert to the risk of missing a curve on the downhill run. This risk was immediately clear as even on the straight bits, both brakes had to be on full strength to moderate my speed. Going round the bend at such speed caused the heavily weighted rear of the cycle to swing out dangerously close to the edge, I quickly gave up on the exhilarating downhill experience, dismounted and walked down.

At the bottom, there was a flat stretch with equally impressive brooks and rocks surrounded by majestic hills. But Wrynose quickly appeared and I was walking again. This climb was slightly shorter than the 1.5 km of Hard Knott but the descent required walking also.

I carried on into Ambleside where I am booked at the hostel. This is one of the very large, hotel-like hostels that are open all day and provide a full meal service. So, I went in early to get rid of my panniers and freshen up a bit.

As this was Sunday, the designated day for ringing home at 3 pm, I needed to find a phone. We had picked 3pm British time to be early enough in the Canadian day to catch Mari before she got away for the day's activities. These calls were never very satisfactory for me, trying to cram a week's worth of news into a half an hour phone conversation and I had yet to be able to ring through without involving both the British and Canadian operators—a very frustrating process. Inevitably, some of her news is bad and my fault but there is nothing I can do at such distance and ostrich-like, I would rather not have worries interrupt my tour. I was using the public telephone in the ante way of the Queen's Head pub and was constantly being interrupted by someone that kept opening the bar door to see if the phone was free. Consequently, I used the excuse (legitimate) of someone else needing the phone to shorten the conversation.

The impatient person's call was very brief. He was a drunken old church organist who had come to the pub straight from his Sunday duties and now wanted his wife to fetch him home. He explained the situation thus: 'Being righteous works up a thirst'. Perhaps his deficiencies will be a conversational topic when she picks him up.

I had a delicious bowl of broccoli and Stilton soup for lunch on the patio of the Priest's Hole, a nice spot where I could keep an eye on the cycle while eating. During lunch a man approached me about it, asking about my bar-end shifters, as he was having a cycle built for him. These shifters are positioned at the end of the handlebars and are designed for touring cycles so that the gears can be changed without removing your hands from the bars. Today, the shifters are often incorporated into the brake levers on higher end bikes.

Wordsworth, Kendal and Kirkby Lonsdale

After lunch I headed off for Grasmere Village and Dove Cottage, Mecca for Wordsworth devotees. The village was streaming with tourists, particularly Japanese. If you see Japanese, you know that you are on the beaten track. Although both attractions were beautiful and worth seeing, the presence of other tourists annoyed me. If I'm honest, this attitude reflects my wish to do unusual, remarkable things that others don't, can't or won't. I don't like thinking of myself as having common tastes. In short, I'm somewhat of a crazy snob. Imagine thinking you are better than others because you take arduous holidays on a shoestring, stay in hostels, and experience physical hardships for the bragging rights! My family certainly thinks I am crazy.

I returned to the hostel on country lanes west of Grasmere overlooking Lake Windermere. The cycling was glorious and parts of the lanes were virtual tunnels of rhododendrons. As mentioned earlier, this hostel was big, more hotel than hostel. I was assigned to room 217 and given a key! It was a new hostel experience to have a key and for a brief moment, I thought the room might be private but no it was only semi-private –six bunks! The choice at dinner was surprising also, four main courses and five sweets.

The next day was spent at the village of Hawkshead, a hard 6 km from Ambleside and at Griezedale Forest. At Griezedale the Centre for the Arts had a cinema, put on plays and had sculpture exhibits in wood. Unfortunately, many of the sculptures gave the appearance of creativity struggling unsuccessfully to emerge.

At Hawkshead I lunched at Whigs on a corned beef and pickle sandwich served on a Whig. This turned out to be a sweet yeast roll with caraway that was delicious. Hawkshead is also Wordsworth country; a cottage where Wordsworth lived while attending the small school (circa 1585) was graced by a gigantic yellow/pink rose bush emitting a sweet natural fragrance. Otherwise, the village offered whitewashed cottages and tiny alleys.

Kendal, on the eastern edge of Lakeland, was my hostel location tonight and as the day was cold and wet; I wasn't upset that today's distance was only 53 km. There I met a Canadian woman from Barrie, Ontario (less than 100 km from Oakville) who is off to Paris and Greece with a boyfriend for a month. At breakfast, I sat with an Australian couple that carry Vegemite with them for breakfast just like my sister's Australian husband. They are off to Scotland, Scandinavia and Iceland.

Kirkby Lonsdale, a spot that appealed greatly during the End-to-End, was my next destination and close enough to permit a leisurely morning looking round Kendal. I visited some of the shops and purchased my lunch from Marks & Spencer's tremendous selection of sandwiches. The variety they offer includes all the old standards but much more that reflects the relatively high proportion of British that are vegetarians. My choice today is indicative: carrot and hummus on sunflower honey bread. This, together with a large bottle of freshly squeezed orange juice made a perfect and healthy lunch.

While walking round Kendal, I passed a butcher's assistant carrying half a longitudinally sliced pig carcass lengthwise on his shoulder. The sliced side was away from me, making the pig look very life-like, particularly since its full tongue was hanging out.

A short eighteen kilometres along the A65 brought me to Kirkby Lonsdale in time to enjoy that Marks & Sparks lunch in the village square's hexagonal stone and timber shelter. There was plenty of time after lunch to explore more before stopping for the night and a quick visit to the Tourist Information office produced a 40 km circular cycle route map.

This route took me right past The Courtyard B&B where I had stayed in 1990 and am booked in to again tonight. Later, just before reaching Sedbergh, Yorkshire a gnarled old man approached me on the opposite side of the road driving a small horse cart. I called out 'Good Afternoon' while passing; this was obviously unexpected and startled him but he tugged at his cloth cap, fixed his crossed eyes on me and croaked out a 'How Do.'

Sedbergh is the main western gateway to the Yorkshire Dales. The town has strong Quaker associations and George Fox preached in the district on many occasions. Two miles away at Brigflatts is the oldest Friends' Meeting House in the north of England. It was built in 1675 and retains many original furnishings in an atmosphere of calm, cool tranquillity. But for me Sedbergh's main appeal was that it provided an excuse to stop for tea and two orders of teacakes—this gluttony surprised my waitress and proved to be almost more than I could manage.

Later, back at Kirkby Lonsdale, Mrs. Green, my Courtyard landlady, served more tea and home-baked pastries in an elegant sitting room and I just could not refuse her hospitality; after all, I tour for teacakes! I had forgotten how nice her home is. The main door to the house is on the side behind an impressive person-high gate. The entrance hall features a stone floor and stairs bounded by persimmon walls. There are many rooms, all of which are very spacious and yet the house was built in 1811 as only temporary accommodation for its owner who was having a mansion built nearby.

Accompanied by my book and newspaper, I took my dinner of lamb cutlets, mushrooms, tomatoes and chips (with plenty of English mustard) at a nice old pub called the Sun. Afterwards, I walked behind St Mary's Church to see the River Lune view that Turner has painted and John Ruskin described as one of the finest in the country. The river makes a horseshoe bend here encircling a cow studded emerald pasture. A stonewall border and distant mountains complete the scene. It must have been much the same when Ruskin was here.

Next morning, I returned to St. Mary's to see the interior of the church. It is very simple without much decoration. Some ladies were busy installing new seat cushions. A group of touring school children came in to be greeted by a lovely older woman who very warmly and capably told them about the building, its current Norman architecture and its Saxon past. I am sure it was as obvious to the children as it was to me that she loved the church and telling people about it.

On the road out of Kirkby Lonsdale, I passed Devil's Bridge, one of the most popular tourist spots here, already besieged by coach tourists stopped for their early morning buns and mugs of tea. The bridge is thought to be thirteenth century. A huge pool beneath the bridge is full of salmon and a favourite spot for aqualung divers. There is a lovely walk from the bridge along a footpath following the river Lune for about a kilometre leading to stone steps up to St. Mary's.

The cycling quickly became superb. The road was narrow with little traffic; the air was crisp, bright with sunshine and redolent with country smells. Sun shining on scudding clouds created moving mosaics of various greens on the distant hills. I was headed towards Dentdale.

Farmer Sedgewick and the Japanese Cyclist

Dent, a partly cobblestone streeted small village, was larger than I expected. There was a stone block monument to Alan Sedgewick, an early 19th century geologist and MP, and some historical information about Dent knitters. Some of these knitters worked so fast that they reportedly had to stop from time to time to cool their red-hot needles. A huge brewer's dray was delivering to a pub and blocking the entire narrow street. Dent 's railway station, on the Carlisle to Settle line, is the highest in the country.

Continuing past Dent on to the intersection at Stone House, I got disoriented temporarily and went the wrong way. I stopped to ask directions of an alert, old farmer standing by a stonewall along the road. He was keeping a close eye on his nephew cutting hay while driving a tractor. The farmer told me that he was 77 and his family (the Sedgewicks) had lived in this area for about 1000 years but recently when some relations sold out to the rest of the family there was no evidence of ownership. Nevertheless, he observed bitterly, the local council continued to charge him property rates. He broke off our conversation abruptly after a few minutes saying it was his turn to drive the tractor.

Following farmer Sedgewick's directions, I was soon headed south on the B6255. The road ran downhill amidst broad, magnificent vistas. My speed, at times exceeding 50 km per hour, made a lovely breeze that completed paradise. Soon, a huge railway bridge came into view with multiple, elegant arches. Somewhere, I read that it took six years to build. This was on the B6479 near Horton in Ribblesdale.

It was clearly a very popular spot for communing with nature as there were several cars parked on the verge. Some of their owners were off hiking; others were simply watching the hills from their cars or on folding chairs outside.

As it was still quite early in the afternoon and my hostel at Stainforth was very close, I chose to have a look at nearby Settle before going to the hostel. Along the way, I met a cyclist who had started the End-to-End last year but had to terminate due to bad weather. He was now in training for the second part aiming for over 100 km today. Today's objective was only half completed and he was already very tired. Having just travelled his route, I knew that the balance of his day's training was up the hills I had just coasted down at high speed.

After a look round Settle, I 'settled' on a park bench at the edge of town to read a newspaper and soon nodded off. The sunshine and exercise combined to induce a delicious marginally awake state in which both the warmth and refreshing breeze could still be enjoyed. Although on this occasion, I did not get much of the paper read, careful reading of the *Times* or *Telegraph* on a fairly regular basis is now an important element of these tours. Both papers are well written and offer interesting and useful information about British issues that provide understanding and conversational fodder as well insight into the British perspective on North American events.

Stainforth boasts a fine arched packhorse bridge over the River Ribble, dating from the 17th century, when it lay on the main route from Ripon to Lancaster. In the autumn, the nearby Stainforth Force is a favourite spot for watching salmon leap on their way upstream. (2)

The Stainforth hostel had been an old estate and was sadly in need of repairs. A disdainful ginger cat graced its entrance but did not deign to be introduced. A large party of school children was in residence creating considerable noise and motion. I got into conversation with one of their supervisors and told her that I had promised Mari I would stop in at the famous Betty's tearoom in York where we had a lovely, but very dear, afternoon tea in 1992. Betty's had been the location of this woman's wedding reception some 37 years ago. She retired last year and took a tour of the Canadian Rockies and the Alaska Passage. Connections like this may be tenuous but they create a sense of community and add interest.

After dinner, I retired to the member's kitchen, about the only place where one could read or write in reasonable quiet. A Japanese guest, seated at another table, was working assiduously on a laptop computer. We exchanged friendly nods but no conversation. However, next morning I chose to sit with him at breakfast and learned that he was a cyclist working on his fourth year of an around the world trip that he started in Alaska. Later, he showed me his cycle, an eighteen-kilogram monster with specially made luggage racks front and back and a four-litre sized water bottle.

He carried the camera stereotypical of Japanese tourists and was also equipped with a tripod. He used his laptop to record the location and date of each picture taken (8500 at this point!) as well as for writing articles that he sends back to a hometown newspaper. Daily route, distance and averages are all carefully recorded and graphed. He plans on spending another two years at this and told me that he had already done a several week diversion in Europe so that his arrival in Africa would avoid some bad seasonal weather. He is anything but a stereotype—Japanese or otherwise.

It is amazing how things and events seem to travel together. Now, after several days seeing hardly any cyclists, they seem to be round every corner. In Hawes, later in the day, I met a couple in their late 50's, a little overweight and not in top condition but they had been on tour for a fortnight already. Shortly afterwards, I met two young men doing a training run for a ten week cycle tour from Istanbul to Amsterdam.

More Dales and the Grange

Today's journey took me back to Settle and then along the Kendal road as far as Ingleton and north to Hawes. This route again passed the impressive railway bridge outside Horton. I stopped for lunch at the nearby Station Inn. It was terrible but the only choice. I ate outside despite the heat to avoid the loud noise inside purporting to be music. The fork was filthy and had to be replaced. Some aspects of British life are so contrary to my admittedly dated and somewhat blinkered love-in that it is sometimes hard to believe that the crudities can co-exist with the refined loveliness in the same country. They do or I would not still want to cycle here. Perhaps it is a case of intermittent reinforcement being stronger than continuous.

The first half of the remaining ride to Hawes after lunch was a hard slog but the effort was rewarded by a good run down into the village. Hawes is an attractive place with stone buildings, a small waterfall and a generally higgledy-piggledy nature. It attracts many hikers during the summer as well as tourists doing the James Herriott tour.

In 1992, Mari and I enjoyed a stay at Hawes in the Herriott hotel. We visited the Force (waterfall) outside the town (accessible only by walking through the back of a pub and paying a 50 pence charge) and cycled (with long periods on foot) the steep access road near the Butter Tubs. We fell in love with an elegant pair of antique blue and white Fenton vases and justified their purchase as our 30th wedding anniversary present to ourselves. They continue to grace the mantle piece of our lounge.

After arranging a B&B at Asygarth through the Hawes Tourist Information office, I visited the Dales Country Museum that offers a chronology of the major changes in people and their way of life in the Dales. I also stopped in at a rope maker's shop and returned to the antique shop, resisting a pair of gorgeous green, sterling silver encrusted scent bottles.

Despite all this 'delay', I reached Asygarth by 5.30, again too early to stop. I carried on to the falls to produce a respectable total distance for the day and, without knowing it, cycled right past my B&B host outside in his garden. Later he told me that he thought it might be me and that I was lost!

When I returned, the Jones received me very graciously. They had made arrangements to store my cycle across the road in a farmer's shed. The farmer was an elderly gent with one long white whisker protruding from his chin. When I walked the bike over, he was gilting the top of an iron fence set in stone round his garden.

Later, over tea with Mr and Mrs Jones, we discussed her professed ability to tell nationality by a guest's choice of beverage and talked about a Torontonian that spends a week with them every year to walk the Dales. The day concluded pleasantly with an expensive dinner of Tikka Marsala followed by gooseberry tart and ice cream at the George and Dragon. James, the publican, was a car buff and answered my question about the Montego, an attractive British Leyland product that seemed to have disappeared. It had. Now the company itself is history.

Next morning, I went back to explore the Asygarth falls. There are three of them with only the upper being visible from the road. These are broad, limestone over shale, stepped falls, not sheer drops that North Americans tend to associate with the term. Access to the other two falls was via a woodland walk graced at the time with a scampering squirrel (the first I had seen on this trip) and several strutting grouse. A collection of scum at the base of the lower falls reminded one of man's effect on the environment, spoiling the picture.

The woodland walk opened on to a pleasant open country footpath that I explored until reaching a stile that I could not lift the cycle over. So, I retreated and went another way, going through Caperby and past the Wheatsheaf Inn where the Herriotts spent their honeymoon in 1941. Caperby was a very natural village with animal enclosures mingled between the houses. It would only require removing the cars and a few road signs to create an 18th century scene.

I temporarily abandoned my aversion to tourist spots to climb a steep hill to the ruins of Castle Bolton. No tour was provided but there were a few run down exhibits and a nasty hole in the ground that had been the dungeon. This was fitted out with recorded, appropriate sounds of inmates being tortured.

I returned to the Wheatsheaf for a cheese and pickle sandwich with a lager and then went back to Asygarth and on a back road to Kettlewell. The farms fronted the narrow twisty lanes maintaining the sense of distant past that Caperby had. From Kettlewell it was a clear gentle slope down towards Skipton. The scenery was great and I managed a pleasant stop for afternoon tea outside in a comfortable armchair in the village of Threshfield. Although the market day traffic was heavy, I still made Skipton by 5.

My B&B's address was Eshton Grange, Gargreave, Skipton. Although this methodology of ordering an address from the most particular to the least particular is also used in North America, I think Skipton would have been left off the address in North America. If it had, I might have gone directly to Gargreave rather than via Skipton. At Gargreave, some six uphill kms away from Skipton along the main highway, it took three tries to get definitive directions to Eshton Grange. These directions required retracing my route back to a village of Eshton where I found Eshton House, Eshton Hall, Eshton Lodge and finally the Grange. From my point of view, the address should have read The Grange, Eshton, Yorkshire---Gargreave and Skipton simply gave a better idea of approximately where Eshton was.

Despite these complaints, the Grange was worth the effort; a large farm with lovely views and a big open area in front that made a square between the barn and house. My room overlooked the garden and was well fitted out. There was a private bath across the hall with all gold plated fixtures. My host then advised me that I would need to go back into Gargreave to be able to get an evening meal. Many country pubs and restaurants stop serving by 7 or 7.30 on a weekday, so I had a quick wash and rode about three km back to the Woods Bistro.

This was a popular and pleasant but mediocre spot that was largely taken over tonight by a big, noisy cricket club party. My Penne Carbonerra and two lagers were topped off with a sundae with "cinder" toffee and maple syrup!

Then it was back up the hill on the bike to the Grange and their dogs who were eager for attention. The sun, low in the sky, cast serene shadows that changed shape and colour as the clouds scudded by. I stood at the pasture fence for several minutes, soaking up the serenity and fresh air before returning to my room.

Next day was overcast despite a bright forecast. My hostess, Mrs Shelmerdine, said 'Not to worry! I have made representations to the authorities for better weather.' She was not heard! My breakfast companions had come in late from London taking seven and a half hours to do 350 km because the traffic was so heavy. They were to spend the weekend at Appleby for a jazz festival and suggested that the terrible litter I encountered during the horse fair could be due to a bomb scare. This could be a possibility as there certainly was a dearth of litterbins. Those that you do see are heavy cast metal with very small cut outs to push the rubbish through. Today, we would almost automatically associate a bomb scare or alert with Muslim terrorists. Then, our automatic reaction was to blame the IRA.

During the day I met a Glaswegian cyclist who had come to York for the cycle festival and was headed home. He had lived for sixteen years in New Zealand building logging roads. Since returning, he was doing a seven and a half month cycle trip round the country. Shortly after talking with him, I was waved down by a very cheerful cycling postie who wanted to chat. He and his wife were off to Shropshire the next day for a week's cycle tour. They put the bikes in the postal van and use hostels in a circular tour. Just about the same time a group of cyclists on top class racing cycles and clad in the latest of colourful gear passed by on a Saturday run. An elderly full white-bearded gentleman riding a three-wheeler completed this sudden concentration of cyclist variety. He gave me a nod, one of those particularly British nods where the chin flips out to the left. I have tried to respond in kind but cannot duplicate this motion; I automatically dip my head in greeting. This cluster of encounters made a cheerful start to the day—other people are just as crazy as I am!

I carried on through nice country and pleasant villages to

Grassington, a popular spot bulging with Saturday shoppers and tourists in the cobble-stoned village centre. A large group of leather-clad, mature motorcyclists was milling about acquiring and consuming refreshment while a woman attracted considerable attention due to her totally transparent skirt and knickers!

I bought some Eccles cakes and a blackcurrant drink and enjoyed them while vicariously participating in the bustling activity from an outside bench on the square.

My Fair Lady

The next stop was to be Pateley Bridge. Its name summoned up comforting images of downhill or at least flat river valleys. Initially anyway, the reality was somewhat different. A strong, constant north wind, accompanied by sheets of mist, swept across the road striking my panniers and me full strength. The temperature had dropped considerably. It took all my strength coupled with a severe lean towards the verge to avoid being blown right into any following traffic. This was a scary but exhilarating challenge ----pitting one's strength against the elements in a setting of broad, desolate moors.

At Pateley Bridge, the Tourist Information Office again came to the rescue, arranging a B&B for me in Harrowgate about 18 km away. They also told me that there was a live performance of My Fair Lady in Harrowgate tonight. Theatre is one of my interests so I decided to try to see it. My new landlady, Mrs. Bell, advised the TIC that she had to go out this evening, so could I please arrive by seven. This left me time for lunch and a quick look round this pleasant old town on the River Nidd.

I left about three and after climbing back up out of the river valley had a downhill run to Harrowgate. I immediately went to the theatre and was able to get a seat for tonight. Later, at the B&B, Mrs. Bell told me that her engagement for this evening was, most appropriately, bell-ringing practice. During conversation over a pot of tea, we learned that she and her entire family had been on Hardknott Pass last Sunday near the spot where the Mini crashed at the same time I was!

The theatre was a bit of luxury, the cost of which had to be partially compensated for by eating at McDonalds. One can question the nutritional value of McDonalds but if you are hungry, they provide the lowest cost. The theatre was a marvellous Victorian, lavishly gilded and boasting colourful boxes and balconies. The cast was amateur but several were quite talented and obviously were enjoying themselves.

I had forgotten how good the music is. Compared to modern musicals that are largely group shouts with perhaps one memorable song, all of My Fair Lady's songs linger pleasantly long after the show is over. I was reminded of a youthful infatuation with Inga, an exotic girl of mixed ethnic origin. Too shy to make a direct approach, I used to cycle by Inga's house, hoping that she would be on the front porch, while singing *On the Street where you Live* under my breath. Needless to say, this strategy was totally unsuccessful.

The next day was bleak and cold so I chose to remain inside by doing laundry. The laundrette was close by—run by a woman who provided change, made the awkward machines work, and looked after your laundry, including ironing if you wished. I stayed put and did my own and after returning it to the B&B, set off on a listless walk round most of the streets and to the 'Stray'. This is a huge sports ground past the first well (1527) in Harrowgate and along the Queen's Parade.

Being Sunday, most places were closed but I did find an open appliance shop. I have no secret passion for appliances but, like the laundrette, the shop offered a temporary warm and dry refuge. Inside, I discovered that while the fridges, washers, tumble dryers, and cookers were narrower than a typical North American equivalent, the British prices were equal or higher. I always enjoy learning the mundane details of British life, regardless of what they are because it helps me better understand them, behave accordingly and appear less of a foreigner. However, I must admit that an appropriate application for this bit of knowledge has yet to appear!

Cold and having exhausted everything of potential interest, I returned to my B&B and read until my scheduled call to Mari at three. I was blue and it must have been apparent but the call did not help. Problems with the neighbour boy hired to do the lawn in my absence, having to alert the police about a wild teenage party at the same neighbour's house and enduring the neighbour father's resulting wrath, did not amuse her or raise my spirits.

By the time we finished, the weather had brightened a bit so I went out on the bike having decided it was now or never. My plan was to do about 30 km but the chosen southbound road (B6162/1) ran so well that I carried on to a pleasant spot at a wide section on the Wharfe River where people were enjoying paddleboats and walking along a river path. I bought a chocolate bar and took my book down to a bench by the river. It was about 5 pm but all of a sudden the clouds dissipated and the sun appeared in a bright blue sky, so I extended my rest for half an hour.

The return journey was on an unmarked north road that took me quite a bit west of Harrowgate to a place called Blubberhouses on the A59. It was uphill most of the way but pretty country and the day was so much improved from earlier that I really did not mind being lost. My 30 km became 48 km by the time I reached Betty's in the town centre at 7 pm. There, I nearly fulfilled my promise to Mari, by buying two of their remaining three sandwiches and a muesli square for my dinner.

These were consumed with great pleasure in my room along with three cups of tea. I finished in time to go down to the lounge to watch the news and see the third of a five-part television drama I have been following called Oliver's Travels. Alan Bates is the main character. It combined a murder mystery with a sort of travelogue. Clues were provided by the daily newspaper crossword, a concept now used very successfully by two US crime writers under the name of Nero Blanc. Despite the drama's unlikely plot, I enjoyed the intelligent dialogue and interesting scenery. Tonight's episode had some good views of Hadrian's Wall and Lindisfarne (Holy Island on the English northeast coast).

Bill Bryson and York

Next morning I went to have a look at Harrowgate's Georgian houses that were my main reason for stopping here. While engaged in this, the weather changed to glorious sunshine, I found an interesting section of town not previously explored and an intriguing bookshop. There I discovered a travel book about the US by Bill Bryson, an American who was then living in North Yorkshire. This proved to be hilarious and very sympathetic to my views about the US. Since then, I have read all but two of Bryson's many travel books as well as his books about the English language. He is a very capable and humorous writer but occasionally litters his text with unnecessary gutter words that mar otherwise excellent works. His vast vocabulary surely has some alternatives!

A few years ago, Bryson returned to the US and wrote at least four more books. In 2004, he moved back to Britain where he is working with the English Heritage Society. I feel him to be a kindred spirit in many ways—a North American that loves Britain for many of the same reasons as I do and has a strong interest in the English language. The main difference is his ability to use it!

My next stop was to be York, England's second most popular city for tourists. I prefer it to London because of its more human scale, and because it has less traffic and noise. York is the former Roman city of Eboracvm that was the capital of the Roman province of Lower Britain. During the later occupation of this part of England by the Danes the city became Jorvik, from which the present name derives. In turn, the Normans sacked the Danish town, establishing their own stronghold. Clifford's Tower is the sole remnant of the Normans' 11th-century castle, but the medieval city walls remain largely intact. The maze of lanes and alleys that formed the medieval street pattern also survives. The great minster (cathedral) was built over the space of two-and-a-half centuries, from 1220 to 1470. York has a strong cycling tradition, with one of the largest everyday cycle usages in Britain and an extensive cycle route network. (3)

For nostalgic reasons, I chose an indirect route, in hopes of revisiting a section of road that Mari and I had travelled in 1992. We were cycling from Beningbrough along a country road on the way to our B&B when suddenly we became depositories for bits of manure-encrusted straw blowing off a farm wagon in front of us. At the time, it was not at all pleasant but later we took considerable perverse pleasure in relating the story to certain friends and neighbours whose idea of travel requires four-star hotels and exercise is limited to golf and bending their elbows.

I wasn't successful in finding this area. I was working from memory (becoming increasingly faulty) and made a number of false starts, changes of direction and finally ran out of road at a river and gave up. My journey could have been a direct 45 km but turned out to be 75 km!

The hostel is located centrally in a section of York known as Clifton. The notice board had an advertisement for "Travels with My Aunt' currently playing at the Theatre Royal. Tonight would be my only opportunity for live theatre in York so I immediately went into the city to see if any tickets were available.

Not only were tickets available for tonight but also it was bargain night. Professional theatre for only £6.50 is amazing value. But, of course, this is twice in less than a week. The budget is under strain so I told myself that since I had not stopped for afternoon tea, I could call in at the nearby Reed's teahouse for a late snack that could double as dinner.

The gorgeous weather required something summery and cool so I had a fruit crumble pastry with ice cream. Cycling back to the hostel along the Clifton Road amidst gracious homes and pleasant looking small hotels, I realised that the distance could easily be walked in twenty-five minutes so I decided to return to the theatre on foot.

The hostel had somewhat of a resort atmosphere with outside tables and umbrellas. My semi-private room had its own washbasin and only three other guests. All the beds were already made up but the room was empty so I was able to clean up quickly without interruption.

My hunger overpowered budget rule and encouraged me to get back to Reed's teahouse in time to take advantage of their pre-theatre special of haddock, garlic mushrooms, and apple pie with ice cream.

My theatre seat, on the very first row, provided an excellent view of this most unusual play. Three actors played at least six characters. The scenery and props were minimalist, consisting of just three straight white chairs and a table. One man would be a taxi driver one minute, the nephew the next and then the Aunt all without any change in costume. It was very well done and amazingly did not confuse because the voices were so distinct. Nevertheless, the combination of the day's sun together with the comfort and darkness of the theatre had me nodding off from time to time.

I walked back to the hostel and although it was only about 11 and the hostel was supposed to be open 24 hours, it was necessary to ring the buzzer and wait for several minutes to get my room key. As I entered the room, I was immediately conscious of an almost overwhelming odour of body sweat. The other three guests were nearly ready for bed. There was no greeting or acknowledgement of my presence at all.

The odour lingered in the air until I fell asleep but wasn't noticeable in the morning. Perhaps my olfactory senses had been totally numbed overnight. A night's sleep did not improve the level or extent of the conversation. One managed to say 'Good Morning' but that was it. The explanation may have been that they were Polish and not particularly capable in English.

The Shambles

Today's plan called for strolling round York's famous Shambles, and fulfilling a couple of commissions for Mari in the morning and then to go to Scarborough by train. Mari's first commission was to find a replacement for a back brace that we had bought in York in 1992 when she was suffering from back pain. I had no clear recollection of the shop's name or location and nothing in the medical supplies section of the telephone directory sounded right. So, I rang one of them and was referred to the 'Able Living Centre' in Walmgate. Walmgate was familiar and very near to Fossgate, home of the Cockatoo Creperie, our favourite restaurant. We ate here twice in 1992 and doing so again this trip was on my 'must' list. It would not have been possible last night as they close on Monday evenings.

Although close, the 'Able Living Centre' was concealed away in a courtyard off Walmgate, making it difficult to find. Having acquired the brace, I went off to the Shambles in search of a V-neck Aran pullover for Mari. Arans are stocked by dozens of shops in the Shambles but not one of them carried the desired style. Oh well, it was one less thing to have to carry.

I should explain about the Shambles. It is a cobble-stoned, multi-laned pedestrian mall of historic timber frame buildings sharing common walls or leaning on each other. Today, these buildings primarily house tourist oriented shops and restaurants. In earlier times, butchers largely inhabited the site and today's name comes from 'shamel', the Old English word for slaughterhouse.

This area is contiguous with a broader, but still cobble-stoned pedestrian area populated with larger, more general interest shops, the famous Betty's teashop and restaurant and outside benches. In summer, buskers, Punch and Judy shows, mime artists and jugglers create a lively holiday atmosphere. Today, a group of violins and bass were performing those international stalwarts of the busker repertoire, *Eine Kleine Nacht Musik* and Pachobel's *Canon* to extract funds from the tourists.

Nearby is the popular and impressive York Minster. Inside, as described by the Automobile Association guide, is a 'kaleidoscope of light (that) explodes from windows of medieval stained glass that are among the art treasures of the world.'

Also within easy walking distance is the Castle Museum where cobbled streets and reconstructed shop fronts represent periods from Tudor to Edwardian times. And there is a not to be missed virtual exhibit of the life of the Danes that settled here at the Jorvik Centre near Coppergate.

Scarborough and the North

My knowledge of Scarborough was limited to the Beatles song "Scarborough Fair" that conjured up visions of warm sunshine and light-hearted activity. Reality, when I arrived, was somewhat different. A cold North Sea breeze struck me immediately as I emerged from the railway station. My cycling jacket was inadequate protection but I was determined to see something of the town.

The sea front was reverberating to the sounds of some ten visiting Scandinavian, mainly Norwegian, bands, some in native costumes. Despite being hopelessly unmusical, even I could tell that they were not very good musically or in marching precision. Perhaps they should be forgiven; it was bitterly cold.

The front was a typically British, somewhat seedy seaside. Amusement arcades, fish and chip shops, donkey rides on the beach, fresh mussels and people sunbathing behind wind blinds. I walked up and down the front pushing the cycle while absorbing the atmosphere but within an hour headed off to find the hostel and hopefully some warmth.

The hostel proved to be about six kilometres north of the city on a dirt track off the main road. At the top of the track, I was greeted by a group of Pakistani youth asking directions to the hostel. They turned out to be part of a school group from Peterborough on a biology field trip. During the day, these students collected things from the seashore, woods and river and made observations. After dinner, they worked until late plotting their findings and making drawings and notes.

I had some conversation with a number of their teachers. One of these was a student teacher that had just been offered a position in a private school in Portland, Oregon. Her boy friend was doing postgraduate work in medicine in Portland. At breakfast, she spread her toast with Marmite and happily told me that it was available in Portland.

The males in the school party were also my roommates. One of the male teachers advised me not to be concerned if there was a little noise early in the morning as the boys were Muslim and would be getting up at four to pray. I slept right through their devotions. Today, given all our concerns with terrorists and the hatred of 'infidels' held by some fundamental Muslims, I might well have stayed awake and 'on guard' all night.

Next morning, I took a short walk along the river because one of the teachers had seen herons catching the jumping fish the day before—I wasn't so fortunate.

Streetscape, Robin Hood's Bay, Yorkshire

The new day was warm, making the North Sea breeze welcome instead of the curse it had been yesterday. I headed north along the main A road towards Whitby. The hills were manageable and so by eleven, I reached Robin Hood's Bay and enjoyed an exhilarating downhill run to the coast from the main road. I suppressed the knowledge that it would be uphill on the way back and set about to explore this narrow-streeted, cliff-hanging coastal village. Robin Hood's Bay is larger but very reminiscent of Clovelly on the Devon coast and has a number of hotels and shops. Cliff walking appeared to be the principal activity for most tourists with nearby Whitby and Scarborough as diversions.

I had a nice tea in a little shop with oak beams and mullioned windows. The proprietress was a graduate baker, whose shop walls were covered with qualification certificates going back some forty years, including one from Hovis.

Some nine kilometres of uphill later, I arrived at the crest of a hill that provided a panoramic view of the river flowing down to the sea and the Whitby harbour. The tide was out, marooning boats in the mud, creating a dishevelled and dissolute appearance.

The Whitby front was much the same as in Scarborough but with a fishier ambience and more people today as the sunshine made everything so much more pleasant. There was a gypsy fortuneteller that claimed to be known round the world. The number of people in wheelchairs or otherwise disabled struck me. Does the seaside attract them, does Britain have a larger proportion of such disadvantaged people than North America or do they just get out more?

Regretfully now, I recall that I did not stay to enjoy the other aspects of Whitby---the old Abbey, the 199 Church steps up to St. Mary's or Captain Cook's house in Grape Lane. Instead, I carried on to Sandsend, a village further up the coast with a lovely bay, and then moved westward across the top of the empty North York moor with its patchy, dark landscape. A mist blowing across the road completed the Heathcliff nature of the scene. These conditions persisted for perhaps two hours but the cycling was fast chewing up the distance.

The ICI Connection

I was headed for Ingleby Greenhow where memory told me my B&B for tonight was located. I had forgotten that the B&B in Ingleby Greenhow could not take me and had arranged a B&B for me elsewhere. There must have been some niggling doubt in my mind that caused me to stop, look at my plan and discover that the new arrangements were in a different village altogether!

The British penchant for naming their houses and using that name as an address, sometimes, in small villages, without further definition, complicated my search for the replacement B&B. I would never have found the house without the help of a friendly butcher. On arrival, no one seemed to be home but finally I noticed a small flat board lying on the door step with 'go round back' written on it. At the back, the doors were wide open and in the garden was a small table with the tea things laid out! I did not feel comfortable enough to actually go in the house and stood around looking untidy when Len, my host, appeared round a shed corner.

Len was a kindly, white-haired 75 year-old. He showed me to my room and generally got me oriented, and then produced a pot of tea with delicious buttered scones to be enjoyed in the garden. It was idyllic. The sun was still warm and my chair faced a low hedge beyond which was a vista of rich green pasture dotted with plump Jerseys and bordered by the Cleveland Hills. Shortly, a Scottish guest named Dave arrived and joined me.

Dave was retiring from Imperial Chemical Industries (ICI) the next day. This provided a common interest as ICI's headquarters are in Welwyn Garden City, Hertfordshire where Mari and I lived for nearly six years. We agreed to go to dinner together and were joined there by Richard, another ICI man who knew one of our friends in Welwyn Garden City. After dinner, Richard and Dave still had a lot of ground to cover but I had spent my budget for dinner so could not afford the extra pints they contemplated. So I returned to the B&B.

There I met Len's wife, Margaret, for the first time. Margaret was a very pleasant and friendly woman whose daughter had run the New York Marathon three times for charity, once in stocking feet it was so hot! The daughter now looks after Mick Jagger's children on weekends including this weekend when Mick would be in Paris. The evening concluded with more tea and shortbread.

The next day's agenda was unplanned except that I was due to reach nearby Thwaites House by teatime. This is the residence of more ICI friends of ours from Welwyn Garden City days. As is often the case, we met through the children. Theirs and ours went to the same nursery school. Gillian was a liberated woman with strong attitudes about politics, men and women's roles. Mari was fascinated, never having met a woman like that before.

We maintained contact with them on a sporadic basis after Mari and I left England and spent a weekend with them in the late 70's while they were temporarily based in the US. Other postings took them to

Brazil and Pakistan but John was now based at ICI's Middlesborough operation, a convenient commute from Thwaites House.

Consequently, I had a large part of the day to explore the area without time pressure. The only necessity was to cash some traveller's cheques and there were two banks in nearby Stokesley. I chose the Midland Bank (now part of the Hong Kong and Shanghai group or HSBC) because they issue my particular brand of cheques and did not charge to negotiate them. Next stop was a well-stocked cycle shop that carried both Treks and Cannondales. I always enjoy looking round cycle shops just to see what is new but rarely buy anything.

Stokesley was a very pleasant and bustling market town with a village green ringed by mainly Georgian houses. The Leven River running behind the High Street was populated with lots of ducks including three brand new ones. The little ones were already preening themselves as if they had been doing it for years

Next, I rode over to see Great Ayton, where other ICI connected friends from Welwyn Garden City had lived for a while. They had mentioned a place famous for an ice cream brand called Sugget. It was certainly popular with cyclists. There were at least eight of them there when I arrived. The ice cream came in one flavour—vanilla, and was good but not really special. Captain Cook's 1736 schoolhouse was next door to Suggets. This wasn't open yet for visitors and his actual boyhood home had been transported to Melbourne for display there.

Mari is much more curious than I am, always wanting to see round the bend or over the crest of the next hill. I most always choose to get from A to B by the route I already know and not to take a road unless I know where it is going. Today, she would have been proud (and surprised). I set out on a road without having any idea of where it went!

The terrain was gently rolling, attractively pastoral and perfect for cycling, as the traffic was minimal to non-existent. Shortly after noon, another cyclist overtook me and rode alongside. He was an anaesthesiologist on his lunch break from Musselborough specialist hospital. Without a schedule to restrict me, I just carried on with him. After about twenty minutes at a good pace, he announced that he would stop for a pint at Hutton Rudby. I joined him and we sat outside, discussing the dramatic changes he has witnessed in the National Health Service. He said that the paper work had increased tremendously and that rationing of health services was now policy. As an example, he told of a young woman who was denied an expensive operation because the chances of success were so small. This caused a great national outcry causing some rich person to buy the operation for her at a private hospital. My companion had to return to work then and I never learned whether the young woman survived.

I stayed on for lunch and another lager. As I was finishing, another chap approached me and carried on a monologue about his cycle holiday in France last year going from St. Malo to the Loire. 'Did it to get away from the Brits'. It was an interesting conversation despite his self-centred, patronising, old school manner.

Now it was time to make a move towards Thwaites House. I went to Carlton in Cleveland, a small picturesque old village and my friends' official address, via Stokesley. No one seemed to have heard of the house. The small shop that also served as the post office had the electoral rolls but my friends were not on it. The postmistress said it must be over the hill, just beyond the Lord Stones café. Three people had now mentioned this café, as it is unique. Planning permission required agreeing to build the cafe into the side of a hill so as not to spoil the natural views. Its name comes from three stones of a nearby ancient monument.

The hill was as steep and long as the Hardknott Pass but largely straight. It was a warm day and the climb was monotonously slow. I kept track of the distance and elapsed time as a mental exercise on the way and calculated that the one in four grade meant a 200-metre vertical climb. Lord Stones was at the crest. Sweating like the proverbial pig despite a short-sleeved shirt, I took advantage of the café's washroom to cool off and clean up. Then, not knowing how much further there was to go, I treated myself to a rhubarb crumble with ice cream.

Two hundred horizontal metres further on, a big gate across a dirt lane and footpath, sported the sign Thwaites House. At first, the gate would not open and I was afraid that something was wrong. There was –my mechanical ability. Eventually, the gate was persuaded to open, leading to yet another gate about one hundred metres on. Finally, the house appeared; it is old smooth grey stucco, sitting at the very edge of the lane. On the other side, the sharply sloping rocky ground was dotted with sheep and cattle and framed by the Cleveland Hills behind.

A beer in the garden helped get us re-acquainted after some eighteen years, Then John and I walked a bit of the Cleveland Way that runs very close to their property. We spent the evening bringing each other up to date on our now adult children and enjoying an excellent late dinner of quiche, fresh cauliflower with cheese sauce, superb tomatoes and new potatoes from their garden, finishing off with a summer pudding that was heaven.

Gillian and John were off to Wimbledon to see the tennis next morning. This was a several hour journey, involving a train to London. An early departure was necessary and I overslept! This left no time for shaving or other early morning functions before breakfast. Despite their timetable, John expertly prepared strawberries and yoghurt, orange juice, bacon, eggs and mushrooms. Would that I was as competent in the kitchen.

They obviously needed to get away right after breakfast. I had hoped to take care of my morning functions in leisure after they left but they clearly wanted to lock up before leaving. I took this to reflect their frequent experience with burglaries rather than an indication that I could not be trusted in the house with their daughter sleeping upstairs. So I gathered up my things quickly, forgoing a shave and another pressingly urgent activity.

This would be my earliest start of the entire trip. At 7.30, we had said our goodbyes and I was back at the Lord Stones café, hoping to use their toilet. As I should have known, the café was closed. I could only hope that some facility would be open in Chopgate, 5 km away.

The morning was cool with bright sunshine and apart from me, only rabbits on the road—they were everywhere. It was a marvellous morning that has stayed in my memory as about the best experience of this tour or any tour. Magnificent scenery, a nice downhill slope, warm sunshine and crisp air combined to make it 'perfick'.

The road ran down to the main Stokesley/Helmsley road at Chopgate. At the front edge of the village, my eye just caught a car park and toilets sign behind me so I doubled back and was grateful to find all the facilities needed. Twenty minutes later, I emerged, a new man-- freshly shaven and with empty bowels. The air was still cool and the warm sunshine gave a feeling reminiscent of camping on a similar morning—that special sort of cleanliness and contented peace one feels washing up outdoors.

Heading Home

Helmsley was little more than an hour away, a perfect distance for a morning teatime stop. The road and scenery continued to be super until a big hill about 8 km out of Helmsley that forced me to walk. This was followed by a downhill and a noticeably gentler landscape. Helmsley is a prosperous town on the main tourist routes because of the Abbey and gardens at Riveaux. Today was market day and the square was filled with a wide variety of stalls selling fruits, vegetables and other foodstuffs.

The square was surrounded on two sides with more permanent establishments including The Police Station, a café where I chose to have my tea and teacakes. This ever-pleasant activity took me until 10.30 when I went across to see the All Saints Church. The church offered a blissful cool escape from the now boiling temperature outside. It was interesting in its own right as well with its ceiling, half in painted wood, the other half in arched stone. A list of all the vicars going back to 1127 adorned one wall!

My plan called for me to return to York. Given York's importance, the choice of routes from Helmsley was extensive. I kept to the B roads and chose to pass through Sutton on Forest where, in 1992, a Shetland pony tried to remove Mari's ankle, getting in a good nip! The pony was otherwise occupied when I arrived at 12.30 so I called in at the Rose and Crown, an upscale pub that provided free bar snacks of nuts and pickled onions. The white linen cloth on the tables was further evidence of this pub's social standing and suggested my appearance might make me unwelcome. Nevertheless, I ordered the only selection on the menu that the budget would allow, a tuna fish and cucumber sandwich with a lager. This arrived garnished with a salad and pickled onions and was definitely a cut above typical pub food. I behaved myself and was not asked to leave for improper attire.

Back in York and before heading off to the hostel, I stopped in at the Assembly Rooms. This is a grand open place with huge marble columns supporting a ceiling perhaps 30 feet high. Massive paintings, many of the Minster, graced the perimeter. An elegant afternoon tea being served in the centre completed the 1920's Palm Court atmosphere. This would be a grand spot for a special anniversary occasion.

A shock was waiting at the hostel, my reservation had been mistakenly cancelled and the hostel was full. There was a lot of ineffectual dithering around trying to determine how the cancellation had happened but I did get a refund and they very kindly made a booking for me at a nearby B&B. Staying in York was crucial to my plan to conclude my tour with a fine dinner at the Cockatoo Creperie.

After cleaning up in greater privacy and comfort than the hostel would have provided, I walked to the restaurant in Fossgate. It was a warm evening but the restaurant's windows were open and the temperature cooled quickly as the sunset or perhaps it was the two gin and tonics that I treated myself with.

The proprietor was new having taken over shortly after our visit in 1992. Andre, the former proprietor, had gone to Paris but became disillusioned and was now working for the Hilton Chain in Egypt. Fortunately, Andre's brother Robert was still chef and most of the menu was unchanged. I had a prawn and buckwheat crepe with salad and a cognac flavoured pie that was heaven. It was a great meal that fully lived up to my expectations. I left telling the owner to stay put for another three years, as I would be back! (As it turned out, it took four years and management had changed again, so had the name. Now it is the Blue Bicycle and the prices are out of my reach).

The next day was largely consumed with the train journey back to Manchester for the flight home. I spent the night at a B&B close by the airport and got a lift there in the morning from my landlady. Thus ended the Peaks, Lakes and Dales tour.

Panniers, Pedals, and Pubs

CIRCLE TOUR

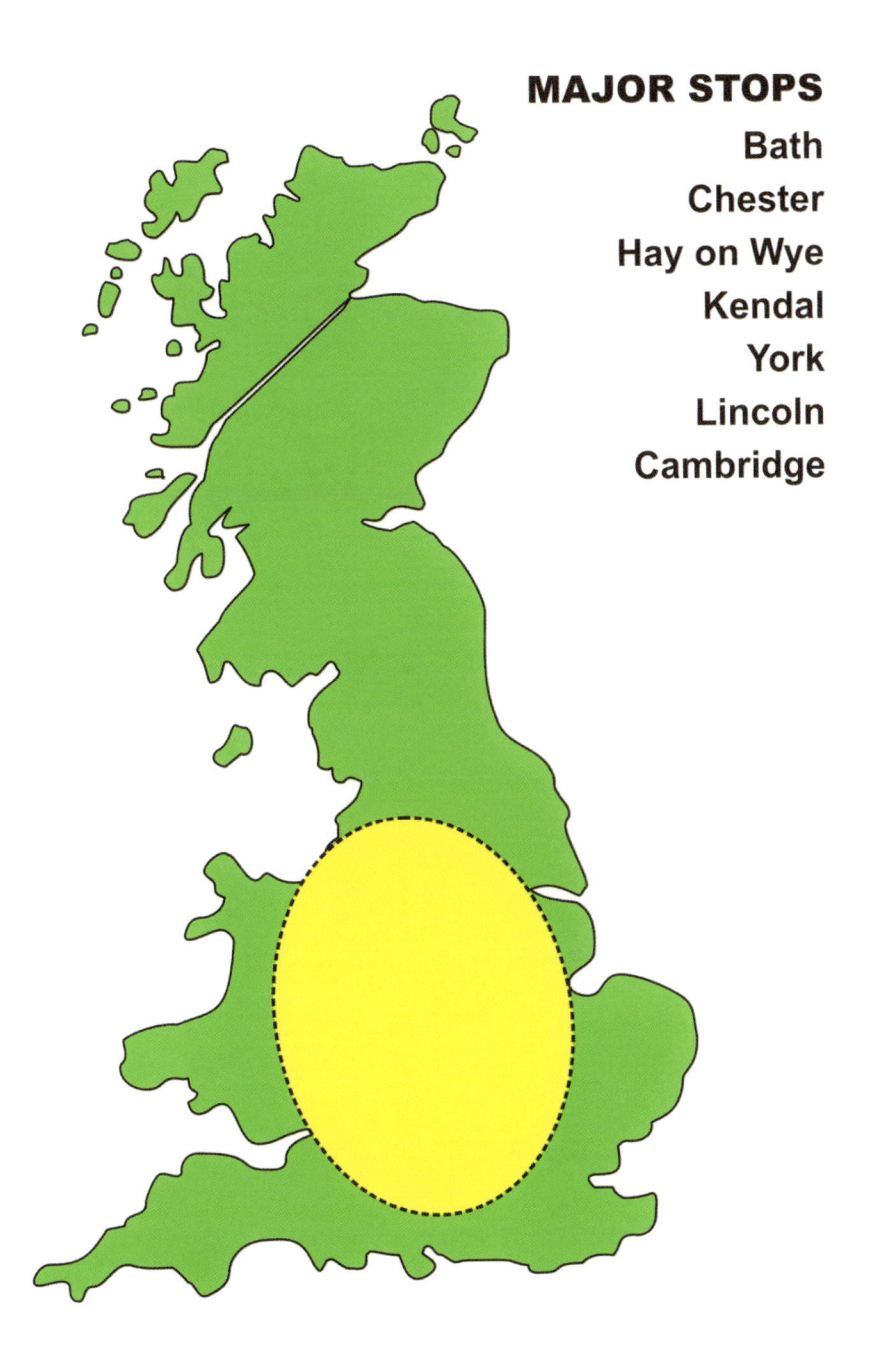

MAJOR STOPS
Bath
Chester
Hay on Wye
Kendal
York
Lincoln
Cambridge

CIRCLE TOUR – 1550 KM

Overnight at	Day's Distance in Km
Storrington, Sussex	52
Overton, Hampshire	108
Calne, Somerset	75
Bath, Somerset	76
Chepstow, Monmouthshire, Wales	63
Hay on Wye, Breconshire, Wales	83
Bridges, Shropshire	81
Chester, Cheshire	110
High Bentham, Lancashire	65
Kendal, Cumbria	36
Dentdale, Yorkshire	41
Keld, Yorkshire	46
Thirsk, Yorkshire	82
York, Yorkshire	52
Lincoln, Lincolnshire	141
Grantham, Lincolnshire	48
Ramsey, Huntingdonshire	101
Cambridge, Cambridgeshire	64
Warley, Essex	110
Seven Oaks, Surrey	60
Horley, Surrey	60

BETTER WAY HOLIDAYS

- TIRED OF "LUXURY" HOLIDAYS THAT LEAVE YOUR BODY BLOATED WITH RICH FOOD, YOUR PURSE RAVAGED BY EXCESSIVE PRICES AND YOUR SOUL EMPTY?

- FED UP WITH THE INSINCERE ATTENTIONS OF SERVICE PEOPLE INTERESTED ONLY IN THE SIZE OF YOUR TIP?

- *BETTER WAY* OFFERS AN ALTERNATIVE. WE HAVE JUST THE HOLIDAY TO RAISE YOUR SPIRITS, RESTORE YOUR HEALTH AND SOOTHE YOUR PURSE.

- THIS IS A 3-WEEK CYCLING ADVENTURE COMPLETE WITH FANTASTIC SCENERY, ALL WEATHER EXERCISE, A DRESS CODE AS CASUAL AS YOU WANT TO MAKE IT, ALCOHOL-FREE CUISINE AND NO FUSS, MINIMALIST ACCOMODATION.

- SHARE THE CHEERY CONVIVIALITY OF HOSTEL DORMITORYS WITH STRANGERS, SECURE IN THE KNOWLEDGE THAT THERE IS A FRESHLY LAUNDERED SHEET BAG FOR EVERY GUEST.

- SAVOUR TRADITIONAL ENGLISH COUNTRY DISHES LIKE "TOAD IN A HOLE" AND "BANGERS AND MASH"!

- DISCOVER MUSCLES YOU NEVER KNEW YOU HAD AFTER AN EXHILARATING 75 KM DAILY CYCLE RIDE.

- FORGET RIGID TOUR SCHEDULES WITH EXTENDED HOSTEL CAFETERIA HOURS TO 8 PM.

- GLORY IN THE SELF SUFFICIENCY OF TRAVELLING WITH THE ABSOLUTE MINIMUM OF CREATURE COMFORTS.

- ALL OF THIS FOR AS LITTLE AS $85 A DAY. TOTAL LAND COSTS ONLY $2100. DEPARTING 15 JUNE 1999.

DON'T WAIT—THIS TOUR WILL FILL UP FAST—GET YOUR RESERVATION IN TODAY.

CIRCLE TOUR

This tour is really mis-named. The route was actually more like an irregular hexagon but that doesn't work too well as a tour name. I spent a lot of time preparing for this trip, cobbling together parts of different routes recommended by 'Cycling Britain', a Lonely Planets guide book and *Cycling Great Britain* by Tim Hughes and Joanna Cleary, published by Bicycle Books, San Francisco.

The Route

From Gatwick Airport, south of London, my route went generally west to Bath, then northwest to skirt Wales and due north to Chester in Cheshire. From Chester, I continued north to Kendal in Cumbria and on into the Yorkshire Dales and York. The trip's final leg was south from York to Lincoln, Cambridge and back to Gatwick. The plan was to combine familiar territory like Yorkshire with unfamiliar Lincolnshire and Cambridgeshire.

The Better Way

For fun, I wrote a mock advertising flyer touting the advantages of my approach to travel, called 'The Better Way'. This flyer incorporated many of the negative comments friends and relatives had made over the years about these trips, as benefits of 'The Better Way'. Perversely, I also stuffed it in a wealthy neighbour's post box, knowing that such a trip would be physically abhorrent to them and never even be contemplated. Unfortunately, their housekeeper put the flyer in the rubbish while they were away and I never got the hoped for reaction. This flyer is reproduced on the opposite page.

Arrival

For some reason, perhaps my advancing age, both Mari and my daughter, Allison thought this trip was doomed. They were more than usually sensitive to the volume and speed of traffic on British roads and thought this time could be my last. This made for a tearful parting at the airport for my late flight via Montreal.

For the first time, I was using a bicycle box that Deirdre, a neighbour's adult daughter kindly lent me. Mari and I first met Deirdre at an Oakville restaurant where she was our waitress for a meal we had during a house-hunting trip. Then Deirdre was a very pleasant teenager who coincidentally lived diagonally across the street from where we chose the house that is still our home. Deirdre's personality strengths continued into adulthood when she and her husband developed a love for hiking and biking the British countryside. Hence her ownership of a bicycle box.

These are hard vinyl boxes with layers of thick foam inside to cushion the bike. This approach actually requires more disassembly than using an old cardboard cycle box or the airline supplied plastic bag. With these hard vinyl boxes you need to remove the wheels, pedals and handlebar stem. But I was not going to risk the bent wheels and frame that my cycle suffered on my last trip.

This arrangement introduced new complications to travel plans. These boxes aren't disposable; they are quite expensive and thus need to be stored somewhere during the tour. Previous experiences proved that the airport left luggage areas were horribly expensive and many railway stations had closed theirs down due to potential IRA bomb activity.

My flight was into Gatwick. Mari and I and our son Cameron had stayed at the Prinstead B&B at nearby Horley in 1997. This time, I wrote ahead to book a room with them for the final night of my tour and asked if they would look after my bicycle box for the four weeks of my trip. They graciously agreed so I hired a taxi from Gatwick to take the bike box and me to Horley. The car was an impressive brand new Renault Espace (a highly regarded French minivan) that had plenty of space but the driver (not English) was very concerned that his car would be marked by the bicycle box in some way and treated me rudely. I returned the favour by withholding a tip.

Due to a connection in Montreal and a late departure from there, the flight did not arrive until late morning. It was nearly noon British time when I reached the B&B. The day was very warm making hot work of the reassembly exercise. It took far longer to put it back together than it did to take it apart. The front pannier rack was particularly difficult, as I had not taken much notice of how it was mounted when I took it off. Then, this nut discovered that he had left two nuts crucial to the assembly behind. The wheels would not run straight and the back one insisted on rubbing against the chain stays. Sweat was pouring down my face and attempts to wipe it off just deposited greasy streaks.

It was half past two when I finished the assembly; I'd had nothing to eat since the inadequate airline breakfast but I was anxious to achieve some distance before the day ended. So, I decided to get underway and stop for tea and teacakes at about four. But when the panniers were loaded on, the bike's weight was almost overwhelming.

Once again, the pressure of work had made it impossible to train properly and I was truly unfit at the start of this tour. I had done no loaded training at all and now could barely move. A few kilometres on, I realised that the back wheel rubbing against the chain stays caused part of the difficulty. After mending that and while climbing a narrow road on the rougher, potholed surface at the road edge, I hit a hole hard, causing the rear wheel to slam against the chain stay, stopping me dead. The traffic poured by but fortunately I managed to stay upright. I overcame the problem (temporarily) by repositioning the rear wheel more to the rear where the chain stays are further apart and tightening the quick release.

Shortly afterwards, on a steeper hill, climbing up in semi-darkness due to a canopy of trees, I was going so slowly that I had no ability to keep the bike balanced. Then the front wheel hit a hole and turned sharply to the left. This and my automatic, still North American, reactions caused me to fall to the right—directly in front of the traffic. Two cars swerved, narrowly avoiding me. Perhaps Mari and Allison's premonitions were prescient!

I was headed in the general direction of Horsham, Surrey but had no map for this first day. At 4.30, when I arrived at Horsham, I was definitely ready for something to eat and a bit of a rest. The combination of jet lag, the heat and events to this point had taken both a physical and mental toll. Some tea and teacakes would put that right but no tearoom appeared so I had to settle for a cheese and pickle sandwich and a Coke bought from a newsagent.

His reply to my request for some directions was 'I've only lived here eight years and don't know the area yet.' Later, others repeatedly gave me conflicting information but eventually I was at least headed in a westerly direction. By now, I was about ready to find a B&B and put my weary, untrained and somewhat bruised body to bed.

Naturally, no B&B appeared. Finally, at Storrington, after covering 52 km, I called in at the White Horse pub to ask about B&B's and wound up staying with them. The price was a high £30 but the room seemed all right superficially. After dinner and a bath, I discovered that neither the teakettle nor the bedside lamp worked. Then I found a lovely gift Mari had hidden in my luggage—a battery operated light that attaches to your book. She was looking after me even 5000 kilometres away.

The White Horse was not a good choice. My tiredness had made me less discriminating. It should have been obvious when they suggested I leave my cycle behind the pub adjacent to the car park footpath. I was alert enough not to do that and carried it up to my room.

Not wanting to give the White Horse any more of my business, I took dinner at the rival Anchor pub across the road. The Anchor served an excellent huge steak and kidney pie that I washed down with a pint of lager. This revived me enough to delay bedtime a bit for a look at house prices in an estate agent's windows and to walk through some lovely residential areas. There was no visible nightlife other than the pubs but the streets roared with a constant stream of traffic.

Next morning, the White Horse continued its shabby behaviour. They had no marmalade or jam for breakfast and all I got when I mentioned the non-functioning items in the room was 'oh dear, I'll have to tell the manager.' There was no apology or apparent concern that I had been inconvenienced. A confirming indicator of the quality of this establishment was that twice when I went to use the toilet reserved for overnight guests, someone had peed all over the seat! Is this really the Better Way?

Galsworthy, a Corgi and Bush House

Now though, the first part of my mix of cycle tours began and I had an adequate map. The route, chosen to be off the beaten track, is marvellous for lack of traffic but also lacks any facilities. Tea and cakes was, as always, on the agenda but there were no tearooms to be found. So, I made an early lunch of another cheese and pickle sandwich at the Holiest Arms pub. This pickle, by the way, is not the bread and butter pickle or piccalilli common in North America but a chutney-like, British pickle relish called Branston. I sat out in the garden on a picnic bench with two old dears, a black cat and a dog at our feet.

Before lunch, at Bury, Sussex, I passed by a manor house where author John Galsworthy had lived for seven years. Now, my route became a footpath, erupting in knarled roots and crossing a narrow bridge over a marsh, which ended in a very steep set of steps.

At the top, the footpath went in two directions but without any indication of where they led. There were some houses in the near distance where I headed to get some advice.

At the first house, after a vigorous and unfriendly interrogation by an aged Corgi, his mistress arrived to help me. She was a no-nonsense, white-haired gardener with a healthy amount of dirt under her nails but a lovely garden. It was her belief that the dog did not like my cycle helmet!

She directed me towards Liphook where I was able to find a road a little more appropriate to actually getting somewhere. It was clear that either I had misread the guidebook or needed to abandon its suggestions altogether. Although now on a more populated road, it looked unlikely that I would find any accommodation before Overton, some 50 km away. This would mean a 100+ km day but nevertheless, I was unable to resist the temptation of afternoon tea at Bush House in Selborne, Hampshire.

This was a proper place—very old, low ceilings, a beam and vine covered back garden, long open porch and locals as customers, no tourists. Quality, however, has its price. My two teacakes, jam and five cups of tea (one pot with extra hot water) came to over C$10! The ambiance held me for forty-five minutes, so it was after four when I left.

The overcast sky threatened rain but within an hour the threat was gone, the sun reappeared and it was perfect riding. The conditions were so pleasant that I wasn't aware that my average speed was only about 15 km/h. So it was nearly eight pm when I arrived in Overton, achieving 107 kms for the first full day. There was a painful price as everything ached, particularly my neck and shoulders.

Changing animals tonight, I booked a room at the White Hart pub. The only alternative to the pub for dinner was an overpriced place and economy was required to offset my afternoon tea extravagance. I settled for an indifferent meal with my book in the White Hart's dining room before a soothing hot shower and bed. Sleep became almost impossible after about 3.30 a.m. as again, my room overlooked the street and was just above the corner traffic lights. It sounded like a racetrack as a steady stream of Friday night traffic passed by, gunning their engines in anticipation of the light changing and then roaring off into the night. Only intermittent pauses punctuated the din, allowing me to just doze off and then be blasted awake again. Finally, I gave up at 6.45 to take advantage of a 7.30 breakfast and get an early start on the day

Young People –Bah!

Part of this morning's ride was along 'Grand Avenue' a misleadingly named narrow road through the Savernake Forest near Marlborough, Wiltshire. The Savernake is a privately owned wood with a magnificent avenue of trees along a restricted speed public road running through it. At 32 km per hour, I exceeded the speed limit three times on the way through. Reaching the outskirts of Marlborough at about 12.30, with no tea break and only an early breakfast to sustain me, I was ready for a stop. A pleasant looking pub, the Roebuck, soon appeared to rescue me. I sat outside with a massive cheese and pickle sandwich (the third in as many days!) and a tall orange juice for over an hour. There were lots of people, mainly women, also enjoying their lunch in the sunshine.

Marlborough claims one of the widest high streets in England and is also home to a famous public school. This area is also a centre for English racehorse breeding. After lunch I explored the High Street for a while, visiting a bookshop and being stopped twice by teenage girls doing a tourist survey. Is it my cycling clothes or are North Americans so obvious no matter what they wear? My attempt to just blend in was not working.

My pre-determined route became a little unclear from here and consultation with the map showed a much more direct route along the A4 to Calne where I decided to spend the night. The A4 also provided better access to Long Barrow and Silbury Hill at West Kennet.

'For prehistoric interest, this part of Wiltshire offers serious competition to the more famous stone circles of Stonehenge further south. The ancient track known as the Ridge Way runs along the crest of the Marlborough Downs.

Silbury Hill, the largest earthen mound in Europe, surpasses all other prehistoric monuments in Britain not only in size but also in the degree of utter puzzlement it has created among those who have studied it. The site bears a superficial resemblance to the many smaller round barrows found in the vicinity of Avebury, and local tradition suggested that a great leader lays buried somewhere in its depths—encased in golden armour, according to one legend. A series of extensive excavations, however, has failed to reveal any trace of a burial or other objects entombed within. So, the massive mound's purpose remains a complete mystery.

But the excavations did reveal a surprisingly sophisticated method of construction. The mound's turf façade hides a series of partitioned circular chalk enclosures, packed with earth and stacked one atop another to create a stepped shape resembling a wedding cake. The smooth finished appearance was achieved by filling in the steps with additional chalk and dirt. In all, it took about 6.5 million cubic feet of material to create the mound.' (1)

Another pub overnight, and another interrupted sleep. This time, it wasn't the traffic but noisy, vulgar kids, some sounding almost pre-teen despite it being two in the morning. Again, I got up early, forgetting that weekend breakfasts start later. During breakfast, a very well-upholstered young woman in clothes tighter than her skin breezed through the front door on the way to her room, promising to be back in time for her work shift. The landlady told me that the girl had been partying all night and wasn't yet 16!

The only other person in the room, obviously single and apparently gay, started a conversation. He was concluding a week's walking holiday from the Cotswolds through Bath to Avebury. He complained of a dull and poorly paid office job in Yorkshire. Nevertheless, he was interesting to talk to and convinced me that Avebury was worth seeing despite the extra 26 km backtracking doing so would require.

Avebury, New Agers and Bikers

Returning to Avebury meant climbing the hill called 'Labour in Vain' that I felt so smug about going down yesterday on the way into Calne but going up provided a good view of the Cherhill Chalk Horse carved on the hillside that I missed yesterday. This horse is a relatively modern imitation of the famous Uffington Horse. The Uffington horse could almost as well be called the Uffington White Cat. It has recently been dated to at least 2,500 years old and is thought originally to have been a symbol of the victory of good over evil. (2)

On the way, I saw again and exchanged 'good mornings' with a traveller outside his Romany caravan across the road in a small pull off. A little further on, there were three beautiful brown and white gypsy ponies grazing beside a folding sign offering Romany Fortune Telling. On my return, later in the morning, the fortuneteller was outside brewing tea, apparently for personal consumption rather than professional purposes as there were no customers.

Three beat up vans filled with dirty young people and some

dogs sullied the Avebury parking area. Rings hung from every visible part of them and they wore their filthy clothes very sloppily. I can't really believe this is their personal choice but one made to elicit the greatest possible disdain and disgust from others. On the path into the village, I saw one older man that looked as if he might be their guru—long flowing white hair, beard, beads and headband; the full kit. At first, I did not appreciate why so many of them were here but later realised the connection with stone circles and new age philosophy. The following day at nearby Stonehenge, the summer solstice was disturbed by some of these types who broke down the protective fence and 'celebrated' on top of the stones.

Avebury is a one street, 17th/18th century village, not particularly notable in itself. However, on Avebury's perimeter is a deep dry moat like structure inside of which huge stones sit in rough circles.

'The Avebury stone circles are the largest in Britain, and considered by many to surpass even Stonehenge in grandeur. ....The first thing to strike visitors to Avebury is not the stones, but the surrounding bank and ditch. Originally, the ditch reached a depth of nine metres and the adjoining mound stood over five metres. While erosion has taken its toll, the henge still dwarfs the nearly vanished earthworks at Stonehenge. At about 1 mile in circumference, the Avebury henge completely encircles a small village, and even the smallest of the three stone circles within is still larger than Stonehenge.

…..so few of the original Avebury stones remain. Of the two inner circles, only four and five stones still stand, respectively. The third circle remains only marginally more complete, with 27 of the original 98 stones still in place.' (3)

Later, on the path returning to the car park area, I passed over a hundred motorcyclists, most attired in the stereotypical black leather. They were probably the perfect antithesis of the new age group suggesting that the situation could become violent quite easily. I was glad to be leaving.

I returned to Calne and on to the National Trust village of Lacock, a totally open, working village, attractive but not as special as I had expected. It was filled with tourists, so I did not stay long. Lunch was at a very pleasant pub, The Rising Sun, perched on top of a long descent. It was very popular and I was lucky to get served. I had a tuna baguette, salad and a glass of orange squash. The orange squash was over C$ 4, which I only discovered when it came time to pay. My complaint was met with 'you are in tourist country now.'

Coming into Bradford on Avon, there was an amazingly steep descent into the city along a very narrow road enclosed between a high wall and buildings. A sharp bend at the city entrance caused the heavy traffic to stack up just out of sight and I had to brake hard to avoid hitting a car. Bradford on Avon is very old but looks to be largely ignored by tourists and so was more appealing to me.

I could not resist stopping here for tea and a teacake. It was the best ever. Toasting the teacake caramelised the currants raising their taste to a new level. Unfortunately, my time to savour this or to explore the town was very limited, as I wanted to be in time for evening meal at the Bath hostel. (If you haven't already noticed, food is a preoccupation of mine).

This objective was not realised; there were no signs in Bath directing one to the hostel and most people that I asked had no idea. It turned out to be at the top of a very long hill and by the time I arrived it was an hour too late for the meal. So I showered and walked into the city, seeking a recommended pub. 'The Greentree' had stopped serving food by the time I arrived. Next on my list was 'The Moon and Sixpence" where the minimum price for a main course was C$ 31. Finally, I found a French bistro where, by eating lightly, I could eat well and have a glass of wine. My meal was a smoked duck breast salad with bacon and walnut dressing and warm celery and Roquefort pate accompanied by a Cabernet Sauvignon. It was superb and enjoyed all the more because each bite had to be chewed thoroughly to extract maximum taste and nutrition and to extend the experience. Mari would say that I should eat all my meals at that pace.

After the long hike back up the hill to the hostel, I met my roommates, two university students from Wisconsin, and one from Salamanca, Spain. He and I spoke a little Spanish combined with English and seemed to understand each other. Now, thinking back on that experience, I realise that my first Spanish professor, at Edinburgh University, had been trained at Salamanca!

Bath

Next morning on the footpath along the canal, I saw a barge coming through the lock. Colourful others were moored alongside. It wasn't clear whether these were on holiday or permanent as there wasn't much visible activity and their owners could have already left for their city jobs or be sleeping late. In later years, living on the water like this became fairly common, as the mooring fees were often cheaper than rent or property rates (now 'council charge').

One of the iconic images of Bath is Robert Adam's Pultney Bridge over the River Avon and the picturesque weir. Buildings filled with shops form the sidewall of the bridge. My hometown in the Finger Lakes district of New York State features a Pultney Park and like many North American towns was named after Bath, England. My brother Byron, who travels widely in the US in a quest to run a marathon in each of the fifty states, arranges side trips to visit as many towns named Bath as possible.

I carried up on the Grand Parade and over to the Roman Baths, meaning only to survey the exterior, not actually visit this tourist-infested attraction. An interior argument was raging, however, chastising me for letting my aversion to tourists and my parsimony deny me one of the principal reasons for coming to Bath. An exterior sign, noting that the Baths were a World Heritage Site clinched the argument in favour of going in but I still winced at the C$16 entry fee.

Once inside, I was pleased at my decision; an excellent audio guide was provided and the tour was well arranged. The 'Sacred Spring' continued to overflow and spill its 46.5 degree Celsius water. This entire complex of baths has only been a tourist attraction since the late 19th century when it was discovered –some 1500 years after the Romans built it. Much of Bath today is about two metres higher than it was originally as newer civilisations built on top of the older ones.

In the Roman times, this facility was known as Sulis Minerva, a combination of the Roman god of healing waters, Sulis with the Celtic god Minerva. The lead walls of the Great Pool are still watertight from the days of original construction. At that time, people had an early version of *Three Coins in the Fountain*, throwing gifts to the gods into the water. According to the tour information, people also sometimes wrote out curses and threw them into the water requesting the gods to intervene in petty crimes. There was no indication of the efficacy of this practice.

Outside in the courtyard with a large appreciative audience, a man was playing a musical saw or at least he made an excellent show of it. He had a boom box, ostensibly for accompaniment, but it could have generated all the sound.

Before leaving the city, I made my weekly call to Mari. The previous week had been our middle daughter's birthday and they had spent the day together shopping for our first grandchild, expected in November. Allison apparently spent several thousand (mentally); I don't know what the actual total was. Son Cameron, a recent MBA graduate, has been offered a job in global market intelligence by a major US consumer products firm based in Wisconsin and is quite excited.

After lunch, I made my exit from Bath up a long and hard hill and along a difficult route to the Severn Bridge at the Bristol Channel so that it was nearly six pm when I approached the bridge. Built in 1966, it was at the time one of the world's largest single-span suspension bridges. (4) Fortunately, there is a cycle path across the bridge as the winds that roar down the channel could easily slam you right into traffic.

Coach and Horses Redeems Pubs' Reputation

My destination, Chepstow, was only a few kilometres beyond the Severn Bridge. Chepstow had no hostel but many B&B's. However, either no one was home or they had failed to indicate no vacancy. Eventually, I found a vacancy at the Coach and Horses pub. Pubs seem to be my destiny this trip. This one was run by a very friendly gnome of a man who gave me a nice double for the price of a single. The only drawback was that the window inside my room served as the fire escape for the entire floor! There was even an emergency key to my room taped to the wall outside. How's that for privacy and security!

After a quick wash and brush up, I came down for an excellent sirloin steak dinner washing it down with two half pints of Stella. The pub had a very friendly atmosphere (no doubt encouraged by the owner). After dinner, at about 8.30, Neil, the cook gathered everyone who was interested for a trivia quiz. Given Chepstow's location, it wasn't surprising that a large proportion of his questions were on Welsh subjects. Neil made it very entertaining and reminiscent of an old time music hall. The participants paid a pound to play and the one with the most correct answers went home with the bulk of the takings.

This time my room did not face the street, there were no noisy teenagers or cars and there was no fire—so I slept through the entire night. At 7.30, a bright and cheery Neil provided a massive breakfast, including what must have been a half-pound of bacon.

Breakfast time, particularly with British fare, is one of my favourites. Despite good intentions, I linger longer than intended. This morning was no exception. And playing toss with Sam, the pub's friendly Labrador retriever, further delayed departure. My cost for this most pleasant stop was £26.50, including dinner. The equivalent cost for my first stop in Storrington had been over 40% higher and could not begin to compare.

Hay on Wye

Progress was very slow this morning. Again, the guidebook route was confusing and included one very blatant error where the wrong town was indicated. Then, I encountered a four way crossroads, with two separate signs for my destination, each pointing a different direction! I used my map and compass to make the choice between them but did not feel especially confident as these lanes rarely run straight.

Luck was with me this time, although the way that these lanes run, both choices could have worked out. I arrived at Llantilio Crossway just at lunchtime without knowing it. There were no signposts and the church that my route noted as a guide for a right hand turn was hidden behind dense roadside hedges.

I called in at a pub for directions and lunch. It was a very old (1459) and perfect pub with an alert, affectionate Doberman in residence. The only other customer during much of my stay was a thin man with terrible teeth and long stringy blond hair. As it turned out, he was the back up barman and when not serving spent his time performing quality tests on the product.

The publican, a man several social stations above his backup, discussed his brand new computer and how he had used it to plan a motoring trip to France. This was the first time I had heard of the route planning capabilities of computer software and was amazed that it could produce detailed maps, driving distances and ferry times. This concept should be extended to back road country cycling!

We also discussed the implications to a country pub like his from the proposed new lower allowable alcohol content for driving. He was afraid that people would choose to buy their alcohol at the off-licence and drink at home rather than go to the pub. City pubs would not be so badly affected because people there have access to public transit and taxis. We also talked about the heavy tax on beer and other business aspects of running a country pub. I find these conversations very interesting and am a good listener because I want to learn as much about British life as possible. People tend to open up a lot more when the focus is on them and your questions show genuine interest. I am careful to ask questions neutrally, without revealing any bias of my own or expressing an opinion on their information. So, they get no clues from me of praise or censure. I think I get a more accurate indication of their true feelings this way. Mari thinks, however, that my face betrays me. I apparently cannot prevent it registering disapproval.

At one pm, I set out again with only 34 km under my belt at this point and shortly came to an unmarked road that might be my turn but I had been advised to alter the route and take the main highway A465. This led to the turnoff to Llanthony where the real climb began. Now pushing the bike became a regular feature and I was soon dripping with sweat although the temperature could not have been more than 17 or 18 degrees Celsius. Hopes of a tea break at Llanthony were dashed, as it was a village of only a few houses. So, I moved my hopes on to the next village on the map, Capel y ffin, five and a half kilometres away, only to have them dashed again. Now there would be no sustenance available before the waiting ordeal of Gospel Pass. There was, however, a lovely cemetery and church at Capel y ffin that looked as if they merited a visit and would provide a short period of rest. The church was very small, simple and peaceful. A balcony ran round two inside walls; the ten or so pews were of dark oak. The former inhabitants dedicated a wall plaque commemorating a previous priest. Outside, there was little evidence of any inhabitants as only one house was visible. Later I learned that this is the smallest church in Wales and the smallest constituency in the entire United Kingdom!

Beyond Capel y ffin the narrow road was wooded and very beautiful, climbing out onto bare grassy hillside, uphill all the way with an average 10-12% grade to the pass at the top---the Bwlch-yr-Efengyl or 'Gospel Pass', so named because in the days when those who wished to practise nonconformist worship were harassed, people would gather at this windswept spot to the hear the gospel preached. The top of the pass is one of the highest roads in Wales at 542 metres and as you broach the top a tremendous view opens over the middle Wye valley and the hills beyond. (5) My spirits soared at the broad vista, populated with sheep and apparently wild horses. Golden shafts of sunshine in the western sky pierced the fresh, bracing air. The only negative was the weight of the panniers.

Then, I experienced one of the best runs of my entire cycling career that was probably made more enjoyable by its contrast with the rest of the day's ordeal. The road became a black ribbon snaking its way downhill for what must have been seven kilometres through a manicured lawn like vista all the way to Hay on Wye.

Hay was immediately attractive. It is an old, clean and moderately sized town that claims to be the second hand book centre of Britain. My first stop to find a room was successful at Skynlas House, an attractive and well-maintained B&B on the main road. Ann, my friendly and competent landlady, gave me a yellow ensuite double room for twenty pounds providing another favourable comparison with the White Horse pub in Storrington.

Ann also has a housekeeping cottage that sleeps four/five that she lets for £200-275 a week. The higher price applies during an annual Book Festival week that I had never heard of. Ann claimed that it is the largest of its kind in the world. This year's festival just finished and attracted 42,000 for readings, talks and concerts. Hay is also a centre for walking, canoeing, and kayaking.

After a nice shower and two relaxed cuppas in a comfortable wing chair with a book, I went off to the town to find some dinner. There was a ruined castle and a full complement of necessary, everyday shops but about every third one was a bookshop! One of these, an open-air establishment situated in the grounds of the castle, was called the Honesty Shop. It operated primarily on an exchange basis and was totally unattended. I had a nice meal of battered cod at the Wheatsheaf.

In the morning, Ann provided a massive pile of strong yellow scrambled eggs served on granary bread with grilled tomatoes and mushrooms -excellent quality and delicious.

Bridges Hostel

Today's route was definitely easier, providing time for a teacake stop but only on the self-promise that my lunch break would be brief. I kept this promise with a chicken and mushroom pie, acquired from a small post office cum general store, that I enjoyed with a Coke on an outside bench while finishing off my current book.

Tonight's destination was Bridges, which I chose only because there is a hostel there. Both town and hostel proved to be extremely well hidden. There was virtually no signage on the road directing anyone to Bridges, no sign to announce that you had arrived and only a tiny sign for the hostel.

Arriving early, despite having covered 81 km today, I found the hostel reception closed. Thank goodness the door to the outside toilet was open—I had been bursting for at least two hours. I rested on an outside bench until the warden and her daughter arrived. They took pity on me and made, guess what, that British cure for every malady known to man, a pot of tea.

Despite its small size, this small, former schoolhouse hostel serves meals. Tonight's meal was simple and of the 'old British school' style with French onion soup, a meat pie with overdone carrots and broccoli, followed by coconut tart and ice cream. Breakfast was also poorly cooked and presented—my sausage went into the dustbin. Penny, the cook, is a second year medical student at St. Bartholomew's in London. She will be successful---she already produces meals that can match the worst hospital! Her younger, cheerier, and slimmer sister took over mid-breakfast and provided me with a five-cup pot of tea!

Over dinner, I talked with the only two other guests, a sixtyish couple doing a pre-ramble scouting trip for a series of walks they are to lead individually next week from Long Mynd. This future activity was our principal subject of conversation and I learned a lot about the skills necessary to lead these walks, primarily map reading and first aid. After dinner they went to meet the hoteliers at the hotel that will be their base for next week's tours.

I was the only occupant of a room called Ashes Hollow so took the opportunity of unfettered access to the washbasin to do a hand laundry that I hung in the special drying room. Drying rooms are one of the useful facilities that most country hostels provide. Many hostellers arrive with muddy boots and wet clothes or just need to dry out some hand washed clothing, as Britain's generally moisture-laden air is rarely conducive to quick drying. These rooms are usually just overheated spaces with clothes lines and racks to lay things on but when you need something dry, the lack of one can seem total deprivation. Larger, more urban hostels may have washers and dryers but the queues can be daunting.

My walking tour acquaintances from yesterday joined me for breakfast and she 'entertained' me with tales of her daughter (job transfer to Geneva), their plans for a round the world backpacking tour and the posh roll-up dress she had bought so they could go to the opera in Sydney. Graham, of course would have to take a tie to go with his non-iron seersucker shirts. All through this conversation, I was reflecting on Mari's travelling preferences. She relies on a personal version of the old American Express slogan—'Don't leave home without it' --the home that is!

Chester

Chester was my next stop but on the way I hoped to make a detour through Church Stretton, Shropshire where my one and only pen pal, Andrew, lived back in the 1950's. The topographical map showed that the diversion to Church Stretton would be very tough, involving a whaleback of a ridge known as Long Mynd that has grades of up to 25%. I had visited Church Stretton back in 1990 but been unsuccessful in finding Andrew's home or his father's parish church and hoped to be more successful this time but the difficult terrain put me off. So, I gave up on Church Stretton, going to Chester through Woolstaston and Leebotwood instead. This still involved a part of Long Mynd and was very tough.

Arriving in Chester at about 6.30, I was immediately struck with how run down it appeared and how many 'undesirables' there were. Do they go together; does one cause the other? Certainly, environment affects one; clean and tidy surroundings are a subtle influence on your own standard of dress and deportment.

I set out looking for a B&B and stopped at a small hotel that looked less expensive than the rest but was charging the equivalent of C$106! Once I recovered from my shock, they kindly directed me to the B&B section of town where I stopped at Duke's Cottage in a mean street just down from the railway station. This turned out to be just a B—no breakfast was provided but the small room had every thing I needed and was about a quarter of the price at the other place. But some loss of privacy and convenience was required to achieve this saving. My German hosts' bedroom was their access and mine to the car park where I stored the bike. They lived in three rooms, one of which contained a big screen television that ran all day.

After a quick shower, I went out for a meal, walking into the city centre through a very unappealing set of subways (underground walkways). Within a few minutes a wealth of pedestrian walkways, shops, and restaurants appeared making Chester much more attractive than I had thought. It is, after all, a walled city with Roman origins.

My plan for tomorrow had involved a side-trip visit to British friends met cycling in France in 1994. However, a bad train wreck today cancelled train services for the line to their home. So, I decided to spend the next day exploring Chester's newfound charms instead. Then like the British, I went out for 'an Indian' (meal). My favourite is a lamb curry with Nan, a green salad and a lager. , The restaurant proprietor turned out to have relatives in Ottawa and was considering setting up a business in Canada. We talked about that for a while then I rang my friend before leaving the restaurant to cancel tomorrow's visit.

On the walk back to Duke's Cottage, I called in at the railway station to check on ways to avoiding cycling through an industrial area and was pleased to find that the disruption in train services did not affect trips to Preston. This would achieve my objective and free up some time to see Chester.

Ah! A day off the bike and with it safely stowed at Duke's Cottage, I was free to roam and do as I wished with no concerns. Despite a late breakfast at the railway station, the walk into town via those unpleasant subways made me hungry again. So, I acquired a copy of *The Times* and climbed the stairs to a coffee house on the second tier of one of the Rows. These Rows are unique in Britain. Dating from the 13th century onward, these are raised covered galleries with two tiers of shops—forming, in effect, a medieval covered shopping mall. (6)

I spent a leisurely hour absorbing information about British life and the interesting parallels with life at home—e.g. the debate about the high proportion of total education spending involving administration and the programming and financing problems facing the national broadcaster. It was interesting that the BBC decided to take the high road, concentrating on quality rather than ratings. It must be recognised that was an easier decision for the BBC than it would have been for the CBC. The BBC doesn't have to rely on any advertising revenue to operate.

After this, I explored the Church of St John the Baptist and its 12th century ruins, the Roman Amphitheatre and walked along the River Dee. The church's origins go back to the 7th century and the Saxons. A guide to the history introduced me to the term Dissolution that apparently is shorthand for the Dissolution of the Monasteries that followed Henry the VIII's break with Rome.

My historical interest had been piqued today and needed additional feeding. This led to the purchase of a walking tour pamphlet from Tourist Information and about two hours strolling around Chester, climbing walls, peering at buildings and trying to absorb the commentary provided by the pamphlet.

Remains of the Roman walls from AD79 are still visible. Later the Saxons and Normans added to the walls girdling the city. Chester had been a great port but by about 700, the river silted up and ships could longer get in. Now the river is largely a canal. There were more than 50 points of interest on the walking tour and with museums along the way, more than a full day would have been necessary to do it justice. My two plus hours wasn't nearly enough but I had passed the saturation point and so promised myself to study the pamphlet and Saxon and Norman history more in the future. You can break those kinds of promises can't you?

Next morning while loading up the bike, I again had to pass through my host's bedroom. On the first trip, he must not have heard me coming as he was watching German television. Possibly, he thought this was unpatriotic, because on my second trip, the BBC was on.

Trains and Cattle

I arrived at the railway station to find that the two-car train only had capacity for two cycles—just enough in this case. My fellow cyclist was a commuter. He cycled thirteen kilometres from home to the station, and then paid Northwest Trains six pounds daily for the round trip into work. We talked for a while about the train service. Northwest was the worst in his view. Since Margaret Thatcher's privatisation program, the railway stations and tracks are owned and operated by one company while several different companies operate the trains. This car was nice inside but the guy selling snacks was very unkempt, despite wearing a suit and tie. He must believe that simply wearing a suit and tie overcomes scruffy hair, dirty nails and unclean, untidy linen—assuming he even thinks about the incongruity of his appearance.

The first stage of this journey ended at Manchester's Oxford station. I climbed and descended another set of stairs to the platform for Preston. Virgin operates this train, the same people that run the airline. This was a much longer train but still had capacity for only two cycles. A couple of young business people and a self-important Virgin railway guy sat close by—I read.

Before noon, I was outside the Preston station ready to roll again with Kirkby Lonsdale as my goal. I hoped to stay again at 'The

Courtyard' B&B, operated by the nurse that had done part of her training in Oakville, where I had stayed in 1995.

Preston was large, heavily trafficked and poorly signposted. It took careful reading of the map to plot the nearest likely route. This took me through a broad residential/commercial section and eventually to my selected turnoff. At Longridge, I stopped for lunch at a pub. At the edge of the car park where I was to leave the bike, a young scummy couple were having a meal, smoking and fondling each other. I took extra time securing the bike in hope that they would leave before I was finished –it worked. Love was definitely blind in this case and all the other senses must have been defective as well.

I had made good time in the past hour and began to wonder if Kirkby Lonsdale might be a little unambitious, leaving too long a run for my following destination. However, while re-checking the map, I discovered that Kirkby was 47 miles further, not the 47 kilometres I thought it was. This left 60 kilometres after lunch, definitely ambitious enough for this terrain.

The road was undulating with a consistent climb. I was very warm which generally saps my energy but the pleasant countryside induced a sense of contentment that energised me. The sheep-spotted basket of eggs topography was blessed with clean air touched with farm fragrant authenticity. Just before Whitewell, I stopped to admire a magnificent multi-tiered garden with a stone patio and humped bridges over a stream. Two people were wandering around so I asked if I could take a picture to show Mari. Gardeners generally love others to take an interest but this lady was particularly gracious, especially so to someone attired in black latex. She invited me into the garden, provided a huge glass of cold barley water and explained that the house was a converted barn. Its beautiful stone and stained wood exterior had been very tastefully re-done.

There were sheep in the paddock along with a playful brood of black Labrador puppies to complete the scene. Most of this area is Crown land but this property was one of the few freeholds in the district.

Stone fences, bubbling streams and tree-canopied tunnels graced the next several kilometres—just ideal! A little while later, I overtook my first touring cyclist—an American on a solo camping tour. We talked for a while but I was put off by his appearance, odour and conversational style. His response to everything, I said was 'gotcha'.

Presumably this meant that he understood but it also conveyed a total lack of interest, as 'gotcha' was his only response most of the time. He claimed to be in theatre arts in Chicago and West Palm Beach and said that if he got to smell too bad, he would stay over in a hostel. Hopefully, this will not be at any hostel I am in.

From Dunlop Bridge, the road climbed steadily and my hopes of reaching Kirkby Lonsdale were fading fast. A herd of cattle was crossing the road at a cattle grid just ahead at close to what looked to be the summit. As I approached, so did the resident bull. It seemed prudent to give him a wide berth and ask his permission to photograph the scene!

The cattle were straying beyond where they should be which caught the attention of a red-haired, massively freckled boy of about 9 or 10 who roared over on a motorbike to guide them back. We had a brief conversation during which I complained about the hills and enquired about the rest of my day's route. His only response was 'you're in trouble!'

His assessment proved accurate. The climb was tough involving considerable walking but this was rewarded by a run of about 4 to 5 kilometres that brought me down into High Bentham at just six pm. High Bentham immediately became my new destination for the day. (I checked the map to assure myself that I could still get to Kendal tomorrow before making this decision).

Emboldened by this decisiveness, I marched into the smartly refurbished White Bull to request a room, to find that their accommodation was not ready to be let and they were not serving any evening meals. So, I wound up at the Coach and Horses and had a lovely Indian curry, even better than the one in Chester.

Kendal, the Dales and York

Kendal, Cumbria was one of the major destinations planned for this trip because my newest niece has been christened with that name. Her Australian father's maternal family, surname Ireland, was once prominent in Kendal, hence her name. Her older sister is called Ireland. So, I thought my visit and perhaps a souvenir from Kendal would be appreciated.

But first I had to spend some time in one of my favourite places, Kirkby Lonsdale. The new day started out beautifully with lovely countryside and nice weather. In less than an hour I arrived at the

Kirkby Lonsdale's stone pavilion in the market place. I sat there writing notes in my journal until eleven when I succumbed to the call for tea and cakes at a nearby teashop.

Refreshed, I revisited some of the lovely spots round the town including Ruskin's favourite view from behind St. Mary's church, discussed in a previous chapter, before rejoining the road to Kendal.

The difficult terrain restricted my average speed to about 16 kilometres per hour so it took almost two hours to reach Kendal. I had planned to ring my Mother upon arrival, thinking it might be a bit exciting for her to receive a call from the town her newest granddaughter was named after. But a Renault dealership right at the edge of Kendal diverted me. I cannot resist stopping to look at cars that aren't marketed in North America. In general, I find the European cars much more interesting than those available in North America, perhaps simply because they are different. Function and economy seem to play a much bigger role in their design yet their designs are attractive, creative, often elegant, and space utilisation is excellent. The current North American love affair with ever increasing horsepower isn't responsible or sensible in the face of growing gridlock, pollution and diminishing oil reserves.

The dealership was featuring a Laguna saloon (sedan) and an Espace van. The Espace was most impressive, particularly with the very comfortable seats that French cars are known for. No salesman bothered me; perhaps they did not accept cycles as trade-ins!

I rang Mom from a car park phone box and disguised my voice a bit. Her response was cool and guarded much like the time I made a surprise visit from England with my son Cameron, then eighteen months. Then, when she opened the door, not expecting me or recognising me initially, she said, 'Yes, may I help you?' My father's first reaction to this sudden visit was that Mari and I were splitting up! This time I was disappointed; the call was appreciated but having it come from Kendal apparently did not mean much.

The hostel did not open until five, so I left the bike in their car park and strolled round the town visiting shops in search of an appropriate souvenir, stopping first at Jackie's Attic for a toastie and tea. Must get my priorities right!

Kendal's High Street is very long so that my search and general exploration consumed a generally pleasant three hours. In that time, I learned that Kendal has a very long history, a 12th century castle and a house where Bonny Prince Charlie stayed during the war with England.

There were no obvious references to the Ireland family but I chose a guidebook that describes the town and its history as the souvenir. It is far too old for my niece now but perhaps will have more lasting interest than a Kendal ashtray. My family rarely receives any gift from me that isn't a book!

The hostel was busy tonight with some sixty-nine members staying. They don't do an evening meal so I decided to try to squeeze in a meal in time to see *The Apt Pupil,* a film showing at the nearby Brewery Arts Centre. Doing so required a quick shower and dining at McDonald's both for speed and to save enough on dinner to afford the film.

The cinema was like some of our new North American ones—spacious, wide screen and elevated seats for a clear sight line. There may have been 30 people in the 250-seat auditorium. It appeared as if this lack of patronage was common as there were lots of promotional events to increase trade even to the point of providing transport for people from rural areas and offering meal and film combination nights. A bar and an outside patio with tables improved the already pleasant ambiance. A very nice centre; it will be a shame if it fails due to lack of support.

Although I had no recollection of ever being in Kendal previously, I was experiencing déjà vu. The exterior of the hostel and the Arts Centre were familiar to me. Now, I realise that my previous visit was only four years ago! My hostel roommates tonight were four walkers from Preston up for the weekend and a sour-faced chap. He never uttered a word that I heard, slept under my berth and was still there next morning after the rest of us had breakfasted and were departing!

The next day's run from Kendal to Dentdale was only 41 kilometres that I thought would be fairly easy but a cold rain and steady climb to Sedbergh made the journey feel difficult. It was still raining when I stopped for tea. I explored a little bookstall to prolong the rest period but was obviously unwelcome to the dour little woman minding the stall. So, I bought a Bounty bar for energy, gave in and carried on towards Dent. The road became fairly flat following the river and through very pretty countryside. Now, rather than spoiling things, the light rain enhanced the atmosphere, providing a more authentic character than a sunshiny day would have. So I wasn't entirely unhappy with the weather at this point.

I reached Dent at 1.30 and quickly chose the King George Pub over the Sun for lunch, as it looked more upscale and offered Roast Beef and Yorkshire pudding. A very traditional Sunday lunch was exactly what I needed to warm up. I persuaded myself that I would forgo the evening meal to appease the budget. Inclusion of a sweet in the £4.95 price eased the decision and given that the remainder of the day's journey was short, I also persuaded myself that a half pint of lager was permissible. Being Sunday, the pub was very busy and I had arrived only half an hour before they stopped taking orders. So, I performed a very abbreviated wash and brush up in the loo and got my order in just in time.

Despite the meal, it seemed even colder when I went back outside, making my long cycling tights a must. I walked round the cobble stone streets of Dent encountering a middle-aged man who was interested in my cycle. He told me that his first frame (a famous Claude Butler) had cost him £23 at age 16 but had been stolen last year. He had just found a replacement frame and was going to fit it out with quality gear.

Unfortunately, all this rain has stopped my computer and I was unable to track my progress. It was only another ten kilometres to the hostel but I am very dependent on that computer to assess distance and speed as well as helping me to anticipate the specified turns on my route. This distance was easy and amidst lovely countryside. This was particularly true of the last half that ran along a rushing brook with glen like topography with huge rocks worn smooth by centuries of water. I met a man and his wife on the last day of a cycling trip. They were upset at the prospect of returning home tonight because he had to be at work tomorrow. (Sometimes, we destroy the joy of the now with bad thoughts of the past or future, ensuring that much of our lives are spent miserable).

I arrived at the hostel about 4.30 and met an English walking couple from Stockport waiting for the opening at 5. The place was thick with midges—the first real insect problem I have encountered. I quickly unloaded the panniers into the entranceway and found an open shed to pop the bike into. The common room and drying rooms were also open so I put my sopping panniers and shoes in there. By this time, the hostel was ready to register its guests

My eight-bedded room was called Inglebrough. My companions were two Englishmen and a Yank from Kansas who now works in Toronto in the organic vegetable business. All the facilities are down the hall. Two sinks, two showers and two toilets.

There were another three Canadians (from the Okanogan Valley), a couple in their thirties and a woman of about sixty. We had dinner together with the English couple and chatted away amiably until about nine. It turned out that I was the newcomer to the group as everyone else had met the previous night at another hostel.

The English couple was very pleasant, refined and educated. He was a semi-retired Economics and statistics lecturer and was pursuing an Open University course in philosophy. 'The course was good value', he said, because it required seven or eight essays and a final examination. Next morning, I got stuck with a shy Englishman who nevertheless proved to be an interesting person because of his knowledge of canals, geography and transportation history.

The new day began cold and wet again. The walkers left but I stayed behind in hopes that the rain would stop. At about 10.30, a crowd of school children arrived creating general bedlam, so I decided to leave despite the continuing rain. I got the bike out of the shed between raindrops but before I could attach the panniers, the skies started dumping bucketfuls. So, I moved back inside to wait out the rain and finally set off about eleven.

My route today went by the 350 metre high Dent Railway station mentioned in the previous chapter. I stopped for a look and discovered a waterfall at the end of the platform. This could easily be a set for a period drama. The road continued climbing for probably six kilometres to the Garsdale Head junction with the Kirkby Stephen Road. The Moorcock Inn conveniently stood at the junction, tempting me to a lunch break. The Moorcock is one of two historic moorland inns that in horse-drawn traffic days were essential staging posts in the bleak trek over the moors—and are still very welcome to thirsty cyclists.

An old gentleman cyclist left The Moorcock just before I did and later I overtook him studying the landscape. He warned me of lots of water on the road at Black Boar Fell but when I arrived it did not seem dangerous. I had to walk a fair bit, particularly one climb that was a 20% grade. At the turn to Keld, there were only three kilometres into Kirkby Stephen where a tea break seemed more of a possibility than if I stuck to my route. This was, after all, a tour for and on teacakes—so a detour was justified.

Kirkby Stephen caters a lot to the tourist trade but is still an honest, natural, busy and pleasant market town. I stopped at The

Mulberry Tree, an upscale tea and gift shop—to be greeted as 'Another Canadian!' by one of their customers. She was a university student from British Columbia, travelling for most of the summer. The tea was excellent and the teacakes were perfect, not over toasted, so good, in fact that a second order was required. This was not a real indulgence as I used the time productively to learn from the newspaper about the latest in British life. Apparently the pound sign is missing from some newly issued notes making the Conservatives nervous that the Labour Party was surreptitiously preparing for adoption of the Euro!

Behind the market entrance was a square of green mown lawn, smooth as a bowling green, surrounded with footpaths bordered with lovely manicured trees. A nice church with twelfth century origins and a lovely wooden ceiling featuring coats of arms at the intersections sat peacefully in the green. The rector stopped to say hello. The market entrance had a historic poster advising fourteenth century charges for stalls and hawkers.

About four, I started the run to Keld Hostel thinking I had plenty of time. The weather had improved considerably; my computer had dried out sufficiently to register speed and distance and my spirits rose. The route was tough but included perfect waterfalls, bubbling brooks and sheep-manicured moors, making this one of the most pleasant two hours of the entire trip. I saw heron, rabbits, sheep and cattle. The sheep responded to my conversational enquiries and the cattle at least acknowledged that I spoke to them. Sometimes if both sets of animals appear in rapid succession, I get my languages confused and speak to cattle in sheep tongue! (This talking to the animals is a harmless foible in my character makeup –it has nothing to do with Dr. Doolittle).

The hostel at Keld was immediately likeable. I wasn't too late for evening meal and there was only one person in my room. He turned out to be from Hartlepool but worked on the Aberdeenshire oilrigs and was walking the Pennine Way. We had a pleasant meal served by a bright, open-faced cheerful woman, my stereotypical image of a happy country wife—attractive in a fresh wholesome way. We were speculating on her accent so I finally asked her and learned that she was from North Derbyshire in Buxton. She said just twelve miles south of there the accents are totally different.

Next morning I spent an unproductive hour trying to improve the power of my brakes. Part of that time was wasted on the front brakes that turned out not to need any attention. I could not get the rear pads any closer to the rims without rubbing. Brakes have been my nemesis for years but this bike's rear wheel and brakes seem to have it in for me. Aligning the wheel properly and getting it tight enough to hold position under a heavy load is always difficult. Of course if it isn't aligned properly then the brakes don't work as they should or the whole wheel slips and rubs up against the chain stay.

Consequently it was ten before I got underway. The day was bright and warm and the road ran flat alongside a nice river, over stone bridges to Thwaite and Muker. Once again, I decided that this day's route was the best yet—particularly around Keld. It was slightly gentler than yesterday and was lushly carpeted in various shades of green. There were deep valleys, streams, stonewalls --- all the features necessary to complete my idyllic vision of rural England. Swaledale and Dentdale are the best of the dales in my opinion. The only possible improvement would be an unladen trip.

Just beyond Reeth, I decided to go further east rather than climb out of the valley as planned. This meant going to Richmond—a nice, relatively flat run. There I requested a Baba ('book a bed ahead') booking for Thirsk at the Tourist Information Office. This would take about an hour to arrange as Thirsk was outside the Richmond TIC district. I waited for the response on a bench in an adjacent park. While enjoying a snack there, I got into conversation with a man who had retired nine years ago from the horticultural business. He told me that he had joined the Richmond Cycle Club in 1947 and used to participate in their 160-kilometre Sunday runs over the dales on fixed wheel (only one gear) bikes! He suggested a route to Thirsk for me that coincided with my plans so I could be genuinely enthusiastic.

After the specified hour's wait, I returned to the Tourist Office and found that they had booked me into Long Acre in Thirsk. I am always just a little leery of the culinary conditions in private homes so declined the offered evening meal. Long Acre specified that they would hold the reservation only until 6 pm and the TIC ladies were concerned that I could cover the 46 kilometres in time (now 1.30).

This did not prove to be a problem. The first 26 kilometres took only an hour and brought me to North Allerton, a large market town without apparent tourist appeal. My speed meant there was time to explore the High Street and find some refreshment. I chose a teashop on the High Street but was disappointed at both quality and price.

The remaining run to Thirsk took only an hour so that by five I was opposite the former home of veterinarian, Alf Wight (James Herriott of *All Creatures Great and Small*). I walked round the market square trying to find a pub that would substitute for the evening meal I had declined at the B&B. Every one of them offered only lunch, so I went on to Long Acre.

The address was 86A Topcliffe Road. After number 84, the name of the road and the numerical sequence changed! I stopped there to learn that Topcliffe Road continued half a block away. Once at 86A, Rose Dawson warmly greeted me. She later brought a full pot of tea and buttered scones to my room even though I had tea-making facilities in the room. I could immediately tell that this was a clean and generous household so I asked Rose if it was too late to change my mind about the evening meal. It wasn't!

After a shower and brush-up, I went downstairs to a massive meal with lots of fresh vegetables including one of my favourites, parsnips. A little later her other five guests arrived for similar large meals. After dinner she asked if I had any washing. When I gratefully brought my laundry down, Rose brought out maps and books to suggest pleasant back roads to York where I am going next.

Next morning, the table was laid with grapefruit segments, strawberries, bananas, cantaloupe and orange juice. This was followed by scrambled eggs on toast and grilled tomatoes.

My laundry was delivered fresh and folded from the tumble dryer and my cycle was brought out from the shed. She filled my water bottle and offered to make sandwiches. I have never had such service in a B&B. The cost of all this was C$ 55, including dinner. She definitely deserved a gratuity but I am embarrassed to realise now that I did not think of it at the time.

Rose recommended that I visit the Herriott museum that she said opened at nine. The museum is at Alf Wight's old surgery. His son, James has taken over the practice but moved outside the village. The museum just opened this April and already had 20,000 admissions. Unfortunately, opening time was actually ten, so I deferred my visit to another trip and went up the street to St. Mary's, the church where Alf was married in 1941. It is a very old church with a castellated tower, wooden ceilings and pews. Two people were worshiping together in a small chapel. (I am happy to report that the museum is very worthwhile, encompassing the living quarters and surgery as well as the studio sets used for the television series and a complete veterinary museum on the first floor. I did indeed visit again).

The day was cool and overcast. I set off towards Sowerby that was largely a long tree-lined residential street, very pleasant and genteel. (I could live here easily). Next stop was Kilburn, another lovely small village, larger than Sowerby and famous for being the location of Robert Thompson's Mouseman furniture

This is traditional oak furniture made special by a small mouse carved into every piece. Thompson was born in 1876 and apprenticed for five years before becoming an independent craftsman. These five-year apprenticeships are still the career path for furniture craftsmen, at least at this establishment. Each craftsman makes his own version of the mouse so you can tell which one made your piece of furniture. I watched two of them and talked to one of them who showed me how a latticework for a chair back was made. This involved four hours of labour. . A small gift shop and museum are housed in Thompson's original home.

Across the road was a modern, upscale furniture showroom where I priced a dining room set very similar to that owned by friends of ours in Hertfordshire. The table and six chairs would have been over C$12,000—out of our league!

Next-door was the Singing Bird, a tea and gift shop. This time my teacakes were spread with a superb lemon cheese. However, the proprietress was unfriendly and she over-charged for her wares—perhaps she was a recent transplant from the urban south of England. So it wasn't entirely surprising three years later on my 2002 tour to find that this particular 'Bird' was no longer singing.

Further along, I stopped in the first Skoda dealership I had ever seen to look at their Octavia estate car. Skoda is a Czech brand that is now owned by VW. The Octavia's VW origins were clearly recognisable; it closely resembles the Passat but sells for about C$12000 less. Car prices in Britain are always a shock even after you make the adjustment for the sales tax that is buried in the price rather than tacked on afterwards. In the UK the VAT (value-added tax) is 17.5%.

I carried on straight into York and decided to have a late lunch at an all day fish and chip place. Just as I was locking the bike, a yahoo walking along the pavement was shouting into his mobile, 'f… this' and 'f… that' and calling the woman he was shouting at, 'a cow'. This was a very upsetting welcome to my favourite city but unfortunately this sort of behaviour is a frequent hazard in the larger centres.

After lunch, I walked round the Shambles and Newgate Market just absorbing the atmosphere. It was impossible to keep all the architectural styles and historical information straight. After very little time, everything was all a jumble in my mind. So at about four, I started to make my way towards the Dairy, a vegetarian B&B that Mari and I had stayed in during our 1992 visit.

Although I had no city map, street name or number, I was able to go directly to the B&B location from memory or would have done if a bicycle shop had not appeared enroute. This required a stop. Inside, the owner, Andy, introduced me to the Gazelle, a Dutch make that he praised highly over Japanese, US and British makes for its quality. He sold other brands as well so I felt that his enthusiasm was genuine

These Gazelles are primarily urban or commuter type cycles with chain guards, generators for the lights, luggage carriers and built in locks. Their purpose-built functionality strongly appeals to me. I would love to have one. I asked Andy's advice on my rear brake problems and wound up leaving the cycle with him overnight to see what could be done.

The Diary was just up the road so I quickly checked in, had a shower and went out again about six as I had a ticket for 'Iolanthe' at the Theatre Royal and needed a meal first. It took twenty minutes to walk to the Café Royal that is in the theatre complex where I planned to have my meal.

With time at a premium, my luck was to get a determined idiot as a server. First, she did not realise that the dish I ordered was even on the menu; then, after a long delay, I asked her to check on my order which she agreed to do but never reported the outcome. I was just rising from my seat to leave when the meal arrived, nearly an hour after placing the order, leaving me 25 minutes before playtime!

It was an excellent meal that unfortunately had to be wolfed down, not savoured. I had chosen a Parmesan cheese and leek flan that was accompanied with a plate of perfectly cooked new potatoes, snow peas and broccoli. Thus, hastily fortified, I walked to the theatre.

The Theatre Royal is very grand in plush, Victorian style but the production paled in comparison to what I am accustomed to at Stratford and the Shaw Festival at home. The sets and costumes were amateurish and I could not hear much of the dialogue (this latter complaint may be a personal issue not a production fault). However, the actor playing the part of the Lord Chancellor was outstanding—

Stratford, Ontario quality.

The next day was full of planned activities. Mari had re-assigned me the task of finding a special Aran type sweater that I had been unable to find three years ago and I wanted to look for some English country squire type shirts. The Shambles area seemed best for both these. On the way I wanted to find the Cockatoo Creperie that Mari and I had enjoyed so much back in 1992. Amazingly, I was able to walk almost directly to it—usually I am extremely challenged directionally. But the Cockatoo has become the Blue Bicycle complete with an elderly blue cycle casually resting against one corner and glowing newspaper reviews displayed prominently outside. According to these the Blue Bicycle is one of the top restaurants in York. Their prices reflected this judgement making an evening meal out of the question and lunch a severe budgetary strain.

After a exploring a number of shops with no success, I stopped in the Edinburgh Woollen Mill and found a special sale of exactly the type of shirts I wanted, so I bought two. The appropriate Aran sweater was not even available let alone on sale.

I headed back to the B&B, stopping at the cycle shop on the way to collect my bike. Andy reported that my wheel had been out of alignment and that the rear brake mounting was at the wrong level. It was intended for a 27" wheel that is nearly extinct and the cycle was fitted with the larger new standard 700 mm wheels. No wonder this has been a consistent concern.

I left the bike and my purchases at the B&B and set off on foot again. It was now noon, signalling the time to head to the Blue Bicycle for my special lunch treat. I was their first customer but it filled up quickly with prosperous appearing businessmen and well-coiffed women. I ordered a goat cheese flan with salad and a glass of wine. This was a meal that had to be savoured slowly to maximise the experience because the quantity of food was never going to fill me up. It was thoroughly enjoyable although more would have been better.

Next stop was a small but elegantly restored Georgian house in Copperfields, called Fairfax House. The house, then a cinema, had been purchased in 1982 for £30,000 and two years plus £750,000 were spent restoring it to its former glory. Fairfax and his daughter had used the house as a coming out residence. Ineffectively, apparently, as Miss Fairfax never met anyone suitable and died a spinster at 68.

During the Civil War, Fairfax had prevented the soldiers from looting the Cathedral (such activities provided the primary compensation for the common soldier). Consequently, York Minster was a generous contributor to the restoration fund. Mr. Terry, of chocolate fame, gave all the furnishings. Apart from these historical connections, the house was interesting for the information provided about domestic life at the time—all of which I have since forgotten!

I then walked to the Railway Museum—the largest in the world. My schedule provided only a little over two hours for this visit and this proved to be far too short. Stephenson's original Rocket, engines back to 1848, Royal Mail trains past and present were all there. However, most interesting to me were the Royal carriages, complete with bathtubs.

My next stop was at York Minster for Evensong. It is a service I've always enjoyed but is typically only available in the larger cathedrals like Winchester, Salisbury and York. There is very little involvement for the congregation so one can sit peaceably and simply let the glorious music and majesty of the surroundings soothe and refresh your soul. Even an atheist would be moved. This service was held in the choir area with seating for visitors right behind the choir. This evening's congregation had a high proportion of foreigners suggesting that many other tourists feel the same way as I do about Evensong.

The service was short, making it too early for evening meal, so I strolled around the Shambles some more. There is always something interesting to see there. However, as soon as the clock struck 6.30, I headed for the Olde Starre in Stonegate, a pub listed in a guidebook my sister, Guila, gave me. This was an extremely old pub but they had caved in to modern pressures, installing games and television and thus spoiling the atmosphere somewhat. I had lamb with rosemary and would have had black current tart also but they ran out before I could place my order.

Lincoln and the Old German

Next morning at breakfast in the Diary, a couple already at my table when I arrived, immediately and enthusiastically introduced themselves as the 'X's' from Philadelphia, apparently assuming that I was also from the US. As soon as I said, 'I am from Canada' they lost interest. Later when their breakfast was served—a skilfully presented poached egg on toast with a sprinkle of sesame seed -- Mrs. X was upset with the colour of the egg. When informed that the Diary was an organic food B&B and that the egg's colour was due to it being free-

Panniers, Pedals, and Pubs

range, she demanded a replacement!

Today marks the start of my journey southward into new territory for me. Tomorrow's destination is Lincoln where I have booked into the hostel; tonight, however, I need to find a B&B somewhere. Access to my route was very convenient from the Diary and soon I was in the countryside travelling the B1228.

This brought me to the port town of Goole in time for lunch. Goole is one of Britain's furthest inland seaports, situated nearly 70 kilometres from the North Sea, where the Don and Ouse rivers meet. The rapid growth of Goole as a port dates from 1826 when docks were built and a canal cut from Knottingley. Cargo was drawn down the canal in square containers, called 'Tom Puddings' that are like floating railway trucks. (7) There is a Dutch element to Goole's history that I did not investigate, as the town was unattractive and did not inspire.

As so many English towns have done, Goole's principal shopping area, the High Street has been made into a pedestrian mall. These are generally very successful, making shopping a much more pleasant activity and creating a stronger sense of community with benches and other amenities sprinkled throughout.

This is market gardening country, with few animals and generally uninteresting homes and villages. But the very flat terrain allowed me to make very good time; so good that it seemed possible that I might reach Lincoln tonight. That would allow me to explore Lincoln for part of tomorrow as well as cut down on the 180 + kilometres gap between Lincoln and Cambridge that my schedule required me to do in two days.

While in the midst of these thoughts and calculations, I suddenly heard the voices of several children at play. This turned out to be a school games day across the road. This seemed a worthwhile diversion so I wheeled the bike across a small paddock to where the parents and teachers were observing the games from folding chairs. The children were in the 8 to 10 age group and were competing girls vs. girls and boys vs. boys at traditional games like three-legged races. The warm sunny day was brightened by the children's joy and the parent's obvious enjoyment. It was very natural and good-natured; the children helped the teachers set up each event and took an obvious delight in everything. In many cases both parents were in attendance. This sort of scene is also part of my idealised vision of England is and how it should be. Alas, the vision doesn't have a lot of truth in it anymore. I don't think similar visions are true anywhere now.

By 5 pm, I was certain that I could reach Lincoln tonight so I rang the hostel to see if they could bring my reservation forward and somewhat optimistically, ordered dinner which is served at seven. I was in luck with the reservation but unfortunately, my estimate of the remaining distance to Lincoln was 13 km short and once there it took twenty minutes to find the hostel. (Again, the hostel was not well signposted and few local people seemed to know anything about it). I arrived at 7.30 to find my now desiccated dinner still waiting for me.

Arriving on time would not have improved the meal very much. The gourmet touch has yet to reach hostel land and probably never will; although, given the high proportion of vegetarians in Britain, there is generally a choice. The dining room was very hot, so I sat in the conservatory where there was a bit of a breeze. This faced out on to a lovely common called South Park.

During my dinner an old German, seated at a separate table with a map, was trying to work how far he had cycled that day. He was talking to himself but in a manner that strongly suggested he wanted an audience so I obliged. Given that he was older and heavier, I was a bit put off by determining his day's distance at 93 km when I had been feeling particularly superior with my 134!

After a refreshing shower, I set up housekeeping in my private room—just seven empty beds and me. All the equipment at Lincoln hostel seemed new and in good condition. I went back to the conservatory to bring my notes up to date, enjoying the lovely breeze.

We had a terrific thunderstorm during the night—the loudest I've ever heard—it was particularly potent in my lonely basement room with the windows open. At breakfast, the old German found someone else to impress with his tale. He was very self-centred—never showing any interest in the other person except to bridge into an opportunity to tell more about himself. He is riding a hired woman's frame Peugeot and heading for Boston today (about 65 km).

Getting into Lincoln proper was very easy after all my navigational activity last night trying to find the hostel. Then Lincoln had looked particularly intriguing. Now with Saturday morning shoppers and traffic, it was less so, seemingly indistinguishable from many other similar sized English cities. I wanted to find out about the cycle museum and locate a tourist information office to do a "Baba"booking (book a bed ahead). Inquiring about the TIC in a bookshop in the first floor of Jews House (a 12th century home at the foot of Steephill), I was asked whether I wanted a TIC up the hill or down. I said it did not matter so she gave me the UP and was it ever!

The street was cobbled and must have been a 1 in 3 ascent. But it was delightfully lined with small quality shops leading to the castle, more cobbled streets, shops and Roman remains. Along the way, I passed the Wig and Mitre pub, one of those recommended in my pub guidebook. Carrying on to the TIC, I made my request for a B&B somewhere in the Grantham area and returned to the Wig and Mitre while waiting for the TIC to make the arrangements.

The pub was an elegant place in a solid middle-class sort of way. Their coffee room was on the first floor in a panelled room with a fireplace. I had my first coffee of the trip with plum bread and jam. The coffee was first rate improving the already very acceptable ambiance. On the way out, I read posted newspaper critiques highly praising the Wig and Mitre as one of those 'surprisingly good little places'. It was a shame not to stay for a more substantial meal.

Wig & Mitre Pub, near Castle, Lincoln

On towards Cambridge

After a stroll round the rest of the cobble-stoned area, I returned to the TIC to learn that they had found me a place in Grantham. As it was near noon and the distance appeared to be about 60 km, it was time to get underway. I wiped off most of the accumulated mud on the bike, lubricated everything and then collected a pre-packaged sandwich and jug of freshly squeezed orange juice from Marks & Spencer for lunch later.

Grantham, the home of Isaac Newton and Margaret Thatcher, was probably less than 5 km off my original route. The terrain was still flat, permitting good speed and allowing time for a leisurely park bench lunch break at Brant Broughton. Despite this, I still arrived in Grantham by four and took the opportunity to see a little of the town before calling in at the B&B. Grantham has an attractive market square, some fine old coaching inns and a lovely riverside walk, some of which is maintained by the National Trust. There are other points of interest such as the 14th century spire of St. Wulfram's Church, a 15th century grammar school north of the church, Grantham House and the Angel and Royal Hotel in the High Street. Generally though, Grantham appeared a bit downmarket and run down.

The Crown and Anchor hotel attracted me with an irresistible offer of refreshments in their lounge. I went in, used their washroom to tidy up, and then enjoyed a languid hour on the sofa reading their *Times* and savouring a pot of filter coffee with a single scone. The incongruity of the experience appeals to my memory even now, the scruffy cyclist wearing questionable gear pretending to be a toff in genteel surroundings!

It took some time to find the B&B because its landmark, the crematorium, was poorly signposted. The B&B was called Robert's Roost and this Robert was assigned to the top of the roost in a tiny room whose only window was in the house roof. Nevertheless, the room was clean, nicely decorated and equipped with all the comforts, tea fixings and television. The *Times* television guide promised a good murder story on ITV later tonight that I planned to watch.

Next morning the landlady gave me a table by myself that I generally prefer as I enjoy reading at breakfast. I had barely opened the book when another man walked in saying, 'my name is David Y. I'm a professor of physics in San Francisco; may I join you?' His business card said Lecturer but I did not point out his overstatement. Learning that I was from the Toronto area, he claimed that a University of Toronto professor had helped organise his current tour of ten universities lecturing on 'The Physics of Magic and the Magic of Physics'. Most of the breakfast was devoted to his story, which was very interesting, so I did not mind doing the bulk of the listening (if he were asked he probably would remember me as a brilliant conversationalist). He was involved in summer theatre with a group of renaissance players doing magic using a learned Elizabethan accent!

There was also an astounding coincidence. His daughter, Eleanor, is the same age as my son Cameron and like him, also a graduate of the San Francisco Conservatory of Music. According to her father, Eleanor is a 'real looker.' I wondered if he were acting as matchmaker. Later in the day during my weekly call home, Cameron claimed no recollection of her.

I got away again at 9.30 and as the run to today's objective-- Ramsay was only 70 km, spent my first half hour enjoying the riverside park. It was pleasant but not extensive. There were a few fishermen on the bank and a few walkers.

Later on in the countryside, I suddenly encountered row upon row of cars along the road with scores of people looking off into the distance at the railway tracks. They were awaiting the imminent arrival of the Flying Scotsman, now 76 years old and recently restored at a cost of £1 million. The Flying Scotsman's run today from London to York was it's first trip since restoration and people had paid up to £300 for a seat. Later when the train passed by, it appeared full of passengers enjoying champagne and nibbles. I got an excellent shot of the engine.

I arrived in Stamford about one and decided to stop for lunch at the Bull&Swan. I initially went up to the bar to ask directions to a particular B road on my route. One of the customers at bar took an interest, immediately branding me as Canadian. He claimed not to know the road but then later realised that it was the road adjacent to the pub and the road that he lived on! Locally the road is known by the name of the town it leads to, not by its official number, which isn't even posted. I have found this phenomenon to be very common.

We discussed my afternoon route. He became concerned that I would not be able to find a place to stay in Ramsay and so gave me the name and telephone number of a woman who could help me in a pinch. I got the impression that they had shared more than a pinch.

After lunch I set off confidently on my now discovered B road, reaching Ramsay before six. My pub acquaintance was right about accommodation here. But I chose not to contact his friend and booked in at the George. That was a mistake. The George was expensive, dirty and obviously not well patronised—there were cobwebs in the bath! I compounded the financial damage with an oversized curry dinner.

Next morning's breakfast was served on a tidy but unclean table. Like the room, all the necessary ingredients were there but the lack of care and cleanliness created a slovenly air that was depressing.

The day, however, was bright and lifted my spirits. I immediately applied sunscreen but after a few minutes of riding the sunscreen was streaming down my face and my arms were coated with black insects stuck in the goo. This was a relatively short distance day (64 km) and I felt no compulsion to hurry. The countryside became more rolling and there were occasional animals to talk to, the villages were more abundant and attractive.

Mid-morning, I stopped at a post office/general store for a bit of snack and used the opportunity to peruse the new issue of *WHICH* car magazine which featured reviews of the best cars of 1999. They were lavish with praise for the new Ford Focus and highly complimentary about the Rover 75. *WHICH* is an excellent magazine that provides very useful comparisons of different cars in the same price/type category. Unfortunately, lack of space and the magazine's price dictated that it remain on the shelf. I took my small snack out to a wrought iron pavilion in the middle of the street and enjoyed it with my book for a few minutes.

My route this morning, based on the guidebook, was again unclear. It is in many ways an admirable guide but seemingly with many errors or at least room for misunderstanding in the directions. I had been slightly uncomfortable with this opinion, given my generally poor sense of direction, until my trip in 2004 when I met an End-to-End cyclist at the St. Just hostel in Cornwall.

We met on the evening before and breakfasted together on the morning of his first day of the trip. To do things properly, he had to cycle the 11 km south to Land's End to actually begin and then return north. I noticed that he was using the same guide and expressed my opinion of its inaccuracies. He agreed and showed me a full-page list of the errors that he had found before even setting out! One needs to study a detailed map when planning these trips and make regular reference to it while enroute.

You need to know where you are going, what other places are on the route as well as beyond your daily destination so that you can make quick decisions when negotiating busy roundabouts. Often the particular road you want will not be so marked or the destination shown on the road sign will not be the one you want but another, either before or after yours.

Another hint: become familiar with the conventions used for road signs. Find out if the order of towns listed indicates their relative distance and if so, which is listed first, the closest or the furthest? Occasionally, and this is particularly true in countries that use the roundabout system, you will be directed to your destination on a road that does not actually go there but leads you to another roundabout where you will be directed to the correct road. The UK often provides a clue to this indirect routing by showing the number of the road you really want in brackets next to your destination name.

The bold arrows often painted on the tarmac are another interesting feature of the UK road system.. I have puzzled over these for years because these arrows appear on bends at the centre of the road but sometimes follow the path of the bend and other times point the opposite way. Today, in St. Ives, I chose to ask someone why and was told that the arrows are guides to overtaking, telling the driver which lane it is safe to be in—much like the dotted and solid lines used in North America.

St. Ives wasn't actually on the guide route but it was so close that I had to make a detour. I'm still not sure whether this is the St. Ives of the famous children's poem—'I met a man with seven wives' or whether the Cornish one is. Now having seen them both, I prefer this one. The Cornish one is too dependent on tourism and does not have the feel of natural town functioning normally.

Panniers, Pedals, and Pubs

St. Ives on River Great Ouse, Huntingdonshire

Today was market day and the place was thronged, giving it a holiday air. It was a beautifully sunny day also which made the riverside location even more attractive. There were handsome homes on one side of the river and outdoor cafes on the other with a 15th Century bridge between the two sides. The bridge was graced with one of only four medieval bridge chapels surviving in England. This chapel was converted to a house in the 19th century.

The different ways that other peoples and countries organise the basics of life has always been of interest to me. One aspect in particular is home construction and design. I am intrigued by the breezeblock exterior and interior wall construction used in Britain, wondering if it is more expensive than the wood structures used in North America and what the relative merits might be. Consequently, I am always on the lookout for model homes that one can visit. After lunch, I came upon a site under construction consisting of a former farm where the barn had been converted to a home with dark brown stained weatherboard on the upper storey and an attractive brick below. The other homes were new and smaller but built in a similar style. I could not go in but walked round looking in the windows. The layouts were very appealing with a comfortable, airy look even though the rooms were generally smaller than we are used to in North America. The ground floor construction was visible on a few homes that were not yet completed. There were solid concrete floors meaning no basement, breezeblock interior walls and plastic plumbing. Despite its reputation for a poor climate, Britain is not so cold that it needs to build basements to get below the frost line.

Despite this diversion and the detour to St. Ives, I arrived in Cambridge by 3.30. Cambridge obviously has a much stronger attraction for tourists than Lincoln; it is more famous and the proximity to London probably adds to its appeal. Strange then that Lincoln had five tourist information offices and I am aware of only one in Cambridge.

Cambridge is one of Europe's ancient university cities. Dissidents who had found the slightly older Oxford inhibited their freedom of expression founded the oldest college, Peterhouse, in 1285. The compact college area in Cambridge's centre is fascinating, well worth a day's exploration of its architectural treasures, ranging from the 13th century to the late 20th. Despite a recent city-centre ban, Cambridge is a city where everybody bikes, with the highest level of cycle commuting in Britain. (8)

The place was overrun with foreigners; US voices were

everywhere but there were visitors from many countries. For me the sense of being a tourist and being seen to be one became very strong and I did not like it. Self-analysis about these feelings is not very helpful. I can't be sure whether I dislike being seen as a stereotypical tourist or want to be considered as an informed and ok near local. Both reasons are probably valid as well as wanting to think that my own experiences are special and some how not attainable by other North Americans.

This was a poor time for live theatre. Shakespeare's "Measure for Measure" at Emmanuel College was the only play on offer. Two days later and Wilde's "The Importance of Being Earnest" would be available. I am booked into the hostel for three nights but my last day is earmarked for a visit to see old friends in Welwyn Garden City, Hertfordshire.

I went along to the TIC, encountering huge queues, checked on train times and bought a walking tour guidebook. This guide was very helpful and interesting but walking along reading it and peering at various buildings removed any doubt that I was a tourist.

The hostel proved to be located conveniently close to the railway station for my journey to Hertfordshire. Slovenian tourists packed the pavement outside the hostel as I arrived. The Slovenians held a religious service in the games room later that night. Their strong and pleasant singing was a nice accompaniment for completing my journal in the adjacent dining room.

Afterwards, I attempted to take advantage of the hostel's laundry facilities but was thwarted by a US woman from northern California who was a real dither head. She monopolised the tumble dryer, delaying the completion of my laundry until 11.30. Unfortunately, you really need to stay put while the laundry is in process so that you don't hold up others and can grab a machine as soon as it becomes available. One washer and dryer for perhaps 100 guests is managing a bit tight. I sat close by and read my book so while the ambience was not inviting or particularly comfortable this wasn't entirely a waste of time. During my wait, Denise, the rather interesting receptionist, came in to collect her smalls from the top of the dryer. The number of guests using the facilities had frustrated her also. I must admit to having checked the tags on those frilly bits, getting a much better picture of her personal dimensions than her loose clothing provided.

Hostel tradition is lights out at eleven. This is honoured more in the smaller centres where they often lock up at that time. In larger centres with lots of nightlife the rule has either been abandoned or is just ignored. I noticed on my 2004 trip that some hostels now use combination locks on the outside doors (changing the combination daily) and give members the combination for late night returns.

Given the time I finished my laundry tonight, I felt bound to get ready for bed in the dark to avoid disturbing anyone in the room. So, it was particularly upsetting to be awakened at 12.30 by the light being switched on and then to have the intruder demand my bed! In my years' of hostelling experience, beds have never been assigned, just 'first come, first choice'. That is, until Cambridge. This room key had a number tag designating which bunk you were to use but I wasn't aware of it.

This idiot woke everyone up and made a fuss to get the bunk I was in although there was a free bunk ready and waiting. I refused, then someone else called out for the light to be turned off and he gave in. But for the next twenty minutes he was in and out of the room, turning on the small reading light over his bunk at least four times. In the morning, I traded keys with him and then asked the receptionist (not Denise) to record that I would be in Bunk 1, not 4, this evening. She said that could not be done, as someone else was booked into 1! I managed to persuade her that the new person could be booked into 4 with the stroke of a pen of which I was sure she was capable. (I don't whether she really was incapable or just bloody-minded, because it did not get changed).

Next morning at breakfast, the Californian dither head asked me to join her and revealed that she had been on a US Social Security disability pension for the past eleven years. She had been a computer systems analyst and developed a bad back. Previously, I would not have thought such a pension would permit a two month long holiday in the UK but perhaps she had saved for years.

After breakfast I walked into the city centre to see the Backs. The Backs are lawns behind the colleges that run down to the river. So the views are of pasture with cattle, punters on the river, beautiful lawns and the colleges. Must be conducive to productive thought.

I went behind Kings and Clare Colleges and then took a path back into the city centre with the Wren Library to the left and Trinity Hall to the right. A tour of Trinity was cheaper than Kings so I chose Trinity. Today their normal tour was reduced to £1 because the Hall and Chapel were closed. Trinity is the largest college with 650 students.

The courtyard is very large (it was used for the famous scene in the film "Chariots of Fire" where the challenge was to run the entire courtyard circumference while the clock is striking noon). The students' rooms surround this courtyard in blocks of about eight to ten rooms per doorway. The ambiance just oozed tradition, exclusiveness and intellect ---at least it did in my imagination.

I circled back and went into the Wren Library which was populated primarily by tourists rather than academics but that may be simply a matter of it being summer. The Wren boasts beautiful woodcarvings and ancient collections, including Newton's first letter regarding gravity, his walking stick and an illuminated bible.

After a lunch on a bench in the market square I completed the self-guided walking tour started yesterday, seeing the Round Church (modelled after the Holy Sepulchre in Jerusalem). C.S. Lewis information and his books were in abundance. C.S. Lewis is of particular interest at the moment as I brought one of his books on this trip intent on studying it thoroughly. Surely good intentions count for something. But so far, spy and high finance novels have won out.

Three different college dining halls stood out as most impressive. One, at Emmanuel College, was decorated in a restful and beautiful cool green and white in Georgian style. The general dining room arrangement is an elevated platform for the top table that is perpendicular to the students' bench style tables on the lower level. Another dining hall with heavy oak panelling was set up for a future meal with all the requisite crystal and extensive cutlery for several courses. I found two discarded menus from the previous day that could have come from a four star restaurant. If one has the ability and opportunity to be an English academic, this looks like the place to be!

I finished my tour with evensong at St. Johns. This was a special experience. The general layout was much the same as York Minster but since this evening's service was in the chapel it involved virtually the entire building making the surrounding long, narrow stained glass windows an integral part of the service. The choir was very good and I emerged soothed and at peace with the world.

It was now time to think about food again. Do I ever stop? Two pubs that I stopped in did not serve food in the evening. A couple of French restaurants invited but their prices repelled. I finally resorted to buying some food to take back to the hostel.

A young Canadian woman was in the members' kitchen preparing dinner for her and two friends that had just arrived yesterday on a two-month research project for their English professor back home.

I never met the others but this young woman was a bit overwhelmed with her situation. She was unable to describe her research project, had no idea where she and her friends might live during their stay and had nothing arranged to access research facilities. I gave her my Cambridge map and the remainder of my loaf of bread; these seemed to cheer her up somewhat, pitiful as they were.

About 1.30 in the morning, the hostel fire alarm went off and all 100 of us trooped out into the street in various states of dress. The fire engine arrived shortly and after a brief inspection, we were allowed to return to our beds. The poor Canadian girl was looking bewildered and as if she very much wished she were back home.

Next morning, breakfast was delayed because a large group of school children was allowed to start early. The children were all in period costumes for a special visit to some historic place. I sat next to two girls who were obviously best friends and very enthusiastic about the outing.

I went along to the railway station, arriving early enough to acquire a paper and join the train at a leisurely pace. For some reason, three different sets of people came on and each asked me what train it was—am I finally blending in?

This proved to be a milk run with frequent stops but still took only about an hour to get to Welwyn Garden City. I had purposively arrived an hour earlier than scheduled to meet my friends. This was to allow time to stroll round our old hometown. The railway station was the biggest change. It is much larger now and encompasses a well-appointed shopping mall. Otherwise, there is little obvious change—it is still a very attractive place if a little less well cared for. An estate agent's window advertised a new home for £235,000 in an estate built on the grounds of the school my much younger sister, Guila, attended while living with us in the early 70's. I later learned that this was a terraced home and that a detached one on the same estate was £450,000! The estate, fitting named Scholars Mews, was very close to my friends' home so I walked through it on the way.

We had a very pleasant visit. Our friends are very comfortable to be around and gracious as well as interesting hosts. Shortly after lunch, their daughter Sarah arrived with her daughter, Francesca, who at that time was my favourite young person. Francesca ('Chessie') claimed to remember me from a visit two years ago, which was very gratifying. She is still a lovely, lively, impish and well-socialised child.

Later, I paid a quick visit to the people that we had sold our home to in 1972. They have made many changes in the past twenty-seven years, making the house unrecognisable inside. They were entertaining former WGC people and my arrival required more tea and cakes.

I walked back to my other friends' home to find my hostess preparing yet another meal. Her husband was in the garden with Chessie helping her to write down a rude poem that her father had taught her which clearly delighted her.

'There was a woman from Leeds
  Who ate a packet of seeds.
  In less than an hour,
  Her face was a flower and
  Her bottom was covered in weeds.'

Her delight was of course focused on the last line. Then grandmother spoilt things by correcting her writing. She crawled up into my lap to be read a book and afterwards wanted to play hide and seek. Later we all enjoyed a salad supper and parted company after walking down to the railway for my 8.30 train. This had been a very different day with good intelligent conversation, ample, well-prepared food, shared memories and a lovely child. All in all it was very pleasant.

The return to Cambridge was uneventful. At the hostel, I had been re-assigned to room 7 that proved to be teaming with noisy teenagers. Youth hostels would be much improved by eliminating the youth!

South to Gatwick

Next morning, I was gratified to find that my pre-planned route back towards Gatwick started very close to the hostel going over a cycle bridge and on to a cycle path. But there were still uncertainties at the intersections that needed frequent consultations of the map. During one such stop, a woman stopped her car and recommended that I go to Fynchfield. I was happy to oblige since Fynchfield was on my route.

There I stopped at a pub called The Fox for lunch. This was attractively situated near a windmill, a nice green, a pond by the green and a clutch of shops arranged around the perimeter. As pleasant as it was outside, I chose to eat in, both to enjoy the atmosphere and to avoid the North American voices on the park benches outside. I find them jarring and incongruous when I am away from North America. As I emerged from the gents after lunch, a chicken walked into the pub. This prompted me to say to a woman at the entrance 'Bit of a turnaround isn't it when the chicken comes into the Fox house.' She did not understand and just stared at me.

I carried on cycling through a district called the Camps and stopped at a small teahouse cum green grocer. You would not think I could eat again but the prospect of teacakes always produces capacity. While there, I overheard a conversation between the lady proprietress and an older customer. They exhibited real neighbourly affection for each other, simple, good natures and an unhurried attitude toward life that was amusing and appealing at the same time.

Next came the Rodings, a series of villages that I had been told were idyllic, best-kept village prize candidates. What I saw of them was very ordinary. By now, the traffic, congestion and noise of London were becoming apparent. It was five pm and I did not want to struggle through London at a peak traffic time nor did I want to pay near-by London B&B prices. So, I started looking for B&B's right away.

There were no B&B's in sight or any pubs offering accommodation. I stopped at one pub anyway to ask if they knew any B&B's. With the help of the telephone directory, we found three in Brentwood, some eleven km further south. A pub in Brentwood gave me directions to two B&B's. Both were full, the second one having let its last room go five minutes before I arrived—so had I gone to it first, the room would have been mine.

The landlord did some telephoning for me and found a room at The Brick Hotel some three miles further on in Warley for £40—just the sort of price I had feared being so close to London. The ride to Warley was pleasant except for the nagging effect of that price. Once there, I found that the Brick had a smaller room for £35 so I took it instead.

It was now after seven and I wanted to watch a program on television at nine. This meant either missing the program or scrimping on dinner. The latter would help the budget so I ordered a toasted sandwich and a beer at the hotel bar/restaurant. The sandwich was a pathetic offering served on a pile of torn up, tired lettuce. If it wasn't obvious before, it was certainly clear now that this hotel would struggle to merit half a star.

Breakfast next morning was in the company of two men

travelling round to work at BP petrol stations. One had just returned from a week's golf in Spain and was interested in golf courses round Toronto. Their work must pay very well.

Consulting my map and guidebook, it seemed that perhaps there was only one route for cyclists across the Thames via the Tilbury Docks. My host confirmed this and said that Warley provided almost a straight run to the Docks.

This proved to be a very pleasant, almost rural, ride despite the proximity to London. I made it to a nearly there spot, Gray, in less than an hour. There I sought the advice about the rest of the route from an elderly cyclist on the cycle path. He grasped my arm and talked right in my face; he was still vital (at 86) and strong with a sparkle about him. Half way through his directions, he apologised that his 'water did not work so well any more so he was just going to go in the bushes.'

His directions did not help much and I had to ask three more times to find the ferry –there was not a single signpost. The route went by one of the construction projects for the new rail link to the Chunnel. Cattle and horses roamed around telephone cable spools alongside the road near the ferry.

The ferry had a capacity of perhaps twenty and seemed to run whenever a few people gathered. No cars could be accommodated. I spent the ten minutes it took to cross talking to the ticket person about the process of laying cables under the Thames. Although he charged me the adult fare, later I discovered that the receipt for the ferry that he gave me was for a child; the difference in price was equivalent only to a cup of tea but repeated several times a day could finance an evening in the pub.

Gravesend, the end point of the ferry run, proved to be a large, well-maintained and very busy town. Although there was little evidence of tourists, they did have a TIC. I used their services to book a B&B in Sevenoaks, a spot within easy reach of Horley for the Gatwick airport and offering a wealth of B roads that could take me there.

After lunch at Gravesend, I followed the Wrotham Road for five kilometres through Meopham ('the longest village in England'). Later I encountered a difficult and busy roundabout with inconsiderate drivers just outside Wrotham. That was a nerve-racking and irritating experience that made the relative peace of Wrotham that much more inviting.

It was a nice old village that was on the Pilgrim's path to

Canterbury, a much quieter road with very little traffic. The old school opposite the square-towered St. George's church had been converted into nice cottages. These cottages looked very appealing. I pictured myself inside with a bread and cheese meal snug in my tattered retirement cardigan.

This vision made me hungry (what doesn't) and the nearby Bull Hotel beckoned. This was a sturdy but genteel establishment perfectly suited for this village. I was their only customer for afternoon tea and enjoyed it thoroughly in their comfortable lounge with a newspaper. There was no time pressure as Sevenoaks was very close.

There was no relevant sign posting from Wrotham, so I chose a road labelled Kemsing Road West simply because a town called Kemsing was closer to Sevenoaks than Wrotham. This proved to be a serendipitous choice; it was a lovely country road, sufficiently curved and rolling to be an interesting ride and with attractive countryside and residences along the way. At Kemsing, I spied a church down a treed lane.

The church had a lych-gate (a small building at the edge of the church boundary formerly used to shelter a coffin prior to the burial service) and a well cared for and well-populated cemetery with an unusual curved brick wall surround. The wall looked much like the famous Thomas Jefferson wall round the University of Virginia. On leaving, I noticed a small lane with a YHA sign; there had been no other indication anywhere that there was a hostel in this area. I really don't understand why they seem to be so shy about telling people where they are.

From Kemsing it was an easy run to Riverhead (the area within Sevenoaks where the B&B is located). I was their first guest in a month. Their most recent previous booking had failed to turn up. Virtually every surface in my room was labelled to identify or instruct--- the sugar and tea containers, a safety warning on the kettle and instructions for operating the shower and the window; all had neatly typed labels in two colours encased in plastic.

The husband was retired and obviously had time on his hands to provide all these little assists for their guests. He was pleasant enough although a bit prissy. I suggested that he had been an engineer. He immediately wanted to know why I thought so. Fortunately my reply of 'the precision I see in your home' pleased him. However, both he and his wife were former opticians. They did everything to make me comfortable from installing a television in the room to providing special high quality jam at breakfast and bringing me cold drinks after my arrival.

From them I learned a lot of the details of running a B&B that don't immediately come to mind such as special insurance rules and coverage, alarm systems and etc. The B&B business isn't the ideal avocation that I once envisioned for myself. My hosts recommended that I go to the Bullfinch for dinner; this proved to be a good choice. I ordered the whisky and ginger that I had promised myself for this trip. It was very good but not as special as I had anticipated—probably too much build up in my mind

Next morning, my host suggested a pleasant route for getting to Horley. But like his other conversations there was so much detail that the main picture got lost. I was only able to remember one bit 'keep Barclays on your left' but that was just about enough to get me underway. An important intersection in his instructions never appeared and I was soon faced with an unappealing choice between two dual carriageways. The map seemed to indicate the A21 as the best choice because there was an intersection with a minor road just about three kilometres ahead. The roads did indeed cross but via a flyover; so there was no way to get on the minor road.

The map showed another possible exit some five miles ahead but I wasn't happy being on the A21 with its very heavy traffic and my rear tyre seemed low. I was not about to try to pump it up on the verge of this road. Suddenly I noticed a lane passing directly under the A21 with a bridle path perpendicular to it that ran parallel with the A21. Access to this was over the guardrail, down a steep hill and then over a chest high fence along the path. I left my cycle propped up against the guardrail and beat an exploratory path through the wild roses and nettle collecting cuts and stings along the way. Next I unloaded the bike and walked it carefully down using the brakes to slow the descent and lifted it over the fence. Then back up the hill to fetch the panniers—what an exercise!

A woman horse rider came along just as I was finished re-loading the bike and offered to help with directions. I declined thinking I knew what I was doing and cycled along a heavily wooded lane to a T-junction where I chose to go right as that was west and in the general direction of Horley. Two kilometres later, I was virtually back in Sevenoaks—nearly an hour with nothing to show for it but an assortment of leg cuts and nettle abrasions.

So, I started again, thinking hard about what I had been told, and eventually found the right road. Finally, this was lovely cycling country, pretty rolling countryside with woods, lots of shade for cooling down and interesting houses. Some of these as well as some barns and churches showed oast house design influence. I stopped to admire a very large new country house under construction. It had a marvellous location sitting high above a broad valley. From this point the road was a 16% downhill grade for a while levelling out somewhat to a 9% grade. Just as this levelling began there was a great noise of something seriously wrong as well as strange behaviour from the bike. The right pannier had jarred loose and been sucked between the rack and the wheel, acting as a massive brake. This was briefly scary as I was still going quite fast (30 km/h). But it was quickly corrected with no apparent damage.

Soon, Edenbridge appeared. I stopped to take my lunch on a quiet shady bench in a lovely churchyard. In a small bookshop on the way out of the town, I found two books of interest for future acquisition: *Devil Take the Hindmost*, a history of financial speculation by Peter Bernstein and *God's Funeral* by A. N. Wilson. It took three years but both these are now in my library. The Bernstein book was published before Enron and Worldcom but probably would have included them had it been written later.

East Grinstead presented another diversion in the form of an estate of new homes where model homes were open for viewing. The reception area was arranged much like similar North American receptions with floor plans of the various models displayed on the walls and samples of alternative kitchen cabinets, tiles and carpets. The attendant was busy with other people so I just wandered off to view one of the homes.

This was very inviting, decorated all in pastels and light coloured furniture with top name appliances, etc. Its four bedrooms were well laid out; there were two and a half baths and all rooms had cornices. The house felt as if it had about 2,000 square feet but the actual amount was 1,312! None of the bedrooms had any closets and there was no basement or other storage area of any significance. The price was the equivalent of C$550,000 with only a small plot of land. But then East Grinstead is a prime London commuting location. The largest home is the development was 1,563 square feet and that was C$600,000!

Five years later on my most recent trip I found that the high house price situation had become worse and spread wider afield. There was pressure on government to do something. Nurses, teachers and similarly paid professions cannot afford homes at these prices. And the wealth of other professions has made the weekend or holiday home feasible in areas more distant from London inflating their prices dramatically. This has made it very difficult, if not impossible, for natives of those places to afford a home. Property rates for second homes are lower, putting a strain on local council finances as the proportion of weekend homes increases. The weekend people want to retain the rural, bucolic features of the village that attracted them and consequently are generally opposed to most economic development that might improve the material welfare of the locals. It is not a happy situation.

Someway out of East Grinstead, I stopped at a pub in Turner Hill. My objective had been tea and teacakes but the opportunity did not present itself. So, I settled for tonic water and crisps for the moment promising myself that I would stop again if possible. Within a few minutes of leaving the pub it was. This was an upscale farm shop for fresh fruit and vegetables, local jams and its own teashop.

This farm was a happy, busy place with a small zoo and play area for children. I had my tea and cakes and bought some lemon cheese to take home. I realised that I was just prolonging the experiences of my final day on the road and had reduced my budget for tonight's final dinner to $12.

It only took a few minutes to reach Crawley from the farm. The B2036 to my destination, Horley, showed up just where the map indicated, bringing me to the Prinstead B&B, where this journey began a month ago. My room was tiny but well equipped and maintained. Now, to get the bike dissembled and packed for the flight home.

After several trips back and forth to the room for various bits and pieces, I got started on this packing task in earnest at 5.45. The job took an hour, presenting no real difficulty except for getting the box closed. It just doesn't look as if the top and bottom could be made to meet, let alone overlap, as the three foam-cushioning layers are each about ten centimetres thick. The additional thickness of the frame, handlebars and wheels create a formidable stack. Even after three trips with these boxes and being proved wrong each time, I still initially fear that the squeezing and strapping process will severely damage the bike.

The rest of my packing, a shower, a cup of hot chocolate from my room's drinks supply, and a two-hour Inspector Morse program meant it was ten before I ventured out for a meal. I had decided to break the budget on this last night with a special final meal but proved to be too late, the nearby Six Bells Pub had just stopped serving meals and my second choice was quite a hike that suddenly was uninteresting. I stopped across the road in a Texaco petrol station convenience store for something to take back to the room.

    Doing so maintained budget integrity but it wasn't how my final meal was meant to be and I still have not had a gooseberry tart or any summer pudding. But then there are more tours to come.

NORTHERN ENGLAND & SCOTLAND TOUR

MAJOR STOPS
York
Newcastle
Berwick upon Tweed
Carlisle
Keswick
Edinburgh
Lochranza
Oban
Tobermory
Portree
Glasgow
Manchester

Robert Adams

NORTHERN ENGLAND AND SCOTLAND TOUR – 2060 KM

Overnight at	Day's Distance in Km
York, Yorkshire	
Thirsk, Yorkshire	66
Carlton in Cleveland, Yorkshire	31
Pickering, Yorkshire	93
Newcastle, Northumberland	63
	(more by train)
Alnwick, Northumberland	77
Berwick upon Tweed, Northumberland	79
Wooler, Northumberland	68
Bellingham, Northumberland	92
Carlisle, Cumbria	80
Cockermouth, Cumbria	80
Keswick, Cumbria	35
Keswick, Cumbria	48
Allenheads, Northumberland	79
Edinburgh, Midlothian	71
	(more by train)
Melrose, Roxburgh	77
Edinburgh, Midlothian	64
Whiting Bay, Isle of Arran	29
	(more by train/ferry)
Lochranza, Isle of Arran	45
Lochgilphead, Argyll	74
Inveraray, Argyll	74
Oban, Argyll	68
Tobermory, Isle of Mull	37
Mallaig, Argyll	97
Broadford, Isle of Skye	76
Portree, Isle of Skye	72
Portree, Isle of Skye	76
Armadale, Isle of Skye	76
Glasgow, Lanarkshire	by train
Dumfries, Dumfries	132
Wigan, Lancashire	by train
Parbold, Lancashire	by train
Manchester, Lancashire	42

NORTHERN ENGLAND AND SCOTLAND

The freedom and release from regular responsibilities has always been a major component of my enjoyment and anticipation of these cycling tours. The first couple of weeks are best; the days are long and varied and future responsibilities distant. Pleasure fades somewhat in the final weeks with the now somewhat repetitive routine and the prospect of facing those responsibilities again looms near. This outlook dulls the last few days and seems to speed their passing.

However, this trip was to follow my retirement, promising freedom from worrying about returning to my interesting but fairly demanding job. And, although living within a budget is always a concern, this time I wasn't also constrained by the limits of annual holiday entitlement. That entitlement was four weeks but I also had one week of carryover from the previous year. This allowed me to stop work, have a tour of five weeks on full pay and not retire officially until the end of the tour!

The months at work before the trip were intense. I was charged with a major review of the firm's pension fund asset mix with the objective of significantly reducing the level of risk. This was early 2002 when prices in the equity markets were eroding fast and the Board was nervous about our large allocation to equities.

This assignment would have been more than enough, by itself, to keep me fully occupied. But, at the same time, we were also trying to dispose of our long-term interest in a real estate joint venture in Alberta with two other pension funds. A large balloon payment due to the several insurance companies that provided the mortgage finance for the buildings established a drop-dead date for completing the transaction. One of our partners was being extremely difficult at least in part because they were the principal tenants and feared a change in ownership.

Documentation for the joint venture proved to be a major problem. Our partnership had been in existence for almost 25 years. During that time one of the other partners had merged with another company but failed to file any documents to acknowledge the change in ownership of the joint venture. And, for a frantic week, my pension fund's crucial files on the original transaction were thought lost. Eventually these were found in the firm's archives.

In the end, we sold the entire property to German real estate interests but with several delays in the closing due to the seven-hour time difference between Germany and Alberta and our difficult partner.

The insurance companies were amazingly uncooperative about extending the deadline for the balloon payment by a couple of weeks, demanding a re-financing fee plus exorbitant interest.

As a result, as Treasurer of the joint venture, I had to arrange an alternative short-term loan of tens of millions to meet the original balloon payment date. The tension was overwhelming and my days were consumed with this deal for weeks.

My successor, Claire Kyle, arrived in early April for a three-month period of training and overlap. We chose to have her take on the department's regular responsibilities and staff supervision while I concentrated on the asset mix review. It worked very well because we already knew and respected each other. Claire is better qualified academically, had similar experience with one of the other large Canadian banks and was then President of our professional association. I had taken the somewhat unusual step of recommending an outsider as my replacement and was most pleased to have the firm agree. The 'bounty' paid by the company for attracting someone from the outside was an unexpected bonus. Net of tax, this paid my airfare for the trip.

My colleagues organised a very moving and memorable retirement party during my last week. Very nice speeches were made and I was presented with a significant amount of cash to purchase my own bike box. Mari, and gratifyingly, a number of the Pension Fund Board members attended but I will always regret not having asked my daughters, both of whom lived locally.

My last day at work was scheduled for the final workday of June, so I booked my departure for the next day. It was a summer Friday and most of the office had left for the weekend before I felt I could finally abandon my post. Truth be known, I was regretting the end of my career and burnishing my reputation for dedication. Not that there was anyone there to take notice!

I returned home to an empty house as Mari had left earlier in the day for a long weekend of kayaking with our outdoor club. The solitude might otherwise have been welcome, but totally wired with the emotions of retirement and the trip, her absence left me adrift with no outlet for sharing those feelings. At that time, we did not own a mobile phone and could not contact each other.

The Route

Once again, my route ideas relied heavily on Lonely Planet's

Cycling Britain. My objective was to see the under populated, hauntingly beautiful countryside of Northumberland that is such a factor in the television dramas of Cathryn Cookson novels. I also wanted to visit the Scottish islands. Having five weeks to work with meant that I could, with occasional use of trains, cobble together five different Lonely Planet routes adding the Lake District and Edinburgh to my agenda. This somewhat disjointed combination accounts for the three separate route area ovals on the map at the beginning of the chapter.

Lonely Planet provides an individual map for each day of their routes and each of these also has the route directions with mileage indicators for the turns. I enlarged each of these directions on a photocopier to a size that would just fit my handlebar map case so that I had a custom guide for each day that was large enough to see easily while cycling. The theory is great. The reality was just a bit different, as we will see.

The first Lonely Planet route that I chose was a circular tour based on York involving James Herriott country and the North York Moors. Next was a combination of three separate tours all based on Newcastle upon Tyne. These tours could be joined together in one amoeba shaped circuit running north along the east coast to Berwick upon Tweed then south and west skirting the Cheviot Hills, crossing the Pennines to the far west of the Lake District finally turning east to re-cross the Pennines and return to Newcastle.

From Newcastle a train journey would take me to Edinburgh for a short local circuit in and around the city before heading west again by train to Ardrossan for a ten-day, ferry-supported visit to several of the Scottish Isles. A final train journey from Skye was to take me through Glasgow and on to Penrith from where I would cycle back to Manchester.

Arrival

The start was not auspicious. My flight was at least 30 minutes late in leaving and sleep was virtually impossible. Then there was a mix-up in the disembarkation arrangements at Manchester. After starting to disembark, we were sent back to our seats and finally had to leave the plane from the rear exit!

I planned to take the train into the city but had an hour wait. While waiting, a woman with a young child started screaming abuse using foul language. This tirade was punctuated with sobs. For several minutes there was no obvious target for her anger. Then a young man appeared but he showed no particular concern, barely responding to her. This scene, coupled with having to lug the bike box and all my gear up the escalator because the lifts to the railway platform were not working, soured my attitude.

The Manchester Deansgate station where I left the train was meant to be the closest to the hostel and probably was but the directions I received, once there, took me the long way round. This route involved a considerable amount of cobblestones that aren't the easiest to negotiate while dealing with a 25-kilo plus bike box on wheels together with a rucksack and duffel bag.

Even without the scene at the airport, the Saturday night litter that disgraced the streets and the damp cold of that Sunday morning would have been depressing. Manchester doesn't have litterbins on the streets because of the risk of IRA bombs and it would probably be Monday before any litter would be removed.

My first sight of a live Rover 75 in a parking lot provided a bright spot. I had seen them in British car magazines and as senior police officer vehicles on British television drama but never in the flesh. Cars are a life long interest and this car was particularly interesting because it was the first new British product since BMW bought Rover. Walking around the car to see it from all perspectives and peering inside attracted the attention of the security guard. He was a bit sceptical about my true intentions but eventually judged me harmless and helped me lug the bike box up some steep steps and gave me better directions to the hostel.

The hostel was located on a canal filled with colourful barge houses and houseboats. Incongruously, many of these were being polished and cleaned despite setting in filthy water.

It was still too early to get into my room so I went out to a large tarmac area behind the hostel overlooking the canal area and took the opportunity to re-assemble the bike. The day continued cold and damp; there was a lot of raucous noise masquerading as music from various marquees that were being set up nearby for a fair that evening. To continue my day on a consistent note, my hands got thoroughly impregnated with grease trying to engage the chain on the rear wheel gear cluster (I've since learned that surgical gloves are a great way to avoid this). At least the hostel confirmed my email understanding that my bicycle box could be stored with them until my return.

Life looked better the next day after a decent sleep although the weather did not improve. Today, I was to go by train to York where my tour really starts. A good breakfast, the comfort of secure accommodation for my new bike box, and a nice clean railway station at Piccadilly largely erased yesterday's irritations.

After arrival at York, I walked in the Shambles area but its attractions were blunted by the continuing cold, wet weather. Despite this, it was bare midriffs as far as you could see. Many of the girls also wore off shoulder blouses. Most wore wide belts as low as they dared to be provocative and better display the jewellery in their navels. Wearing 'the gear' seemed all-important even if they were grossly fat. It seemed to provide some assurance that they were OK. Their posture and behaviour put the lie to that.

As many Canadians do, I wore a 'Maple Leaf' on my cycling jacket to reduce the likelihood of misplaced antipathy. The full weight of Canada's much-vaunted multiculturalism soon became evident as a Pakistani man stopped me in the Shambles exclaiming, 'Here's another Canadian'. He was from Hamilton, Ontario.

Earlier, a very apologetic, impoverished and self-effacing Irish cyclist of perhaps 50 stopped me to ask for directions to the Lake District. It was almost as if he thought it was just round the next bend but he appeared harmless and poorly equipped so I hauled out my maps to help.

The Triplets

One of my objectives on this trip was to see the Herriott Museum at Thirsk that I had missed on an earlier tour. Thirsk was an easy 41 km from York so it made an excellent destination for my first day on the bike. I chose to stay at the Lavender Inn next door to the museum because my brother Byron had stayed there a few years earlier. Although it was fine, I wish I had returned to the Long Acre B&B of my previous visit.

My route along the River Ouse was more footpath than cycle trail. I was soon covered in insects and had to abandon this off road route. The cold and wet continued but the countryside was lovely and traffic was virtually non-existent.

As mentioned in an earlier tour account, James Herriott was the fictional name chosen by Alf Wight for his veterinarian stories. The Royal College of Veterinarians would have considered using his own name as advertising, which was banned. The real Herriott was a top footballer.

The museum was very worthwhile with a balance of displays about the television program and of historic veterinarian instruments and animal protection legislation.

From Thirsk I returned to our friend's home in the North York Moors, approximately 60 km away, at least by the route I took. I got thoroughly confused with my pre-planned route and took my chances on the A19, a dual carriageway (four lanes), for about six kilometres to an intersection with the A172 that led directly to the turnoff to the road leading to our friend's home.

This was over three kilometres of what felt like straight up. Fortunately, the nearby Lord Stone's Café was open and I could wash off the dust and sweat before arriving on their doorstep.

We had a pleasant tea in their garden, fed John's outdoor goldfish and enjoyed a leisurely dinner together bringing each other up to date on our children's accomplishments. It was pleasant, yet not entirely comfortable. There was an underlying tension between them which flared a number of times when Gillian made a pronouncement or observation that the normally imperturbable John could not allow to pass unchallenged.

At breakfast, they congratulated me on our national birthday, confusing, as so many British seem to do, Canada with the US. Both countries are simply 'America'. This seems strange to me given Britain's historical and continuing ties with Canada. But perhaps I am mistaken on this. We had met originally when I was still officially an American and I was still not officially a Canadian. Nevertheless, the tension remained, perhaps even intensified. I was not unhappy to leave.

Another television related objective was to see Goathland, the Yorkshire village called Aidensfield in the BBC television series *Heartbeat* about police officers and villagers in the 1960's. Goathland is located about twenty kilometres from Pickering where I was booked in a B&B. I reached Pickering, via Helmsley, about 2.30 in the afternoon, so dumped my panniers and after a cup of tea in my room, headed out. The outward journey was largely uphill and took well over an hour. As soon as I turned off the main road towards Goathland, the countryside seemed to go back a century or more, displaying railway over bridges, humped back bridges over rocky streams and sheep grazing in the open with their lambs—they were more afraid of me than of the cars! The village looks exactly like it does in the opening credits of each program and I found a number of the buildings that are regular features

Although Goathland is bigger than is apparent in the television program, it is a normal functioning village apart from the tourists that show up to have a look. There were no signs or other indications of its TV role but the local shop had some relevant souvenirs.

The ride back to Pickering was much faster. I showered, had another cup of tea and went out for dinner. The first pub was full, the second was a Best Western and I prefer not to patronise US firms when there is a British choice. The third pub was not serving evening meals. This left a café where the only other customers were a family with triplet boys of about three and a half. Each of the boys, in turn, had to explore the toilet. It was fun hearing their chatter. They were fairly well behaved and their parents were very good with them. But the boys seemed to take an interest in my appearance and my mint ice cream. Much to their parent's embarrassment, one of them called out 'Mom, he's got green cream and some hair'. I chose not to believe that this in any way referred to my follicle-challenged appearance.

Old Tom

A southwesterly route from Berwick upon Tweed took me through lovely countryside that was more rolling, greener and less desolate than the North Yorkshire Moors. My first overnight was at a hotel in Wooler—a marvellously inexpensive place—just 15 pounds for a twin-bedded, en suite room with television, tea making facilities and lots of towels. In Wooler, I met James Noon, a cyclist from Musselburgh, near Edinburgh. James travels with a flask of hot water for tea or soup and carries spare food to save money. Initially he was reticent and dour but later became very friendly and shared his extensive knowledge of the area while we had some meals together.

James suggested I detour to see a castle and some rare wild cattle at Chillingham. I took his advice but never saw the cattle, as the farm was only open to tourists on one day a week-- yesterday. And the castle did not open until two hours after my arrival. So, I returned to my main route and, relying on my memory of it, took the turn to Eglingham. After two or three kilometres, I had a sense that something was wrong. My compass showed that Eglingham was east when my destination was west. What a difference a letter makes—I wanted Edlingham, not Eglingham. This error cost me over half an hour.

Nevertheless, this accidental side trip was not a total loss. It was a pleasant ride and I met someone who could tell me about the cattle that I missed. Chillingham cattle are white, appearing somewhat like small Charlois. There were about 70 of them at the farm and a few more in Scotland where they had been shipped to avoid last year's outbreak of hoof and mouth disease.

My destination for the day was the hostel in Bellingham. This proved to be an old red cedar scout hut located just a couple of streets away from the High Street. I arrived about five to find a grey, gnarled and rheumy-eyed man seated at one of the picnic style tables that served as the dining room. He brusquely instructed me to complete the sign-in book but strongly objected to my filling in the date --'Trying to do my job, are you'-- lingering evidence of the British union mentality.

Then he took me on a tour of the facilities providing totally unnecessary instructions on how to use the cooker, the shower and the rubbish bin! This tour was followed by a long monologue on how difficult it was to run a hostel; the record keeping was murder. I was trapped—an audience of one. The only other hostel occupant, a woman from New Zealand, had wisely made tracks—perhaps she had been subjected to the same treatment earlier.

Finally, I made the excuse that I had to take a shower. I guess I did not reappear as soon as he thought I should so he came looking for me. I was doing some hand wash laundry. Again, I was a captive audience for his stories and complaints. He was proud of the hostel, built in 1936, and particularly because he claimed that its only alterations from scouting days were the new toilets and showers. This wasn't totally true as he took me to another building to demonstrate the hostel's latest acquisition—a small spin dryer. He chose to demonstrate this with my hand laundry. The dryer whizzed the clothes round, squeezing out the water into a compartment that then had to be emptied on the ground. It was a fairly basic appliance but got enough water out that the drying room would finish the job. Tom was proud to have something else to demonstrate.

Now, fortunately, Tom's stomach called him home for his tea and I could get on with mine. Knowing that there was no meal service at this hostel, I had bought a wedge of steak pie and a wedge of ham and egg pie and two yoghurts at a small shop before arriving at Bellingham.

I managed to burn the pies slightly (no doubt, due to inadequate attention to Old Tom's instructions earlier) but they were still good and the yoghurts (mango and orange were superb—my wife would say that means they were sweet, not proper yoghurt).

I had a brief conversation with the woman from New Zealand and learned that she was an English graduate of the University of Otago. She is the first Otago person I have met since I left my lecturing post there twenty-six years ago! She had worked as a newspaper journalist for three years after graduation but got fed up and came to Britain for a cycling holiday. She had completed nearly 1800 kilometres in six weeks and was now looking for work in the Lake District.

After my meal, I made myself some instant coffee from a nearly empty jar left behind by a previous visitor and stayed at the picnic table writing in my journal and reading my book while she enjoyed a six-year-old magazine in one of the ancient easy chairs. The room was warm and comfortable providing a nice sort of quiet domesticity until about ten when Tom came back.

My New Zealand companion quickly got up; said 'goodnight' and I was stuck. Tom started to repeat his complaints about the administrative burdens of the job—but in greater detail. In the process, he told me that his wife was the official warden of the hostel but that he helped out in the evenings and with the lawn mowing and so forth.

He said he was 79 but his wife was quite a bit younger: 'she keeps me young!' This launched him into what must have been his favourite story. Before coming to Bellingham, he lived with his adult son in another village. They had a live-in housekeeper. Tom's son and the housekeeper became engaged but the son later got cold feet and moved out of the house.

The housekeeper then felt compromised so she left and moved to Bellingham where she got a job cleaning out the pub. Tom followed to persuade her to return to her housekeeping job with him. She did and he later decided to take over his son's role and marry her.

I have severely condensed Tom's story but when he was finished, he said, 'How old do you think she is then?' I knew I had to come in low—his ego demanded it. So, I said 'about 45'. In glee and almost shouting he roared out 'NO, she's 35!' My face must have registered disbelief because he jumped up from the table and said, 'you don't believe me, let's just call her!' He rang her up and told her that there was a guy at the hostel who did not believe how old she was --would she speak to him? I came to the phone and without prompting; Allison proudly confirmed that she was indeed 35. That story seemed to be the foundation of their marriage and probably has been told hundreds of times to hostellers like myself that could not escape.

Next morning, Tom's wife appeared at the hostel about 7.30, on her way to her other job of cleaning out the pub. After the pub was clean she moved on to yet another job--the school where she served lunch. Allison may have been 35 chronologically but 50+ would better describe her appearance. Although she could not smoke in the hostel, like her husband, she reeked of cigarettes. School lunches are bad enough without servers like this!

Mayflower Connection

A wet, cool and overcast morning extended last night's bleak mood as I left Newcastle without breakfast. After a few kilometres, however, an unexpected brief spate of bright sunshine coincided with the appearance of a restaurant cheering me with the prospect of breakfast outside on a picnic bench. The sunshine disappeared with the breakfast but the pleasant stop restored my spirits so, re-fortified, I headed north towards Alnwick about 80 kilometres away.

Later that morning there was a dead magpie on the road. The death must have just happened as another magpie was standing on the verge, staring at its dead partner and looking very puzzled. I later saw a dead fawn. There have been a number of pheasants and rabbits running across the road. It is a wonder that none of them has been hit.

Next I saw a blue heron at Warkworth, a picture postcard perfect village on the Coquet River. Warkworth is home to Warkworth Castle, the 14th century birthplace of Hotspur (Sir Henry Percy). Sir Henry was slain at the Battle of Shrewsbury in 1403, when Henry IV defeated the Percys. For more than four centuries Warkworth was one of the most important castles in the north of England.

The castle seemed worth a visit and I was not disappointed. Rather than a human guide, I was given a hand-held device with commentary keyed to numbered positions throughout the castle that corresponded to buttons on the hand-held. This is a great idea, allowing visitors to tour at their own pace and sequence. The commentary can be ignored, or replayed as you wish. It provided lots of interesting details about domestic life at that time and about the family history.

Two bits of trivia intrigued me. While visiting the buttery, I learned that contrary to popular thought, the name buttery refers to the butts that liquid was stored in, with no connection to dairy products at all. The other interesting bit concerned a small, special room called a garderobe, which functioned principally as a toilet. However, people also stored their clothes in these rooms thinking that the smell would keep the moths away! I imagine that this is the origin of the British term 'cloakroom' for ground floor half baths that sometimes also house coats and jackets.

When I arrived at my Alnwick B&B, my hosts advised me that some long-term clients had decided to stay an extra night; consequently I had to be put in a very small room. However, to compensate they were going to only charge me half price. They were most apologetic, not realising the joy this brought to my Scottish soul. I made appropriate grimaces at the inconvenience but 'graciously' accepted their solution.

With this boost to the budget, I treated myself to an excellent steak pie dinner and then walked round the very active town centre watching the pub-crawlers. The women gathered in flocks –for courage or companionship? Most of them were really tarted up, even the middle-aged ones. Their attempts to attract male attention with forced hilarity as they swooped in and out of the several pubs were pathetic. The men were also primarily in all male groups but weren't obviously seeking attention. They were all similarly dressed in short sleeve shirts worn outside their trousers.

My next day's destination objective was Berwick–on-Tweed but first I wanted to visit Lindisfarne, or Holy Island. Lindisfarne lies off the east Northumberland coast perhaps 16 kilometres south of Berwick. *Missionaries from Iona settled here in the 7th century but were driven out by the Danes in CE 875. The ruins of a Benedictine priory built in the 11th century and a small 16th castle are on the island. The limestone cliffs and sand dunes of the north shore are a playground for the warming bird life from the Farne Islands and seals can often be seen offshore.* (1)

Breakfast at the Alnwick B&B was in the company of a large group of smoking Scots at one table and a refined couple from St. Andrews at mine. The latter told me that Prince William's presence at the university had improved the policing and raised house prices. They seemed grateful for both outcomes.

My route ran close to the coast, passing Bamburgh, its imposing castle standing high on the horizon, and brought me to the causeway to Lindisfarne. Access by land to the island is only feasible when the tide goes out uncovering the causeway. I had forgotten about this and turned up an hour and a half too early. There were lots of people hanging about for the tide to go out and taking advantage of the crab sandwiches at the inevitable food wagon. Waiting would make me late for my weekly call to Mari and there was no phone box anywhere. So, I decided to carry on to Berwick on Tweed and return to Holy Island tomorrow.

Once I got to Berwick, I could not find my hotel reservation confirmation or remember the name of the hotel. After my call home but before looking for alternative accommodation, I stopped at a coffee shop called 'Sinners' for the pastry they offered. I indulged in a coffee and a superb fruit pastry then toured the town a bit finally choosing to stay at Miranda's B&B.

Angela, a single mom, now ran Miranda's. The interior was a bit worn and bleak but it was half the price I remembered the hotel wanted and had all the facilities I needed. During my roaming earlier, I had selected a pub called The Leaping Salmon for dinner and went along there after my bath.

As soon as I arrived, I noticed Chris, an American cyclist I had met in Thirsk. We were both staying there at the Lavender B&B next door to the James Herriott museum. We had a most interesting dinner together. Chris was a twenties something Bostonian who claimed that his mother had direct lineage back to Priscilla of the Mayflower. He also told me that he had been a software programmer for start up technical companies and had made so much money by selling his stock options before the crash that he had made a deposit on a house and been able to take a year off for this trip. The story made for lively conversation but other aspects of what he told me indicated that perhaps the option profits were a bit more modest than he suggested. His Wal-Mart quality cycle was a bit of a giveaway for a start. Still, where else but on a holiday like this would you even meet such a diversity of interesting people?

Gross Girls

On my first visit to Newcastle on this trip I was booked into the hostel but no one could direct me to it. There were no signs near the railway. The traffic was heavy and some signs had been altered deliberately to be confusing. After ninety minutes of following a variety of tentative directions, I finally found the hostel only to be told that there was no record of my reservation! I was sent off to their 'annex', one of the university residence halls. This was 'only five minutes away'.

Thanks to some hair-raising motorway roundabout situations when I could not turn where I wanted to or had to turn when I did not want to, to a total lack of hostel-related signs and conflicting directions from three different pedestrians, it only took half an hour to find the annex.

The young woman manning the annex was friendly enough but she could have passed for Dracula's wife—totally dressed and made up in black, including black lipstick. My room was on the top floor, four storeys up and, like most university residences, totally without character. I had been looking forward to a hot hostel meal like the one in preparation at the main hostel but the annex provided no food and had no members' kitchen.

So, I went out for a meal. The city pedestrian mall area was impressively clean but the night scene of young teens larking about was depressing, particularly the girls' ostentatious dress. Bare midriffs (the temperature was about 12 degrees)—tight tops with their breasts spilling out and close as skin jeans with wide belts round the hips. Some of these girls would have been attractive dressed more normally but now looked like cheap tarts; others were absolutely gross—just fat and ugly. Their style of dress only emphasized how ugly they were.

Dave the Warden

Today started well. It was finally warm enough to wear shorts and I enjoyed a relaxed breakfast with my book in the pedestrian mall nearby the Carlisle hostel, another no meals university residence. The restaurant radio was tuned to a talk program promoting a contest in which the prize was a pack of condoms for the weekend. The female host was using all kinds of double entendres about the prize and its use but principally was talking rubbish –failing to complete sentences because there was no thought behind them—she just filled the airwaves with noise that she thought was clever and trendy. She was clearly an, 'on-air' head.

My destination for the day was Cockermouth, about 80 kilometres distant from Carlisle in the Lake District. I stopped mid-morning in Wigtown to buy a newspaper and encountered another example of Britain's multi-faceted personality.

The shop, run by two middle-aged and apparently respectable women, openly displayed copies of the gutter press featuring virtually naked women on the front pages in lewd poses. This doesn't seem to faze anyone.

Robert Adams

I took my respectable *Times* newspaper to a seedy little café for tea and teacakes and later added a cheese pie because the paper proved to be so interesting. There were articles on revenue inflation in financial statements and one on US vice-president Cheney being sued for accounting fraud at his former company Halliburton.

For some reason, these articles stimulated my thinking about statistics. Later, my mind struggled with fat tails and normal distributions while I pedalled and I probably even talked out loud trying to convince myself of some conclusion just reached. Statistics had been a major aspect of my final asset mix project at work and it fascinates me generally. I vowed seriously to study the subject upon returning home. This promise joined the ones on calculus and French all of which are still waiting for action!

The hostel at Cockermouth had been a mill. It is a stone building set on a riverbank at the foot of a rocky path off the main road. I had stayed here in 1995 when they had a full time warden and served meals. Now it is run entirely by volunteers and provides no meals.

After settling in I walked back into town for an excellent steak and ale pie at the Bitter End pub. It claimed to be the best pub in Cockermouth for several years running. For a town of 5000, Cockermouth is well supplied with places to eat. There were seventeen of them.

Dave, the acting hostel warden, told me that most of the people that make their money from the tourist trade in Keswick actually live in Cockermouth. Dave has been retired from teaching for ten years. Now, he says, his worldly mobile possessions would fit into two cases. He bought a farmhouse in France following retirement and stayed there for four years. This was followed by three years with the Arts Council in Whitehaven on the Lake District coast and he has been with the Hostel Association for the past two years. He loves the nomadic life and is moving on again at the end of this year, either to Cornwall or Spain. I never meet people like this at home!

There was only one other man in my dormitory room. He didn't talk unless you can claim the one word 'hello' in response to my greeting. He slept a full twelve hours. The other guests were a party of five female cyclists and a group of schoolboys from Leeds with their supervisors.

I have cut off the Whitehaven part of the Lonely Planet's route, as my visit there in 1990 did not produce any desire to return. Instead, I planned a leisurely day, visiting Wordsworth's cottage and exploring at random before going on to the hostel at Keswick.

The cottage was Wordsworth's birthplace. His father was successful and prosperous so the house was large and comfortable with a formal garden, a separate section for vegetables and a raised terrace overlooking the river at the bottom of the garden.

I was particularly intrigued by Wordsworth's father's journals in the library. The dates (mid 18th century) were written in the current North American style showing the month before the day and words like favourable and colour were written without the 'u'.

One of the letters was not very legible and someone had later written it out to be readable. But they had not been faithful to the original and altered both the way the date was written and the spellings to conform to current British usage. I also found a late 18th century document in which the dates and the spellings were in the current British fashion. It seems likely that sometime in the latter part of the century, the practice changed. Although Noah Webster certainly played a major part in defining American usage, perhaps current American practice reflects the revolution as well as its timing.

Allenheads, Northumberland

I had combined two day's routes into one for today's run from Keswick to Allenheads. The distance and the route description convinced me to brave some A roads to save time and my legs. Being a Sunday, the traffic was light at first and I was planning on having a proper roast and veggies Sunday lunch at a pub until I saw a sign for the Brief Encounters teashop. The name reminded me of the play and the shop was aptly situated in a working railway station for the Carlisle and Settle Line. I could not resist. The shop and station were in superb condition making for a very pleasant interlude but killed the budget and time for lunch.

From this point, the road began to climb and there were ominous notices that the road rose to 570 metres and winter conditions could be treacherous. I struggled away stubbornly refusing to get off and walk but just keeping my head down and pedalling while noisy gnat-like groupings of motorbikes roared by. Shortly before the summit, I ran into a group of four guys cycling up a side road to the main road.

They were pushing their unladen bikes up. The last one of the group, very much overweight, looked at my fully loaded bike and me and gasped, 'you must be insane.' A few metres further, at the very top, was an obviously popular café where all the motorbikes had gathered. Outside in the car park, I admired some excellent scenic photographs offered at a mobile shop. The couple managing the shop earn much of their living taking and selling these photographs. They explained that they were very much hostage to the weather having to wait for just the right light conditions to take these photos. I stayed for a snack and chatted with a cycling couple that arrived about ten minutes later.

From this point the road ran downhill to the intersection with the road to Allenheads. It was briefly difficult again but then levelled out and I arrived in Allenheads about five pm. I had booked in at the inn that was at the far end of the village. The current owners, Steve and Sue, were very pleasant and welcoming. They acquired the inn last year just in time to suffer the double-barrelled effects of the foot and mouth outbreak and the drop in overseas tourism due to the Twin Towers attack in New York. These events had pretty well put paid to the village. The village shop and post office were both closed.

Allenhead's Inn was most unusual; collectibles of all sorts were on the walls, floor and ceiling, covering all available surfaces. There were even banknotes from all over on display. My room was a good-sized en suite and I welcomed the privacy after several days in hostel dormitory rooms.

Next morning, as I was about to rouse myself from bed, there was a knock on the door and a voice called out 'Here is your water.' That did not make any sense but when I opened the door, there was a large flask of water waiting for me.

Later at breakfast, Steve explained that the village was totally out of water this morning. Allenheads' water supply comes from a spring that continuously feeds into a reservoir through an exposed pipe. During the night a cow had knocked the pipe sideways so that the water spilled on to the ground instead of into the reservoir. You never know what sort of problems you will encounter when you go into business for yourself!

Edinburgh Crystal

After Allenheads, I headed northeast back to Newcastle for a train journey to Edinburgh. Arriving at the railway station just after two, I bought my ticket (an astounding C$80) got a sandwich lunch from across the road and ate it on a station bench. Although there was lots of activity to witness, my attention was riveted on a passionately kissing couple on an opposite bench. It was in no way a turn on—quite the reverse. The woman was just so ugly! At least that was what I thought until I realised they were both women! As I walked past to retrieve my bike to join the train, one of them was fondling and flipping the other's breasts. I suspect a large part of their display was intended to draw attention and disgust. Worked for me!

At the very last moment there was an announcement that my train's platform had changed. As rapidly as is possible with over 25 kilos of bike and gear I lugged myself up and down the steep steps of the bridge to the correct platform. I arrived in time but had to lay the bike flat in the goods van as the designated cycle spaces were already occupied.

Otherwise, the journey was fine. The train was well appointed, smooth and very fast. I enjoyed a coffee and piece of fruitcake from the trolley and read. Arrival was at Edinburgh's famous Waverly Station on Princes St.

'Edinburgh, Scotland's capital city, lay originally in the English kingdom of Northumbria and only finally became Scots in 1341. The old part of the city lay south of the castle, now visible in the cobbled streets of the royal Mile and Grassmarket. The modern city layout is Georgian, the architects leaving the view from the main street, Princes Street, open toward the castle, perched high on its volcanic rock. The oldest part of the castle, St. Margaret's Chapel, dates from the 12th century, though most is much more recent. One of the more fanciful names for elegant and neoclassical Edinburgh is "the Athens of the North," and it has been an academic centre since 1582, when the university was founded. The annual Edinburgh Festival of arts and performance in August attracts tens of thousands of visitors.' (2)

My city map eased the task of finding the hostel but it was still difficult, as the YHA seems loath to provide more than the barest of directional signs. Unfortunately, it was one of those big city hostels that have little character and less warmth. This one was filled with undisciplined kids on some school outing. The lobby was sandwiched between the entrance to the male rooms and the common areas. Access to the common areas required use of a combination door lock that rang a chime every time it opened. These kids travelled in packs resulting in the door opening two or three times every minute. The constant chimes combined with the noise of the kids in the lobby created bedlam. It was a relief to learn that I had to go out for a meal.

Robert Adams

For my first breakfast in Edinburgh, I went to a convenient pub adjacent to the Edinburgh Bike Cooperative and very close to the hostel. I ate dinner there last night and noted that they offered breakfast all day at £3.95. As it turned out, breakfast at breakfast time was £5. I was assured that the breakfast quantities were bigger but I suspect that the real difference was the cost of the tea!

While I was there, a postman interrupted his morning deliveries for a couple of sustaining pints before continuing his route. I listened to him describing his recent holiday to Western Canada to the barman. In his opinion, the natives were friendly but the place was far too quiet.

After breakfast I spent a lot of time in the bike shop, marvelling at the much higher prices Britons pay for cycle equipment and at some very interesting products that North Americans never see. This stop was partly an attempt to wait out the drizzle that was now falling.

The rest of the day was spent revisiting former university haunts such as the 'Old Quad' where I spent many evenings in the library and where one of my close friends was an extra in the 1959 Jules Verne film *Twenty Thousand Leagues Under the Sea*. The building is now almost totally devoted to Law and was largely closed for the summer. Consistent with the cool, wet day, I also visited the very austere Church of Scotland (Presbyterian) St. Giles Cathedral.

For breakfast next morning I went to the Doctors pub, on the edge of the big Edinburgh park known as the Meadows. In my days at the university this spot had been 'The Barbecue', a popular student café. It conjured up special images for me of my brief romance with Kathy, one of their waitresses. Head over heels at this relationship with a "mature" woman, I was oblivious to and unaware of the facts of her life. Some months later, I learned just how mature Kathy was--- six years my senior, a mother of several children and already divorced!

Another part of the Doctors' appeal was its advertised breakfast for £2. Like the previous day, this turned out to be somewhat misleading as the tea was an extra pound. But they provided the morning *Scotsman* and a reasonably quiet atmosphere in which to enjoy it.

As I was headed for Melrose today, it was fortunate that the rain stopped after breakfast. The run was fairly easy alongside the Tweed River for much of the way. The countryside is noticeably different from Northern England; it is subtler with rolling but lower hills. There were lots of pine trees but disturbing evidence of clear cutting.

My first stop was at a Rover dealership to examine the Rover

75 close up and without a security guard to question my motives. The interior was a very dated, British sports car style that did not match the elegant, conservative exterior. I have since seen an alternative interior that is much more suitable. Even though this car was developed under BMW ownership, they managed to retain a very strong British identity.

Shortly afterwards, I came across the new (since 1969) location of Edinburgh Crystal. Apart from my university association, Edinburgh crystal is meaningful to me since my parents gave my wife and me a collection of Thistle pattern goblets shortly after we moved to Britain.

I went in to visit the showroom and stayed to take the tour of the works. My guide had been one of their designers and a number of his pieces were on display. One of these was a special wine decanter made for Prince William's birth with a stopper in the shape of a small liqueur glass. The rest of the tour involved seeing various stages of manufacture. Most interesting for me was a personal (I was the only observer) demonstration of cutting by George, a veteran of 42 years. He showed me the several different cuts that form the Star design and completed a water goblet while I watched.

He told me that this goblet would be recycled afterwards so I asked him if I could possibly have it as a souvenir of his demonstration. He agreed but only on the condition that I would not let the people in the showroom know. What a treasure – a very personal and special reminder of this trip! I wrapped it carefully and stored it in my handlebar bag for the rest of the journey. The great thing is that my goblet survived that journey coming safely home with me. The tragedy is that while unpacking at home, it fell out onto a hard surface and broke the foot. I was devastated.

No Room/Food at the Inn

After a final Edinburgh breakfast at the Doctors Pub, I cycled off to Waverly Station and by 10.15 was on Scottish Rail west to Glasgow on the first leg of the journey to the Scottish Isles. On these trains, the cycles go in the cars for the disabled, which are labelled 'facilities'. The system is quite good providing places for up to three bikes per car. The train was clean, modern and comfortable.

The ferry to Arran left from Ardrossan. The train for Ardrossan goes from Central Glasgow station, requiring a short walk from Queen Street station. On the walk over, I stopped at a fruitmongers to buy a banana. As I was about to lock up the bike, another cyclist stopped to offer to watch my bike while I was inside. He was from Halifax, Nova Scotia and had noticed the Maple Leaf on my jacket. He told me that he was working (illegally) as a bike courier.

At Central, I discovered that there was a three hour wait for the train to Ardrossan Harbour leaving me only six minutes after arrival to buy my ticket and get on the ferry. Any delay in this part of the journey could cost me a full day and mess up all my accommodation arrangements! Further study of the timetable revealed that there were three different stations in Ardrossan and that they were all close to each other. The next train to any Ardrossan station left within the hour. I was quickly on it dealing with yet another system for carrying bikes.

This was a milk run calling at all stops along the way but in less than an hour, I was cycling along the sea front at Ardrossan, energised by the change in atmosphere –a sudden but welcome foreignness that I had not yet experienced on this trip. Globalisation, particularly in large population centres, has produced more and more similarities across the world, making many foreign places seem familiar.

First stop was the ferry terminal where I bought a special, several trip, book of tickets called 'Hopscotch' that represented a considerable discount on the single fares. Bikes travel free.

Since there was close to two hours before the ferry departed, I set out to explore Ardrossan. My lunch break was in a café whose ambiance and clientele were very reminiscent of a similar café in a similarly poor town in Saskatchewan that Mari and I visited last year. The patrons were smokers and primarily at the lower end of the socio-economic scale, reflecting the general ambiance of Ardrossan, but the service and atmosphere were friendly.

Back at the terminal, there was a lot more activity as departure time approached. There were many cars and some huge lorries. Cycles were loaded last. As the journey was very short, I immediately went up to the top deck and was soon engaged in conversation with another man that noticed my Maple Leaf.

This man had been raised in my town of Oakville, Ontario but now lives in Sapporo, Japan running a food import advisory service. His entire family now lives on Arran and he was back for a visit. We had a short chat until his mother arrived. They had been into Glasgow for the day.

My hostel was at Whiting Bay, a difficult but short 13 km ride from the terminal. When I arrived the hostel was swarming with teenage girls—there were 32 of them plus their counsellors. There were only two males in the hostel. Priority for all the toilets and showers had been turned over to the women and my room door had no lock. Not that there was any chance of my being at risk—more's the pity.

In fact, one of the counsellors would have been an ideal candidate but I had to content myself with conversation with her about the Duke of Edinburgh awards. The girls had just completed a four-day camping expedition as part of their requirements for the gold award. The counsellor spends a great deal of her teaching year working with the girls on the program and was specially qualified in outdoor recreation. From what she told me, it seemed that the Duke of Edinburgh program is very rigorous and demanding.

This hostel was totally self-catering, so I rushed off to find some food before the local shop closed. Although this was a small convenience type shop, I found pea and ham soup, cheese, nan and yoghurt for dinner plus a tin of grapefruit sections for breakfast.

My sole roommate was Hailey, yet another cycling Otago graduate! Hailey was following the same Lonely Planet tour of Western Scotland but making a diversion to see the island of Harris. He earned his degree in History but is currently working in a local council planning office in London.

The next day was cool and wet so I deferred my start until about 9.30. Lochranza, tonight's destination, is only about 45 km away, so there was no rush. There were some hard climbs right away but little of historic note apart from the 'Standing Stones' that did not appeal enough for me to take the dirt track side-trip.

Just about lunchtime, I reached Machrie Bay, site of a coastal golf course and tearoom. The golf course operated an honour system for paying course fees. You simply put your money in a wooden box. There were a few cars pulled off on the verge but since it was not a 'pay and display' system there was no way to tell whether these golfers were honourable. But it was the tearoom that really attracted me.

Initially, I was the only person there so my order for tomato and lentil soup with a cheese scone arrived quickly. However, by the time I finished this and was ready for something sweet, a swarm of cyclists from a triathlon club had started to arrive. When the last stragglers stumbled in, there must have been a dozen of them. Two of them were women of 50+. Seating was very limited and inadequate to accommodate all of us in comfort so I left sooner than I wished.

Arran was a tremendous change of scenery. The sea air was bracing, emphasised by a strong head wind. Visually, the sea, rocks and mountain views were stirring, very reminiscent of the Otago peninsula on the South Island of New Zealand but perhaps this thought has been influenced by recently meeting two Otago graduates.

The hostel at Lochranza was alongside a sea inlet that was a gorgeous golden blend of autumnal and seawater colours in the sunset. It was a view that could be enjoyed even after 10 pm at this northerly latitude. Lochranza is also a self-catering hostel, so I made another trip to the local shop to get supplies for dinner and breakfast. My choices for tonight's dinner were tinned tuna, sweet corn, and fresh tomatoes. The grocer told me that he swims in the sea almost every night despite a maximum temperature of only 12 degrees Celsius.

Lochranza Inlet opposite Hostel, Arran

Next morning, Hailey and I breakfasted together then packed up and headed for the ferry to Claonaig on the Kintyre Peninsula. The ship was at anchor in the harbour but did not move to the loading dock until after the scheduled departure time. However, once in position, it was very efficient and we were barely on before the ferry was underway.

The views over the stern were magnificent. Arran is very impressive with high hills that dominate its profile. The ferry trip was special also, adding a dimension that seemed to change the character of the trip but then I have always loved travelling by sea.

By 10.20 we were ashore again. Hailey and I decided to cycle together awhile before he deviated from the main route. I was headed for Lochgilphead and Hailey was bound for the Isle of Harris. The day was lovely and sunny and I enjoyed the conversation but after only 16 km, our paths parted. Just at the crossroads, there was a tempting place to stop for coffee but I chose not to as I had not yet earned a rest!

Besides, the next village, Kilberry, was only another hour away and a stop then would be much more justifiable. The road to Kilberry was a B road with hardly any traffic or road signs. It appeared as if I were returning towards the ferry terminal, just on the opposite side of the loch—and that was exactly the case. I motioned one of the few passing cars to stop and got them to confirm that I was indeed on the right road to Kilberry.

Precisely at one pm, I arrived at Kilberry and was immediately faced with a white, cottage style country inn that advertised Sunday lunches. This was a great find as Sunday service can be very spotty, particularly in the west and Highlands of Scotland. This was the prolonged reward! Alas it was not to be. There, posted on the door, was a small notice announcing 'Closed today for family visit'.

That inn was virtually the sum total of Kilberry—I had no snack food and my water bottle was half empty. The guidebook showed that the next possible stop was a further 25 km away with lots of 'moderate' climbs. Fortunately, there were also some good down hills. One of these must have been nearly 4 km.

This next leg of the journey took two hours but it did produce an open café at Ardrahaig where I had two big mugs of tea and two cheese and pickle toasties. These are a Scottish version of a grilled sandwich. They were absolutely delicious but then anything would have been at that time.

My next stop was at the tourist information centre in Lochgilphead to find out the location of the hostel. 'But, there is no hostel here.' Another senior moment! Sure enough, my itinerary says that I am booked in at Mrs. Sinclair's B&B. This was about three km outside town.

My arrival really surprised the Sinclairs because they had

no record of me and no vacancies. They were very apologetic and rang round to find me an alternative spot at the Victoria Hotel back in Lochgilphead. The Sinclairs call their B&B 'Corbiere' after a spot on the island of Jersey where they spend their holidays. The name was an interesting coincidence for me as the land conservation charity of which I was then Treasurer had bought a large tract of land on Manitoulin Island in Lake Huron from a native Canadian named Corbiere. I was making monthly mortgage payments to him for the charity but had never encountered that surname before.

The Victoria proved to be a dump! My room's carpet was frayed and laid in great lumps in the middle of the floor; two of the three lamps did not work and the shower was nearly inoperable. But by this time, I was more than ready just to clean up and have a meal. The Sinclairs had recommended the Vic as a place to eat. It wasn't clear whether this was based on an absolute standard or one relative to the alternatives in Lochgilphead. Either way, the Vic had to be the choice and I was encouraged that there other diners were in the restaurant but found the food just satisfactory.

Afterwards, I walked round the town a bit. Lochgilphead was poor and down at the heels. This showed in people's attitudes and their interaction. The young boys were loud, rude, foul-mouthed and disrespectful of females. The odd thing was that the girls appeared not to mind but almost to welcome the attention. No evidence of the strong, fearless Highland spirit here!

I came down for breakfast the next morning at 7.35, found no one around, rang the bell, read yesterday's paper and rang the bell some more. About eight, the cook entered the front door with the shopping! So much for my planned early start. Perhaps it was just as well; once again it was raining.

My cycle had sat outside, uncovered, all night behind the hotel amidst its discarded flotsam and jetsam---what a depressing hole this place is. The saddle was soaked. I wrapped it in a plastic bag and headed out into the drizzle.

First stop of the day was a side trip to the historic fort at Dunadd. This was in use between 500 and 1000 AD and is considered the capital of the first Scots settlement in Scotland. Dunadd was a natural rock feature rising high above the surrounding countryside. On top, where the timber dwellings used to be, were an ancient footprint, a basin and a carving of a boar (that I never found). Boars are now extinct, as

I discovered an interesting museum about eight kilometres away at Kilmartin.

The whole Kilmartin area is rich archeologically with cairns and standing stones. The museum featured a time map showing what was happening in Argyll at various times, including the animals that were in existence at different times but are now extinct. I took advantage of their very pleasant but pricey tearoom for a scone and lemon curd (superb).

Returning to the official route along the B840 bordering Loch Awe, I spent another couple of hours cycling with a break to visit the Renault showrooms and see their handsome Laguna. My hostel tonight was at Inveraray, a larger, touristier place than Lochgilphead. Inveraray has a castle (headquarters of the Campbells), a gaol, a Bell Tower and a very tired ship museum. There was also a Scottish Episcopalian church. Although Canada uses the term Anglican, both the US and Scotland eschew that term probably because it suggests Church of England.

In the grounds outside the hostel, three English cyclists on the End-to-End tour for a men's cancer charity were trying to fix a broken spoke without success. Tonight's other occupants were two Slavic girls, five French people, a couple of Germans and a Scottish man with his three children. It is a small, intimate hostel and I enjoyed the domesticity and self-reliant activity of preparing my own meal.

In the morning, I was first up and was enjoying my breakfast of beans, sausage and stewed tomatoes on crusty bread before any one else stirred. The next person to make an appearance was one of the English cyclists who was searching the phone book to find a place to have the cycle repaired. He was fuming about the poor service provided by the Cycle Touring Club (CTC). The CTC doesn't do repairs and wanted over £0.50 per kilometre just to transport his bike to the repair shop! My brief time in the region was enough that I knew the location of a nearby cycle shop and the comparative distances. It felt good to be able to help.

I ended my stay in Inveraray with a trip to the Bell Tower that had an interesting display about bell ringing music in the ground floor lobby. The music notation was written in numbers from one to eight, corresponding to the different bells and ringers. All the bells are suspended upside down—the first pull takes them anti-clockwise and the second clockwise, etc. There were records of concerts lasting three to four hours on special occasions.

The Ceidleh
My next stop was Oban, on the coast at the northeast corner of the long finger of land that juts southward ending in the Kintyre Peninsula just west of Arran. Oban was a relatively short ride from Inveraray continuing along Loch Awe, then River Awe and through Glen Lonan. Oban's active boat filled harbour was ringed with rolling hills.

That evening, on my way to dinner along the sea front, a pair of small gull-sized birds was making raucous comments on life in general. This exposed the bright red insides of their mouths that matched their red legs and feet contrasting sharply with their black bodies and white splashed wings. I imagined that they were cliff dwellers as their home was a hole in the wall under the pavement.

After dinner, while returning to the hostel, I stopped to enjoy a pipe band giving an open-air concert. Several of the band members were the epitome of the strong, silent, dour Scot with serious beards and full Highland kit. All their pieces were well performed but I was especially moved by *Green Hills.*

In the morning, I experienced an attitude that while fairly common in Britain is incomprehensible to me. The hostel offered a cold breakfast that I had paid for when I booked in. This gave me a choice of cold cereals. The young chap at reception laid out his display of the available cereals and I chose my favourite, Alpen. 'Oh, sorry sir that isnae available, we are out of Alpen'. My response was 'Well in that case, I'll have this one from the display'. 'No, I couldnae give you that one,' he replied, 'then I couldnae display it.' The concept of not displaying what you could not offer totally passed him by as well as any thought of customer satisfaction.

Today's ferry took me to the Isle of Mull, where my destination was Tobermory. While waiting for the ferry, I met a Dutch woman cyclist who was also travelling solo on a tour of about 1500 km but camping rather than hostelling. She was a very self contained and assured person but not particularly gregarious. So, I was surprised when she suggested that we stop for a coffee at Craignure where we disembarked. Food is always a good idea and we spent a companionable half an hour together before heading out on our separate itineraries.

By the time we finished the ferry traffic had dissipated making cycling a lot more pleasant. My route to Tobermory was on the A849 along the western coast of the Sound of Mull. At Salen, where the route turned north on the B8035, I stopped to visit a silver shop. The artisan was in his workshop when I arrived, as there were no other visitors. He came out to open the adjacent display shop. The work was not attractive or inspired but he claimed to be the world's largest maker of Celtic Crosses, exporting to the US, Spain and Germany. He doesn't like that aspect of the business because the pricing is too fine producing only about £25 profit per week.

He relies most heavily for profit on the coach tour traffic. We spent about an hour together discussing tourism, taxation, UK economics and the meaning of the curved arrows on the road. I felt guilty at taking up so much of his time without buying anything and was relieved when a few others arrived allowing me to leave with no purchases but some grace.

This hour's conversation took me to lunchtime and I was pleased to find a very attractive café, called the Coffee Pot, in Salen. There was only one table free when I went in but the place was very well maintained and inviting so I stayed and stayed and stayed. It took over an hour and a quarter for my simple pot of tea and a toastie. A couple of elderly ladies joined my table due to the lack of space, received the same swift service and vowed never to return. The serving man was clearing table and generally hovering ineffectively and irritatingly like a sorry imitation of John Cleese in Fawlty Towers.

Shopping and Business District, Tobermory, Mull

From Salen, the route formed a rough upside down U, skirting the coast of Loch na Keal, Loch Tuath and Calgary Bay. Tobermory was another 20 kilometres beyond Calgary and appeared suddenly at the bottom of a very steep hill past the distillery. This first view was broad, encompassing almost a full sweep of this candy shop village of bright or pastel coloured houses and shops ringed round its semi-circular harbour.

My interest in silver work, ignited by the earlier visit, caused me to stop at a jeweller's window display showing more beautiful, quality pieces than I have ever seen anywhere. I went in and after much deliberation, chose an amber necklace in an oval sterling silver setting as an anniversary gift for Mari. I thought it was beautiful and would suit her very well. I was so eager to give it to her that a day after my return I took her out to dinner at the Twisted Fork, a new restaurant on our harbour. We had a lovely, relaxed meal that provided an appropriate atmosphere to give her the necklace a month early. Most husbands will recognise that this is not prudent behaviour from a budgetary standpoint.

Memories of early anniversary celebrations and remembrances can fade significantly in a few weeks.

Continuing my stroll along the high street, I found the hostel, a faded pink building, not far away and just around a corner. No one was about when I arrived but I was able to leave my panniers in the lounge and put the cycle under cover. Unencumbered, I went out again to check on tomorrow's ferry north to the Ardnamurchan Peninsula. Departure was at 7.20 am!

I was sorely in need of a haircut so an advertised £6 cut attracted me to a barber's shop on the High Street. A gorgeous, dusky brunette with a superb figure greeted me at the door. My spirits rose at the thought of her hovering close and immediately decided to extend the experience with a shampoo, but it was not to be. She was leaving for the day. My male barber had been a hockey player, which was unusual and mildly interesting but hardly compensation for the alternative! I changed my mind about the shampoo.

My next stop, at a grocer, procured pea and ham soup, potato scones, apricot yoghurt, strong Orkney cheese and grapefruit segments for my next two meals. It was now 5 pm and possible to check in at the hostel. A very efficient, no-nonsense, slender blonde conducted the checking in process. She reminded me very much of Erin, a young woman that guided a week-long kayak trip that Mari and I took in the Georgian Bay of Lake Huron. We both believe that Erin's principal leadership experience was with teenagers for whom a command style may have been necessary but it did not sit well with our 50+ group. A few days into the trip, after a series of her arbitrary decisions, her order to visit the woods for nature's call in pairs because of the risk of bears was the last straw. I rebelled. Can you imagine, waking up someone else in the middle of the night to accompany you to the 'toilet'.

However, this woman at the Tobermory hostel was invisible apart from her reception duties.. So this hostel retained its homey feel with free cups of tea and a friendly atmosphere. The facilities are very good, particularly the toilets and showers although from my room you had to go downstairs and outside to reach them.

During my walk round the town earlier I had noticed signs for a ceidleh tonight, so I got cleaned up and had my dinner early enough to attend. On my way there just before eight, I watched a class of about seven children on windsurfing type boats running races in the harbour, apparently oblivious to the frigid water. I also ran into another Dutch woman cyclist that I had met in the Lochranza hostel and suggested that she might wish to attend the ceidleh also. Her travels alternate between cycle tours (which she does solo) and jaunts to Africa! She said she could not come right away but might later.

So, I paid my fee and went into the upstairs hall where the ceidleh was to be held. This was obviously a local function, not set up for the tourist trade, and all the better for it. White-haired ladies and elderly men were managing the ticket table and dispensing complimentary cups of tea. I was the first to arrive and took a seat at one of the tables around the perimeter of the room, reading until the performance began.

It was a heart-warming family type event—all ages, fathers dancing with their young daughters and very old couples clearly having a good time. It was amusing to see teenagers trying to cope with a waltz. But then if I had the courage to venture on the dance floor –everyone would have been amused or appalled. The entertainment consisted of two accordionists, one acting as compere, together with a piper.

My Dutch acquaintance joined me about an hour later. After the performance, we both felt that we had experienced something both natural and special. Tobermory, by night, enhanced this feeling. The village was truly magical with its ring of lights round the harbour, small vessels bobbing on the waves and the pastel buildings. The face of the tall village clock, standing at the centre of the harbour curve, was illuminated also, creating one of those nostalgic Christmas card type pictures. We walked to the far end of the harbour and back to prolong the spell.

Early to Bed/Early to Rise

Given the evening's entertainment and the walk afterwards the first part of this subtitle is definitely not accurate. But I had still to rise very early to catch the first ferry; necessary as today's cycle route is one of the longest on this part of the tour.

The window in the dormitory room was at the back of the building facing the hills and thus let in very little light. My roommates had closed the curtain so it was impossible to see my watch.. I stumbled out of bed at 2 am to drain and to check the time. Apparently this made others suspicious of my intentions, particularly when I parted the curtains to see a little better---some one grumpily called out 'what are you doing?'

So it was a bad night, waking every little while to avoid oversleeping, wondering if it was time to get up. Finally, when my watch seemed to say that it was 5.30, I got up, packed as quietly as possible, dressed in the dark and moved my gear out to the reception room -- then washed up and went out to check out the bike. I was worried because my bike lock key was not in its regular place in my belt bag. This led me to fear that I might have left the bike at risk with its key in the lock. I hadn't.

The key might have fallen out in the dormitory room but there was no hope of finding anything there without turning on the light, which would probably get me lynched. I was in a real tizzy but gradually convinced myself to do a calm, unhurried search of all the other possible locations for the key. As usual, this approach worked far better than the frenetic, hurried approach, and the key was soon found. Then I discovered that I had arisen at 4.30 am, instead of 5.30. I wasn't going to miss that ferry!

This gave me plenty of time to enjoy a leisurely breakfast but by 7 am, with breakfast over, the bike packed, and the book read, I could not delay leaving for the ferry any longer. With some trepidation, I buzzed the receptionist to return the room key so that I could reclaim my YHA membership card. She was still in bed and decidedly cool at having her sleep interrupted. She could not complain vocally as reception was officially open at seven but her body language was very articulate!

At that hour, there certainly was no crush of passengers on the ferry. One car, two other people and a dog were the only travellers. This was definitely the low end of the ferry fleet. There was no cafeteria, observation lounge or bar, just a wooden bench along two walls of a very narrow enclosure. But the trip only took half an hour.

Good Samaritan Stan

This ferry took me back across the Sound of Mull to the mainland at Kilchoan. From there, my generally northern route of nearly 100 kilometres led to Mallaig. Given today's distance, I did not stop at any of the guidebook recommended historical spots along the way. Thus I missed the natural history centre, Glenborrodale Castle (formerly owned by Jesse Boot, pharmacist and founder of the Boots chemist chain), or the Seven Men of Moidart Memorial (they joined Bonnie Prince Charlie's 1745 uprising).

I stayed overnight in Mallaig at the Moorings, a B&B. This was a welcome luxury with privacy, a television and although not an en suite,

I had exclusive use of the adjacent WC because there were no other guests in my section of the B&B. The landlady even offered to dry my wet clothes.

After a pleasant dinner of fish and chips washed down with a very refreshing sweet cider, I went back to the room to watch an interesting sounding film on television. I got myself comfortable in the bed and read with the television sound off waiting for the film to start. Two and a half hours later when I woke up the film was of course over.

Three women from Glasgow 'graced' my breakfast table next morning. The youngest one was wearing an Arkansas sweatshirt--- giving it a fair old stretch. Arkansas was my mother's birthplace and where I earned my first university degree. I wanted to ask this woman how she came to be wearing the shirt but the right opportunity never presented itself.

Today's ferry ride from Mallaig to Armadale on the Isle of Skye was very short, so that it was only about two hours since breakfast when we arrived. Nevertheless, the wet weather made the café at nearby Armadale Castle irresistible. I stopped for coffee hoping that the depressing weather would improve while I waited.

Once again, I decided to deviate from the guidebook route. This time the objective was to visit the Kyle of Lochalsh and Plockton, sites of a very popular British television drama in which Robert Carlyle, plays 'Hamish Mac Beth', the local policeman trying to adapt normal police routine to a very independent fishing folk.

This change of route provided the same distance for the day as the Lonely Planet route and an opportunity to see and traverse the new bridge that now connects Skye to the mainland. On the near side of the bridge was the little village of Kyleakin that was just in time for lunch.

After lunch, I stopped briefly at a village centre designed to teach children a bit of local history and something about animals. The centre is run by a charity that partners with the Born Free foundation in maintaining the island's former lighthouse as an animal refuge. Gavin Maxwell, the author of *Ring of Bright Water*, lived there and his favourite otter is buried there.

The Skye Bridge is the most expensive toll bridge in the UK but thankfully its officials consider cyclists as pedestrians and do not charge us. As I was going across, an approaching car suddenly stopped. The people in it jumped out yelling, ' A Canuck' (having seen my jacket flag). They were from Vancouver and wanted someone to take their picture on the bridge. Fortunately, traffic was light as they left the car right in the roadway while I took their picture.

Shortly afterwards, I met a gnarled and grizzled English cyclist of about 70 who now lives in Christchurch, New Zealand. He turned up later that day at the Broadford Hostel where I was staying, getting the very last bed.

Kyle of Lochalsh was at the other end of the bridge and Plockton a very tough 10 kilometres further on. It was a worthwhile effort as Plockton was very picturesque. It essentially was a string of joined up buildings around the bay. The gardens for the houses were on the opposite side of the road closest to the sea and were very well maintained; some were quite lush. At the time, the tide was out and a number of unattended cows were roaming about on the pebbly beach. Although I could not recognize any of the scenes from the TV series, I was glad I had come, as it is one of the prettiest spots yet (being temporarily dry may have affected my judgement).

It was now 4.30 and there was another 26 km to the hostel at Broadford but I could not resist stopping at a lovely restored railway station that is now the Off the Rails café. I enjoyed tea and scones on the former platform. Including a stop at the Broadford COOP for provisions, this delayed my arrival at the hostel until seven.

Tonight I was the beneficiary of a promotional program that YHA operated in 2002 that made the sixth night of hostel stay free! Another cyclist from Norwich provided some instant coffee and I chatted with him for a bit and with a woman from Las Vegas who is on a 'do it yourself' tour using local bus services.

From Broadford, I headed to Portree. The direct route was via the A87 but about 13 km along, I turned off on the Moll Road, a narrow, low track that followed the coast of Loch Ainort and avoided the hill looming just ahead. This was a peaceful and beautiful choice dotted with an occasional farm and with sheep, gulls, orange brown seaweed, grass and water.

However, this bliss ended abruptly when I heard the sharp twang of a broken spoke. This put the rear wheel sufficiently out of true that it was rubbing badly against the chain stay, making progress very slow.

After considerable indecision, I chose to return to Broadford for help, as it was closer than Portree. Initially, I thought I would have to walk all the way back, making it difficult even if I found help, to get to my prepaid B&B in Portree tonight. But, once back on the main road, although the wheel still rubbed, I could cycle slowly and thus got back to Broadford before noon.

A pipe band was playing near the Fig Tree Café as I came into town; I stopped briefly to listen and then decided to ask where I could get a repair done rather than simply cycling round the town looking.

The post office/shop adjacent to the Fig Tree suggested that I try Stan Donaldson at the Fair Winds B&B and Bike Hire. This was literally just round the corner. When Stan answered my knock at the door, he said that he was just off to take his wife to the local gala but agreed to return and try to fix the spoke. 'Just leave the bike, go off and have a cuppa and I will have it ready when you get back.'

He could not have said anything that suited me better. What luck! So I went off to the Fig Tree and enjoyed a coffee and piece of carrot cake. This was a reasonably pleasant stop but it was marred for me by the presence of four US tourists having a noisy good time

I returned to the Fair Winds to find Stan just getting started. He did not have a stock of new spokes—just old ones—all but one of which were too short. In the process of fitting this one and truing the wheel, he discovered another broken one. But he said I could get to Portree with this repair and there was a good cycle shop there that could help. While we were chatting, I noticed a triangular cycle banner sporting the words Mississauga, Ontario, tacked to the wall of his shed---what a surprise. Stan could not recall how he had acquired the banner.

The next surprise was that Stan refused to take any payment for his help. I felt so fortunate to have found him, have an excuse to stop for coffee and cake and be back on the road again by two. I was musing on how much goodwill he generated and on my own contrasting bad, unreasonable attitude about the US tourists when the heavens opened up delivering a downpour that lasted the full three hours it took to get to Portree. My Presbyterian upbringing made me think this was my payback!

Glasgow Hotel

My last overnight on Skye was at the Armadale hostel near the ferry dock. From there my plan was to travel by rail down to Penrith in Cumbria and cycle the rest of the way to Manchester for the return flight home.

I breakfasted on an emmental cheese and ham bun with fresh apricots and tea and quickly made my way down to the ferry that was due to depart for Mallaig on the mainland at 9.20. While waiting for the ferry, I met a couple of young German cyclists that were on their way home after twelve days of camping. All the visible flesh on one of them was covered in fresh midge bites. Thank goodness I wasn't camping out! The Germans were also travelling south by train via Fort William and Glasgow. We arrived in Mallaig in plenty of time for the 10.30 train to Fort William. This train journey is considered by some to be one of the ten finest in the world for scenery. I certainly rank it very highly.

By chance, I sat on the north side of the train, which proved to have the best views. They were absolutely marvellous with almost continuous gorges, surging water, deep green mountains and glistening lochs. I doubt any other journey could pack in so much beauty over such a short distance. Even after leaving Fort William the views continued with an impressive gorge featuring sheer, steep cliffs and rushing water at the bottom, again on my side of the train.

Shortly before arriving at Glasgow, the train stopped at a station and all the passengers were asked to leave, as the Glasgow platform that we were headed for was flooded. The rain was bucketing down as the Germans and I manhandled our bikes and gear off the train getting soaked in the process. The less laden passengers got out faster and took all the available cover. Another already partially full train arrived in about ten minutes so, sardine-like we sloshed our way onto it.

At Glasgow, even the alternative platform was flooded, making the lift inaccessible forcing us to heave our bikes up the steep stairway. Glasgow has two railway stations and trains headed further south did not depart from this one. So, the Germans and I headed off to Glasgow Central. They already had booked their journey through to London and had reservations for their bikes but I had no ticket or reservation. So, we parted company while I went to acquire a ticket

Since it was just coming up to 5 pm closing time, the woman at the ticket counter claimed that she could not access the bike reservation information on her computer and therefore did not know whether there was any space remaining for bikes on that train. It could be that she was just about to clock off as she suggested that I not buy a ticket, but just see if there was space on the goods van for my bike on the train. This is what I did. She also said that I would be able to buy my ticket on the train, after departure.

I found a space for the bike in the goods van and, by coincidence, chose the same passenger car as the Germans had. About twenty minutes after the scheduled departure time, an official came on to announce that now the tracks were flooded, making the train journey impossible and Virgin Rail was arranging transportation for us by coach.

After another hour, the official re-appeared to advise us that journey by road was now also impossible --'Scotland is cut off!' Any of us who lived in the Glasgow area should proceed to their homes— tickets would be honoured the next day. Virgin Rail would find accommodation for the rest of us. Then Virgin set about finding whether we needed single or double rooms.

Another hour passed. I was offered a taxi to Penrith (which did not make any sense given the road conditions) but I had no accommodation there either. Just after eight, I was sent to the George Hotel, a few blocks away. This turned out to be a four star hotel in one of Glasgow's most prestigious locations.

The rain continued so that I arrived looking like a dog's breakfast. Even unsodden I would not normally have ventured into such a hotel dressed as I was. Despite this, the reception clerk was very gracious, telling me to just give my dripping cycle to the concierge. She proceeded with the booking-in process, advising me somewhat sorrowfully that unfortunately, the hotel had no more single rooms, 'would I mind a suite?'

I bore up manfully and said I could accept that under the conditions. As I started to leave the reception desk, she inquired, 'Will you be dining with us this evening?' She then told me that Virgin was providing twenty pounds each for their passengers' evening meals. Twenty pounds was my budget for an entire day's food! 'Yes', I said. 'I might just do so.'

The room was massive with a totally separate lounge with television, huge bedroom with another television and a luxurious bath. Unfortunately, I could not savour the shower and thick towels too long as the dining room closed at ten

My best clothes were decidedly downmarket for this place but what could I do? Despite my appearance, the service was impeccable, if a little slow given the number of other late arrivals like myself. Thank goodness, Virgin provided the twenty pounds. The cheapest salad and entrée on the menu absorbed almost the entire allowance. Very interestingly, Virgin stipulated that none of the £20 could be spent on alcohol. No reason was given.

Next morning, I enjoyed a fabulous breakfast in the conservatory overlooking George Square, watching people on their way to work –the rain had stopped momentarily. There was the most extensive buffet selection of cold meats, cheeses, fruit and cold cereals that I have ever seen. They also offered hot breakfasts so after enjoying a plateful of items from the buffet I ordered scrambled eggs and bacon as well. Newspapers were provided—I could not have been happier.

While checking out, I casually asked the clerk how much the room I had generally went for. Virgin had paid a staggering £235 (including breakfast) and I had yet to buy a ticket!

I felt honour bound to do so right away and proceeded directly back to Glasgow Central but I could not buy a ticket---the trains were still not running. I had no spare time. There was nothing to do but cycle south. Naturally, as soon as that decision was made, the rain re-started.

It was a long way to Manchester but a planned visit with an old friend near Wigan and my scheduled flight home left no time to stay in Glasgow. I just put my head down and pedalled, heading on A roads towards Dumfries, braving the lightning, thunder and drenching sprays from the lorries roaring by. This lasted for about two hours when I saw a welcome fast food restaurant at Kilmarnock. Here, at least, was an opportunity to dry off and have a quick meal.

As I got off the cycle, I saw that the tops of my once white socks looked as if they had a black decorative edge. This, I quickly realised was a collection of the dirty water I had cycled through, drenching my feet and leaving a thin black line around my socks. I looked worse than when entering the hotel last night but I was not as much out of place.

After that rest and re-fuelling, I cycled another three hours, promising myself that if I could average 18 kilometres an hour and find a teashop about four pm—I could stop. At 4.01, the Burnside, a teashop attached to a petrol station appeared. I stopped. I desperately wanted to continue with my book for the few minutes it would take to consume my tea and teacakes but the only other customer in the shop wanted to talk. He was a man of 62, retired due to a leg injury. We talked but I managed some reading without offending him and left at 4.35.

Shortly afterwards the rain stopped and a faint glimmer of blue appeared on the western horizon. The road became a gentle downhill for the most part thanks to tracking the river Nith. It was very pretty, gentle country making this a fun part of the day. The 43 remaining kilometres to Dumfries were covered in just over two hours.

Dumfries was larger and more prosperous than I remembered and was graced by a large statute of Robbie Burns in the centre. A circular flowerbed and attractive river scenes complemented the statue. I stopped in a pub to inquire about bed and breakfasts. They recommended one to me along the River Nith but the directions soon felt wrong so I stopped at the Coach and Horses to ask again. This time the barmaid kindly looked up several and rang round to find a vacancy that I could afford.

The one she found was the Waverly Hotel, right by the railway station, which was very convenient as I planned to compete my journey by train. The unshaven, greasy-haired and emaciated check – in clerk advised me not to leave the cycle outside even for the few minutes it took to register. The bike spent the night locked in the lobby. What a contrast to my Glasgow hotel!

The Canal and Parbold

Given this introduction to the Waverly, I was surprised that my room was an en suite, clean and had all the necessary facilities. The only real inconvenience was the absence of a shower. Advancing age makes it harder and harder to take a regular bath, particularly kneeling under the tap to rinse my hair! Breakfast next morning was another pleasant surprise. There was waitress service, cereal, grapefruit segments, and a full cooked breakfast.

Today's plan calls for a train journey to Wigan near my friends Colin and Connie's home in Parbold. There was over an hour's wait for the train so I cycled back to explore the River Nith section of town, crossing a suspension bridge to a footpath on which I rode in each direction for some minutes before re-crossing the river on an arched stone bridge.

I returned to the station about 15 minutes before train time carrying the bike up and over the platform bridge for the platform to Carlisle that is the first part of the journey. The platform was packed with women and retired people; it appears that many people make day trips across the border to England for shopping as it is only a 30 minute run. The train was over five minutes late and when it arrived, I was at the wrong end for cycles so had to run to get on.

This short delay at Dumfries caused me to miss my connection at Carlisle and to wait a further two hours for the next train to Wigan.

Take advantage of the situation, I told myself—use the time to see a bit of Carlisle. As I walked round the pedestrian precinct, everything seemed vaguely familiar, the hanging baskets of flowers, the brickwork of the walkway and even the shops. Suddenly, I realised that it had only been three weeks since I was last here! The only difference was my point of entry. I have only just retired and already my mind is gone!

The journey between Carlisle and Wigan was a milk run but went through some beautiful Lakeland-like country near Penrith and Oxenholme. There had been no tea trolley on the train and despite the steady drizzle outside I felt parched on the inside. I wandered around Wigan, dodging under any available awning or overhang to stay dry and eventually stopped for tea and an Eccles cake in a large modern mall.

The rain just would not quit so I decided to go back to a Pub type B&B just opposite the railway station. They proved to be fully booked but the publican recommended the Charles Dickens and gave me directions. Either the directions were inadequate or I was. The Charles Dickens just wasn't visible. Neither people on the street or in another pub had ever heard of the place. Finally, my persistence paid off and I found a person with precise knowledge of it.

Once there, I wondered why I had bothered. The state of repair was not encouraging and their rock bottom meal prices were strong evidence this was a 'no star' restaurant. By this time however, my spirits were pretty low and at least the Charles Dickens was dry. My dripping and none too clean cycle was stored in the dining room. I remember thinking that perhaps the intent was to maintain the hotel in a condition that would feel like home to Fagin and Oliver Twist.

The breakfast itself next morning was acceptable but the dismal atmosphere of the dining room/cycle store and an insipid and imbecilic breakfast television program marred the experience. I could not find a remote control and short of climbing on a table to reach the overhead set, could not turn the program off.

My plans for the day were to find a TIC, book a B&B in Parbold, and then head off on the canal towpath to Parbold that Colin had suggested I use.

Finding the TIC took an hour even though there were plenty of signs pointing the way, somehow I kept going round in circles missing it. (It was the signs' fault –honestly). Anyway, the TIC people found me a B&B for a reasonable price and gave me directions for the towpath.

This too proved to be difficult. The TIC was located right on the canal or a junction off it, which made getting going in the right direction on the path difficult. I received three sets of instructions, none of which was totally accurate. Once on the path, it ended abruptly, necessitating lugging the bike up a steep set of stairs, to cross a bridge, lug it down another set of steep stairs to return to the path. Now, surely it would be smooth sailing.

Very shortly, I encountered an elderly couple negotiating a canal lock with their barge. The woman was opening the gates as I arrived. I stopped to watch the process and once her husband had guided the barge through, helped her to close the gates again. She showed me how to secure the gates against vandals with a special tool that they carried on the barge.

There were no other barges on the canal during my journey but I enjoyed the ducks and swans and the very pretty pink and white-blossomed plants that liberally cloaked the canal banks. A number of men, apparently unconcerned with the murky water, were fishing on the opposite bank.

After about two kilometres, the path deteriorated from macadam to dirt, spotted with mud puddles, and was suddenly barred with daunting gates every few kilometres. These gates had to be designed to prevent cycles passing. I worked out a way round the first gate only to find that the next gate had a different design, making it necessary to lift the entire laden cycle over a metre high!

Parbold appeared shortly after my lunch at the Railway pub along the canal and far too soon to stop for the day. So I decided to cycle some more. The countryside surrounding Parbold was very pretty with well-to-do villages and very expensive homes. After a couple of hours just wandering around with no particular destination, I returned to Parbold to find Colin's house so I would know how much time it would take to walk from my B&B this evening. Then I stopped at a supermarket for a paper and snack.

My B&B was conveniently located and very private. The room was totally self-contained with coffeemaker, en suite, soft armchair and private entrance. So, it was a perfect place to enjoy a quiet hour with the paper. But again, there was no shower. After another session of contortions in the bathtub to make myself as presentable as possible, I set out to walk to Colin's.

Within less than a block, he passed by in his car looking for me. Although nothing had been said about it, Colin and Connie had assumed that I would stay overnight with them and were concerned when I had not arrived in time to clean up and change before we went out to dinner. We spent the first few minutes apologising to each other for the failure to communicate clearly.

This is a new home for them. Like my friends' place in North Yorkshire, this home is stacked with books. Colin reminded me that I recommended William Manchester's *A World Lit Only by Fire*, which he thoroughly enjoyed. It has been seven years since we last saw each other but there was instant rapport. Colin is a very natural, likeable guy—despite being a managing director and major owner of his company.

We enjoyed drinks and an excellent meal at an Italian restaurant about twenty minutes away. We talked families. His son Mark is a freelance focus puller currently under contract to the BBC and John is a surveyor/engineer. Neither is married. Colin and his partners did a management buyout of their company and now operate as a finance company funded by the big banks. They had an IPO in the works last year and actually printed the prospectus on the 11 of September 2001. Needless to say, the deal was pulled. If and when it is re-offered, Colin will be a very wealthy guy.

Given my interest in British home construction methods, we talked about the timber frame houses that are starting to show up in various pockets of the country. Colin's firm finances one such developer that imports pre-cut homes from Sweden. He told me that the big issues in this business were getting the building regulations changed to make this style of construction acceptable and to locate workers with the necessary building skills. As one would expect, timber frame construction, particularly pre-cut, is much cheaper than the traditional British double wall brick and breeze block method. However, timber frame homes sell for much the same price so there is more profit.

After a nightcap back at Colin and Connie's, he walked back to the B&B with me. On the way, we passed a branch of the Royal Bank of Scotland that had been a Williams & Glyn branch years and years ago. Colin was proud to tell me that he was made manager of that branch at age 19. I can't imagine a person that age today that would have the maturity for such responsibility or that any company would offer it to them.

As we parted, Colin suggested a route for my run to Manchester tomorrow but advised that the Parbold Hill was a killer and doubted my ability to climb it. His doubt of course, just intensified my desire to do it. It was a struggle, but using my lowest gear, I managed to climb Parbold Hill without getting out of the saddle. The rest of Colin's route gave me more trouble and took much longer than it should have. But these were directional rather than stamina problems.

My final night was spent at the Manchester hostel where my bike case has been stored. After re-packing the bike in its case, I walked over to the railway station to check on departure times for the airport and to assess how long it would take to walk there from the hostel in the morning. Twenty minutes seemed adequate but that did not allow for the rain that developed or the extreme weight and clumsiness of all my gear.

In the morning, to make things worse, I was so distracted by the unexpected effort of this short journey that I turned left where I should have turned right. That error and its correction added about eight minutes to the trip (more directional dysfunction). This delay was further lengthened because the main road I had to cross happened to be the route of the cycle segment of the final triathlon event of the Commonwealth Games then in progress. The colourful but damp female cyclists flashed by as two bobbies on crowd control checked round the bend until the way was clear, then waved me across. If I had to wait for something, nothing could have been more appropriate than a damp cycling event, particularly one involving athletic young women in latex.

The train was five minutes late, offsetting my other delays, but was packed with people on their way to various final Games events round the city. So there was standing room only in the entry/exit zone. Both hands were required to hold my bike case and other gear, making maintaining my balance very difficult. Every stop along the way required shifting position and gear to let people on or off. Once at the airport, I had about a kilometre walk to the check in.

There was a huge queue at check in and totally inadequate numbers of serving staff. It took about ninety minutes to get checked in at which point I was told that I had better rush as they were already loading my plane. There was a huge queue at security. I abandoned all pretence of courtesy to jump close to the front of this queue, arriving at the gate about fifteen minutes before scheduled take-off to find the flight delayed for 'technical difficulties'. This turned out to be that day's euphemism for 'we are still loading the luggage'.

Then, I discovered that all today's delays had been worthwhile.

Economy class was oversold and being one of the last to check in, I was assigned to first class! As you no doubt know, first class brings wider seats, more legroom, better food and service, a choice of films and free drinks.

My seatmates were a 28-year-old policeman and a 45-year-old Austrian based in Scotland that had the same good luck. These two seemed to get better service than other first class passengers and were taking full advantage of the free whisky. As the trip progressed, they became very friendly and loquacious. The reason for superior service became clear when I learned that the policeman's girlfriend was one of the first class stewardesses. The other man's mellow mood was due to the whisky and the fact that he was going to see his Canadian girlfriend---all through the journey he kept saying, "I'm so happy!" to the point where his whiskey dulled brain appropriately rolled out "sappy" instead.

The now relaxed policeman pulled up his trouser leg to show me an injury caused by a criminal on a motorcycle. Although now healed, his lower leg was red and raw-looking as if it had been recently gnawed away by a bear. This accident was responsible for his premature retirement. He also expressed frustration and dismay at the state of criminal justice in England resulting from political correctness and strict rules on admissible evidence.

As the flight wore on, my two increasingly inebriated companions became very complimentary about my friendliness and appearance. Plans were made to get together in Toronto the next evening with girlfriends and spouse. Sobriety must have changed their minds and opinions, as I never received a call to say when and where this get together would be.

So ended a very interesting, rewarding, frustrating and wet trip.

CELTIC TOUR

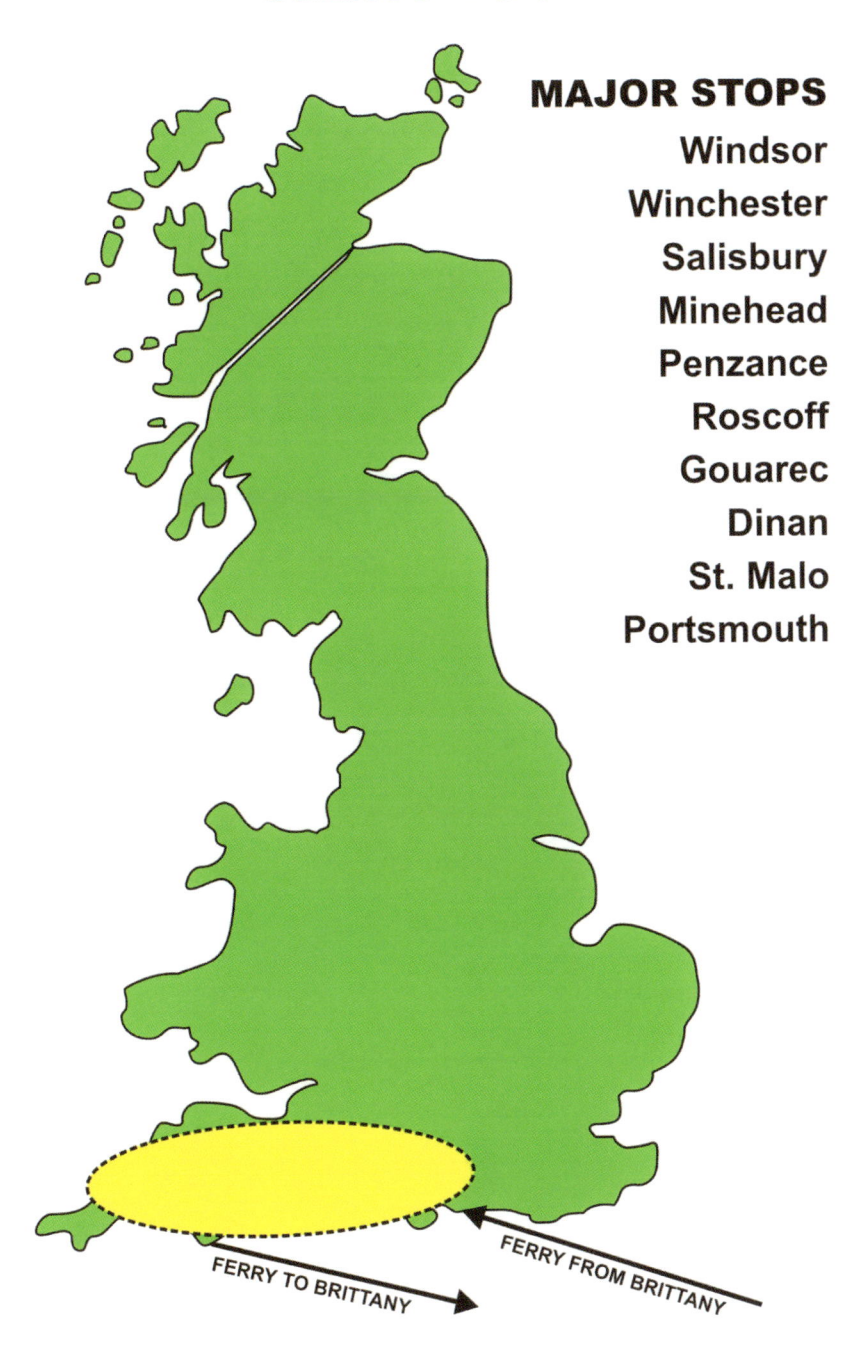

MAJOR STOPS
Windsor
Winchester
Salisbury
Minehead
Penzance
Roscoff
Gouarec
Dinan
St. Malo
Portsmouth

FERRY TO BRITTANY
FERRY FROM BRITTANY

CELTIC TOUR – 1570 KM

Overnight at	Day's Distance in Km
Windsor, Berkshire	26
Winchester, Hampshire	121
Salisbury, Wiltshire	47
Street, Somerset	95
Minehead, Somerset	68
Lynton, Devon	47
Holsworthy, Devon	74
Padstow, Cornwall	84
Perranporth, Cornwall	54
Penzance, Cornwall	58
St. Just, Cornwall	43
St. Just, Cornwall	56
Roscoff, Brittany	19
	(more by ferry)
Huelgoat, Brittany	61
Gouarec, Brittany	65
Group Camping Tour (6 nights)	222
Val Andre, Brittany	90
Dinan, Brittany	60
Cap Frehel, Brittany	55
Cap Frehel, Brittany	63
St. Malo, Brittany	76
Portsmouth, Hampshire	(by ferry)
Windsor, Berkshire	85
	(more by train)

CELTIC CYCLE

My previous trip was the longest in duration of any so far and at the end, I felt a bit jaded with Britain. My familiarity with the country makes me feel at home, enlarges the scope of conversation and generally eases travelling. But, this familiarity, while comfortable, reduces the opportunities for new adventures and for experiencing different cultures and architectures. Thus, there is less of a challenge to reconsider the 'normal' approaches to organising life. That previous trip had been the wettest ever. I longed for better weather and vowed to choose the continent for my next trip.

However, eighteen months later, when it came time to start planning the new trip, I realised that there were still parts of Britain that I wanted to see, the rugged west coast of Cornwall in particular. As my thinking progressed, it became tinged with the Celtic aspect of Cornwall and led me to think of combining Cornwall with Brittany. This connection became the basis for the planning and the title of my most recent tour.

Cycling Britain, the Lonely Planet's guidebook that I use most often, offered a seven-day Southwest England tour, incorporating the coast of Devon and Cornwall that seemed a good foundation. This tour headed northwest from Weymouth on the south coast but I chose to cycle west from the Heathrow area and join the guidebook trip mid-route on day two.

The next step was to see if the Internet would be of any use in planning the Brittany part. Almost immediately, I stumbled across a website for Breton Bikes, a cycle/camping touring company based in Brittany. Most of the time, Breton Bikes simply provide all the gear and the routes for their customers but twice a year they offer a tour led by the owner. As most of their customers are Brits, this seemed an ideal way to explore France in the company of a knowledgeable, bi-lingual guide and with others that I could converse with

The first of these led tours was timed perfectly to follow my intended time in Cornwall so the next step was to organise transport between England and France. Here again, the Internet was invaluable. I could check the railway and ferry timetables, book and pay for my tickets online. Such activity may be commonplace for many of you but it was a first for me.

In order to have the best chance with the weather yet still travel cheaply, I delayed my departure date until virtually the last day of the low season airfares winding up with a 27 May date. An expected income tax refund and enough Airmiles® for the low season fare provided the finance for a month's trip which I split nearly 50/50 between England and Brittany.

Now, detailed planning could begin in earnest. Hostels fill up quickly in the UK with school field trips in the late spring and people trying to avoid the summer crowds. Based on past disappointments, booking the hostels is usually one of the first tasks on the agenda. But the very first task was to find accommodation close to Heathrow that would agree to store my hard vinyl cycle storage box for the full month.

The British hostel directory showed a perfectly placed hostel at Windsor. Alas, my directory was out-of-date and the Windsor hostel was closed (This also proved true for Plymouth, the embarkation point for the ferry to Roscoff). So, I began an Internet search for B&B's in the Windsor area. Initially, this was discouraging, as the available websites do not cover the universe of available B&B's, only the more expensive ones. Eventually, however, I discovered that Windsor has its own website with a link to a Tourist Information Centre B&B booking service. I was able to ask them to find me a reasonably priced B&B that would be willing to store the cycle box. They quickly responded with an acceptable choice and sent me both a confirmation and a map of the Windsor area marked with the location of the B&B.

The Internet hostel booking system proved unequal to my route, being able to deal only with the hostels in Winchester, Penzance and Portsmouth. The Penzance hostel organised my bookings at St. Just (near Land's End). Other bookings were made by a snail mail request to the hostel association's head office in Derbyshire. That said, I must report that they treated me with great courtesy, to the point of a long-distance call to confirm my bookings.

From a budget conscious point of view, it probably would have been better to plan my route around hostel locations in the rough vicinity of my route but I let the guidebook route dictate and wound up having to find another three B&B's to fill in the gaps. One of these was in Street, Somerset where another hostel had been closed. In this case, the central hostel office recommended a B&B that proved to be a good choice.

After Street, the terrain looked tougher and it was hard to

anticipate what sort of daily distance might be achievable, so I decided to be flexible and rely on the resources of the local TIC offices to find the other two B&B's when I knew where I needed them.

The French hostel bookings proved more difficult but I did manage to book with St. Malo, the port city from which my return ferry departed. They sent me a very long email (in English) that began with a confirmation of the booking. As with the English requests for a booking I had included my credit card details. Given my abysmal French, I pleaded with the Paris central office to book Cap Frehel, a small hostel near Fort Latte and the Cape lighthouse that only accepted telephone bookings. In mid May, the Paris office did so and confirmed my booking, probably muttering 'imbecile' under their breath. Later, at Cap Frehel, there they had no evidence of my prepayment nor did I, as the booking was too late to appear on my bill before departure!

Just before departure, in the process of checking all the accommodation correspondence to confirm dates and evidence of the bookings, I discovered that the very last sentence in the St. Malo email response requested a deposit before the 9th of May as they could not accept credit cards. Some quick emails followed and under the circumstances, St Malo re-instated my booking without a deposit so long as I arrived by 6 pm.

As you can see, pre-arranging the accommodation can be challenging. Let's move on to a quick overview of the route.

The Route

The tour began at Windsor, in Berkshire; went southwest into Winchester, in Hampshire. From Winchester, the route continued generally west to Salisbury in Wiltshire and northwest to Street, in Somerset, across to the coast at Minehead, Somerset. From there it was a generally southern route, partly inland and partly coastal through Devon into Cornwall, touching at Padstow, Perranporth, Penzance, Land's End and St. Ives.

The Brittany portion of this trip, as you will have noted, is not shown on the map at the beginning of this chapter. My Brittany travels included both coastal and inland topography. Brittany Ferries took me from Plymouth to Roscoff, a two-day cycle from Gouarec in central Brittany where the group tour began. This tour centred on the Nantes-Brest Canal, visiting Josselin and Pontivy before returning to Gouarec a week later. On my own again, I headed north to Val Andre, Dinan, Cap

Frehel and St. Malo for the ferry ride back to England.

Arrival

Mari dropped me at the Toronto airport just after six pm on the 27th of May. She was very concerned at the weight of all my gear. There was the cycle case, of course, plus a medium sized duffel bag absolutely stuffed with clothing, panniers, helmet, extra shoes, maps, daily route cards, tools, spares and rear rack bag. In addition, I had a rucksack as my carry on bag. This held camera, book, tickets, passport, and handlebar bag. The cycle case weighed in at 25 kg, so I imagine the total was over 40. While unloading the car, the hard edge of the cycle case lock hasp fell against my hand. I took no notice but Mari immediately saw blood spurting from the top of my hand and became certain that her old man could not cope with all of this!

Check in was a breeze. After the attendant provided some tape to secure my cycle case address labels that were falling off, I wheeled it over to the special section for large luggage and in less than fifteen minutes, my load was reduced to the rucksack, now comfortably on my back.

This good feeling gradually dissipated as the flight was delayed by well over half an hour due to the late arrival of one of the flight crew! This wasn't announced as the reason, of course, but an exasperated other crewmember told me. The seat was uncomfortable; the dinner was poor, the film dull and breakfast pathetic.

But we arrived on time and landed very smoothly only to be held up at the gate by a late departing United Emirates flight. This delay was compensated for by the luggage and cycle case arriving very quickly. I rang the taxi company recommended by the B&B at Windsor and requested an estate car (station wagon) to carry the cycle case. They told me where to meet them, told me what to look for and promised to be there in twenty minutes. I began to feel that the trip had really begun.

The taxi arrived as promptly as promised and my driver, although seriously overweight and unfit, at least feigned an interest in my upcoming adventure. After finding the B&B, I spent the next few hours unpacking and re-assembling the bike and organising the panniers for balance and ease of finding things. I had left behind a crucial tool to mount the handlebar bag bracket doubling the time required for that job. And the brakes would not function properly. There always seems to be some aspect of re-assembly that defeats me.

My host, an amiable Italian with a strong interest in cycling but limited English, advised me that there was a cycle shop just 500 metres away. Three thousand metres involving roundabouts and subways (underground walkways) would be more accurate. But he wasn't alone in inaccuracy. While attempting to find the shop, I was told once that there was no cycle shop in Windsor and once that it was just another 400 metres when 1500 was more like it.

Without functioning brakes, this was a walking expedition. Along the way, I tried to dismiss thought that when/if found, the shop might not be open. But it was and they cheerfully, and quickly fixed the brakes. It was embarrassingly simple. The brake cable became disengaged from a support when the handlebars and stem were removed for packing and I hadn't noticed.

While at the shop, I asked about my continuous problem of the rear wheel slipping out of position and rubbing against the chain stay when heavily loaded. They recommended changing my axle and lock nut to a stronger material, to which I agreed.

It was now after three pm and my planned forty-kilometre trip round the picturesque Thames villages nearby seemed doomed. So I cycled into the city to scout out a place for dinner this evening and while there picked up a map of the Great Park that the taxi driver had suggested as a good spot for cycling. I should have also taken a map of Windsor---getting back to the B&B, which should have been a twenty-minute walk, took twice that time on the bike!

A quick change into cycling clothes and I was off to explore the Great Park. These are Crown lands open to the public, providing a fabulous amenity for the people of Windsor. The Park is huge with an immediate rural feel, a village post office and some homes. There are ponds, swans, statutes, a polo ground and large estate like buildings involved in various activities for the Crown. The lattice-like, sporadically signposted, network of lanes disoriented me as many of the lanes went to the same place. The map only seemed to add to the confusion. Perhaps jet lag was a factor.

After about 25 kilometres of this, I was truly ready for a meal, having had nothing since the dry bit of banana bread and cup of coffee that Air Canada had the nerve to call breakfast. So, I went back to the B&B, showered and put on the dark blue sweat shirt and khaki cargo style trousers that were my sole go out to dinner clothes for this trip.

My intention was to go back into the city to one of the bistros that looked so inviting this afternoon, but I got no further than a brand new contemporary Indian restaurant that was only about three minutes away. In previous trips, one of my absolute favourite meals has been lamb and onion curry with Naan bread and a lager. So, finding this place seemed a propitious start to my gastronomic experiences for this trip. It did not disappoint. I had my favourite meal masquerading under a new name but with a sweet coconut flavoured Naan and an excellent salad that improved the experience. The ambiance, cool Mediterrrean with fresh white linen and brushed stainless cutlery, was a refreshing break from the stereotypical heavy red décor of Indian restaurants in Britain.

Continuing the delights of British cuisine, my B&B breakfast next morning included grapefruit segments (that I can never get enough of), kadota figs, prunes, muesli, eggs, tomatoes, beans, sausage, bacon, mushrooms, toast and tea.

Where Is the Hostel?

Getting round that breakfast and paying another visit to the cycle shop to better inflate the tyres and make sure my brakes were properly adjusted delayed my start to 10.15. The weather was cool and rain seemed likely but the terrain was accommodating, allowing me to cover 48 kilometres by about one pm when I stopped for a sandwich lunch in a roadside parkette outside a strip mall in Hook.

The distance to tonight's destination at Winchester was proving far greater than indicated by my advance planning so I decided to forgo my planned stop at Jane Austen's cottage in Chawton near Alton. It was half past three by the time I was in striking distance of Chawton so there might have been enough time for a tour and even a tea break before they closed. But doing so would have made a 7.30 or later arrival at Winchester as my reading of the map showed forty kilometres left. So I chose to press on, even abandoning my planned backcountry route for a busier, more direct one down the A32 to the A272.

Along the way, I stopped at the Watercress Line station in Alton for directions. This preserved steam railway runs to New Alresford, a watercress-growing centre near Winchester. This salad plant is very sensitive to water pollution and can be grown successfully only in broad lagoons or 'beds' fed by the clear waters of chalk streams, such as the infant River Itchen here. (1)

The ticket agent at the Watercress Line told me to 'turn right'; I should have realised he meant his right not mine. I had gone some distance feeling more and more that something was wrong when I stopped a man on the street and was amused to find myself asking directions of another North American. Alton was home to a Coors Brewery so I suspect that this man was one of their imported employees. Anyway, his detailed and accurate directions got me out of town headed towards Winchester.

The altered route reduced the distance to Winchester, so in less than two hours I was there even with the delaying mistake. I stopped at a petrol station convenience store to find out the hostel's location. The recently emigrated attendant had no idea but one of the customers was able to send me very close to the right spot. Nevertheless, once there, there were no signs for the hostel. Every other place a tourist might be interested in was signposted but not the hostel. So, I stopped in a pub. They did not even know there was a hostel in Winchester so I asked to use their telephone directory.

After trying every possible permutation: Youth Hostel; International Hostel; Hostel, Winchester Hostel, I finally found the address just as the publican re-appeared having found someone who knew where it was. The directions were very convenient; 'just follow the path behind the pub, cross the river, turn right and Bob's your uncle'. (Even though I am Bob and my uncles were called Malcolm, Fred and Fount, this was not a mistake—see glossary).

I got to the end of the indicated street without seeing anything remotely like a hostel. So, I asked again. There it was right in front of me! I had been standing virtually looking right at the side of the hostel. There were no signs in the street and only one on the front, inconspicuously flush with the wall and above my line of sight.

Once in, I complained about the situation. Lawrence, the somewhat pedantic warden, explained that the hostel was leased on a year-to-year basis from the National Trust, making any permanent type arrangements such as expensive signs a non-starter. On my return home, I consulted one of my reference books and found that the hostel had been in this same location for over thirty years!

Now that frustration was out of my system, I could enjoy this most unusual hostel. It shares the building of a former 18th century mill on the River Itchen with a National Trust museum. The dining room, one end of which also serves as a museum, is directly over the roaring millrace; outside its backdoor is a small island park crammed with roses and bluebells. Ceilings are low and timbered, apart from the bedroom I shared with eight others. This is reached by stairs up, then down, to a two basin washing area along one wall and a little humped bridge into the bunks area. A timbered, vaulted ceiling encased the lot. The showers and toilets are located in the basement that must have been below the level of the river. Thank goodness, I did not have to use them during the night; that would have been some expedition in the dark.

Before dinner, I walked round the cathedral's extensive grounds. Although the grounds are immediately adjacent to the busy pedestrian mall, there was an almost instant and palpable hush as I entered them. This and the tree-canopied walks created a sense of peace entirely appropriate for a cathedral and a tremendous contrast to the noisy, secular and materialistic behaviour close by. I wondered at the time how many young residents valued this serenity and beauty or were even aware of it.

Breakfast at the hostel was continental style with a curious mixture of formal and casual. We all sat together on long picnic type tables and the food was served boarding house fashion but with each member's place marked by a place card! No names, that is, the members that were using the kitchen to make their own breakfast, were to sit all together at the end of one of these tables and had no place cards.

Hostels regularly post the weather forecast—this morning's predicted a sunny start followed by rolling showers. By the time I went to retrieve the bike from the shed, the sunny part had ended, so I quickly changed into my raingear. Immediately the rain stopped. It continued to threaten all day and but made good those threats only intermittently requiring a lot of stops to change.

Magna Carta

Today's route to Salisbury was short, allowing time for side trips. The best of these was to the village of Crawley. This proved to be a very upscale bedroom village with no shops or post office, just expensive homes and a pub appropriately called the Fox and Hounds. Entrance to the village was on a narrow road alongside a lovely pond surrounded by wildflowers and hosting some uncommon ducks. One of the ducks was black and white and another a rich brown. The homes were so impressive that I must have taken pictures of at least 30% of them. Many had thatched roofs.

Salisbury is much like Winchester with a great cathedral and lovely river walks. Its pedestrian area seems much bigger however. At the cathedral, I mingled with a tour group that was to be the last group of the day allowed in to see the Magna Carta that is housed in a special Chapel. The display was of one of the forty Magna Carta copies that had been made to distribute round the country at the time. The writing was so neat and the lines so straight that it could have been run off on a press had Gutenberg's press been available over 200 years earlier but this work was hand done. Translations were available in several languages for visitors to read as the writing was so small and the style so dense that one could not read the 'original'.

The Carta was forced on King John in 1215 by English barons fed up with his appropriation of others' lands, the failed war with France and heavy taxation to support the war. 'The Carta's sixty-three articles covered every conceivable aspect of feudal dues and rights down to those of widows, hostages, and dispossessed Welshmen. Some of the articles, such as the ban on trials without witnesses or the condemnation of the arrest of freemen "save by the judgement of their peers", were to be fundamental to the subsequent growth of the rule of law. Indeed, the basic idea underlying the charter, that good government depends on agreed rules of conduct observed by all, is the cornerstone of constitutionalism.' (2) A year later King John tried to break the Carta, starting a civil war during which he died. It is not known whether his death was natural or assisted.

After leaving the cathedral, I walked along the riverside for a while, encountering St. Thomas Beckett church where an evensong service was just concluding. I stood just outside the sanctuary doors for a few minutes soaking up the strains of the final hymn and felt better for having done so.

Swedish Steven

My memory of the Salisbury hostel is strangely very dim. The layout of the dining room and member's kitchen is clear, possibly because I had several free cups of tea there while writing my notes. As usual the continental European members that prepared their own evening meals did so at about nine, so there was plenty of activity. Cooked plain pasta accompanied with wine seemed to be the most popular choice.

However, my memory of the morning at Salisbury is very clear. Emerging from the men's bedroom on the way to the washroom, I was stopped by an attractive, young Swedish woman just leaving the women's bedroom. She was a major distraction in her nearly transparent, baby doll pyjamas but I managed to feign no unseemly interest as she asked, 'Is Steven up; may I go in and see him?'

I told her that many of the men where not up or were dressing so it was best that she not go in but I could do it for her. I had to ask, 'which one is Steven?' She told me which bunk he had and asked that I wake him and tell him that Vicky wanted to see him. I did so somewhat tentatively, half expecting to be attacked for disturbing him, and quickly returned to tell Vicky that he was now awake. She remained outside in the corridor, apparently unconcerned at her state of undress, so I fought off my urgent need for the washroom and stayed happily chatting with her until Steven appeared.

Breakfast was with a young German that had recently left high school and was taking a break from his national service as a civil servant. According to him, young Germans have the choice of nine months of military service or ten months of civil service. He was working with disabled and mentally handicapped children before going on to university. I don't know how well this scheme works but it seems a great idea in theory.

Somerton and Street

Today's journey to Street in Somerset appeared long, so I decided to forgo any of the potential side trips. The first part of the morning was basically westward through rolling, slightly climbing country. The scenery to the south was beautiful, with a sweep of apparently manicured pastures bordered by a soft sculpted ridge topped with clumps of canopy trees. This ridge stretched almost the entire 34 km to Shaftesbury.

At Shaftesbury, I headed north and had an exhilarating eight kilometres down hill run to Gillingham. My reading of the map showed another 64 km for the afternoon with no likely spots for a stop before Somerton, just 10 km south of Street. So I settled for a quick sandwich on a bench outside the Gillingham supermarket.

Later in the afternoon, it became clear that my inexpert map reading had exaggerated the distance by about 16 km, making tea and teacakes at Somerton a definite possibility!

The diversion into Somerton required climbing an additional steep hill but the prospect of my first tea stop of the trip offset the extra effort so I cycled up. At the entrance to the village, there was an open house sign for homes developed from an old Red Lion coaching house that looked worth exploring later. Next came a nice little market area, benches and a teashop.

The shop proved to be popular despite the uninterested and perfunctory service or perhaps that was reserved for disreputable looking cyclists. I rose above the waitress's bad attitude and enjoyed my tea and teacakes with my book.

The intermittent rain that had been a feature all day returned adding a practical reason for visiting the open house. Here, I was treated cordially despite my appearance and a forthright declaration that I was not a potential buyer. There were some seven homes on show of varying sizes developed either inside the original inn or in a townhouse arrangement in what must have been the stabling area at the back of the inn. All featured fully fitted kitchens, huge original fireplaces, and solid wood barn-like doors. It was interesting to note the differences from a standard North American design: the electrical points in the wall were much higher than we are used to-at about 45 cm above floor level; the refrigerator and the freezer were two separate units placed in different locations; and none of the bedrooms had built in closets, so installing free-standing wardrobes would reduce their already limited floor space even further.

I was very impressed with the idea of preserving the exterior façade of a historic building in such a tasteful way. There were no gardens or garages but otherwise the development offered character and convenience. Prices began at the equivalent of C$550,000 for the small two-bedroom unit.

Then it was back down the hill in a rain shower that lasted the full ten kilometres into Street. Sally, my landlady, welcomed me with a pot of tea and biscuits that I could not (i.e. did not want to) refuse. She served this in their guests' lounge that also served as her husband's library. He favoured naval stories but had a fairly broad collection of popular fiction that impressively was all organised alphabetically by author.

After a shower and change of clothes I walked through Sally's pleasant back garden into a laneway that led to a pub she had recommended for dinner. I was pleased to find an Indian dish on the menu at a reasonable price but found it bland and undersized for my appetite.

It was still quite light at about nine when I finished dinner, so I explored the High Street (of Street!) getting drenched by a yahoo that drove pell-mell through a large puddle left by the earlier rain. During this stroll, I came upon a small cycle shop that I decided to visit the next day to have my luggage rack mended. The screws on the brace holding it to the cycle had come loose and none of my Allen keys would fit.

Next morning when I called in to this very small shop, the owner was able to help me immediately. While he worked we had an interesting discussion about the sorry state of British cycle manufacturing—much of it is not British anymore. I learned that he had just bought the shop earlier this year after looking for several years and missing out on a few others. It was also interesting to see that he wore surgical gloves to do the work. Not only did they keep his hands free of grease but also they protected him from the carcinogens that cycle lubricants contain. This was my first experience of this approach but I encountered it again in Windsor later.

Since I was there I took the opportunity to have the front pannier supports altered also. They were attached to the upper part of the forks with an awkward brace that made it impossible for the pannier to sit securely on the support. He replaced the braces with stainless steel bolts that screwed into braze-ons built into the forks-- a much tidier and more secure arrangement.

This stop made a pleasant diversion and I felt much more secure about the front panniers now. The past three days had involved re-positioning them several times a day when road bumps dislodged them. Bending forward to do this while cycling was a little unnerving.

Families and Economics

Today my route and the guidebook route merged about five kilometres out of Street. At this point, I changed my odometer back to zero so that the guidebook's mileage indicators would be consistent with it. Initially this worked well; the turns appeared just when the odometer indicated they should. Then minor differences began to develop between the odometer reading and the guide-indicated mileage for a particular turn.

At first, the difference was only .16 km and could be adjusted for as a constant discrepancy. But the differences grew, and were followed by a specified right turn that should have been left. I, of course, blamed these differences on the book, not my transcription of the directions that I had copied to bring with me. Later in the trip, I met a cyclist at Land's End who was about to start the End-to-End using the same guidebook. He already had a full page of mistakes found in the book. (But there is another possible explanation for the apparent differences in distance. Odometers are calibrated for wheel size---if my odometer was mis-calibrated, the difference between a 700 mm wheel and a 27-inch wheel could easily account for my situation).

So, from this point on, I relied much more on studying my map than on the guidebook. From my lunch stop at Bridgewater, I used the A39 most of the way to my destination at Minehead. Normally, A roads are much too busy but traffic is lighter in the West Country.

This road was busy but not excessively so and the scenery was fine. At one point, the road went through a forest of trees whose leafy canopies created a dark tunnel but for the lacey traceries of light formed on the road surface. Outside the tunnel, the landscape presented a tidy set of jigsaw puzzle pieces in multi-shaded green and yellow.

On a whim, at Nether Sowerby, I turned south off the A39 into the lanes of the Quantock Forest towards Crowcombe. This was both a good and a bad decision. The lanes were quiet and the landscape more rural with tree-canopied, cool tunnels and lots of visible livestock. But the terrain was immediately much hillier than anything encountered so far. This proved to be just a preview of what was to come for much of the balance of the trip. The six kilometres to Crowcombe took an hour but then I turned west again on the A358 to rejoin the A39 into Minehead and was rewarded with a gently down sloping run.

The YHA at Minehead was signposted. Unfortunately, the sign was positioned some distance beyond a major fork in the road and I missed it by choosing the wrong fork. Once found, the hostel sat high above the town in a forest-like situation at the end of a forest trail. It was immediately a pleasant place. Later it became clear that this was largely due to the warden.

His guests today were several young British families and a group of young foreigners. He helped develop a sense of community by changing the table you sat at for meals, creating an opportunity to meet several different people. He asked your permission to do so in such a way that it would have been churlish to say no.

My first family was a teacher father with two pre-school age children. They were doing a few days together on a cycle built for three. Mum was to join them later in the week but for now, Dad was coping very well. He was patient and kind, yet firm when required. Despite the attention the children required, the two of us had an interesting discussion on British economic life over dinner

This is a topic that I introduce to many of my conversations, as I can not understand how, with incomes no better than the North American average, the British manage a cost of living structure that is nearly twice as high. He said that most people were heavily in debt, living beyond their incomes but of course that is also true in North America. As an example of one of his own economies, he said that their one family car, a Toyota Corolla, had been bought at auction for the equivalent of C$5000, about one sixth of the cost new in Britain. My understanding increased only marginally. I would have loved to do a detailed budget analysis with him but of course had to restrain myself.

At breakfast, my new family was complete with both Mum and Dad and two children, one just ten months. I tried to discuss British politics without much success, as they were uninterested having decided that all political parties are much the same.

On my way out, about three-quarters of the way down the forest trail into Minehead, I discovered that I had come away with the key to the cycle shed. Fortunately, just at that moment, the laundry service van appeared on its way up and the driver agreed to return the key for me.

I went down to the seafront where a few people were wandering on the wide, sandy beach. Many more people were milling around the tourist shops and amusement arcades. I have never understood why British seasides seem joined at the hip with such arcades. Why do people go to the seaside and then spend their time in these places? I could understand if the weather was poor but this was a pleasant, sunny day.

Revising my Will

After cycling round the rest of Minehead for a while, I left at 10.30, eager for the open road. Today's destination is Lynton, a 45 kilometre run. The warden at Minehead had offered a number of alternative routes but mentioned that Selworthy had an excellent teashop. As Selworthy was already in my plans as a possible side trip, this additional information cemented the decision.

Within an hour and a half along the A39, I reached the turn-off and steep climb to Selworthy, a National Trust village within the Trust's 20 square mile property. At the top of the climb, a church and a number of thatched, creamy yellow cottages overlooked a broad sweep of valley at the edge of Exmoor. There was a parking lot near the church and some walking trails but no sign of a teashop.

After visiting the church and spending a few moments on a bench absorbing the valley view, I returned down the hill, tea less and disappointed, passing by a hillside track off to the side. I decided to investigate and after a few minutes climb was greeted by a small green ringed with more creamy yellow cottages. One of these was the teashop!

Its fame was justified. The teacakes were huge and stuffed with juicy currants. I sat out in the garden, overlooking the valley and observing the interactions of other guests. A mother was chastising her unrepentant son for kicking her. A multi-generation family arrived next, complete with matriarch in a pushchair. Two family members manoeuvred her up the hill, the flagstone path and finally to the table. Worn out with their exertions, they made many solicitous enquiries about her comfort as if competing for her estate. The men looked as if missing this meal and many more would do no harm.

I stretched out the experience as long as was decent, squeezing nearly three cups from my teapot and enjoying my book, the scenery and human dramas around me.

This village, the best example I have seen of the work the Trust does to preserve British history, confirmed my decision a few days ago to leave a bequest to the National Trust in my will. This decision was strengthened when later, in the information centre, the young woman attendant told me that Selworthy was doubly protected from British housing development pressures by being both National Trust and part of the Exmoor National Forest.

Stop and Stare

The next place of interest was Porlock, a pleasant small village, famous for the steep hill that begins just south of it on the A39. This road is so steep that two toll roads have been built to the sides to reduce the strain of climbing it. I chose to use one of them and quickly realised how tough Porlock Hill must be if what I was doing was easier. A sign at the beginning of the toll road specified various charges depending on the nature of the vehicle and surprisingly included a one-pound charge for cycles but there was no visible tollbooth.

This road was nearly 7 kilometres long and heavily forested but with occasional glimpses of the sea off to the right. The accompanying bird song was glorious. After about 5 km, I came upon a little brown hut at the edge of the road that I assumed must be the tollbooth but seeing no signs of a collecting person, thought that I was lucky and would not be required to pay. However, just as I drew abreast of the booth, a man appeared at the doorway and waved me on.

This was a pleasing but humbling experience. It made me slightly cross with myself for thinking that I might get away without having to pay when the operators were gracious enough to waive the toll. It's interesting how my sense of well-being is so dependent on behaving in accordance with my conscience yet how powerful financial considerations are in determining that behaviour. A constant battle between my conscience and my wallet---is that a *civil* war?

A little further on, at a cattle grate, I stopped to admire the now broad view of the sea across a steep valley populated with grazing sheep. A bird watching, hiking couple had stopped at the same point. We chatted for a few minutes during which she quoted a line from a poem she attributed to Walter de la Mare—' what value is this life of care, if we cannot stop and stare'. This appealed to me so I asked her to repeat it in order to remember it long enough to record in my notes. It has more meaning for me than the hackneyed 'stop and smell the roses' but perhaps it is just less familiar.

I rejoined the A39 for the remainder of the now easy run to Lynmouth. This is an unexpectedly beautiful spot with a magnificent rocky river running through abruptly rising soft green grazed hills and forests. One thing it did not have was any YHA sign.

The hostel was known as the Lynton hostel, but I had been warned that it actually was in a place called Lynton Hill. I misinterpreted my directions and wound up spending a good half an hour round tripping on the wrong road. The correct road ran the opposite direction from Lynmouth and went straight up. There was no opportunity for a flying start and any momentum gained could not have been maintained more than a few seconds. I walked.

When the road eventually levelled out, I saw another cyclist ahead just abreast of the landmark indicated for the turn-off to the hostel. Seeing him turn, I breathed a sigh of relief that this must be the place. It was, but the access road was steep so more walking was necessary to get there.

I was gaining ground on the other cyclist and could see that he was thin and quite frail looking, perhaps in his seventies. His bike, an old Claude Butler, was in sad shape. Although the day was warm, particularly climbing those hills, he was wearing two sweaters under a jacket and had a reflective belt on top of all that.

Since we shared the same room, I later observed him dressing and discovered that there were three sweaters, not two, as well as three pairs of underpants. The latter, I imagine, produced the comfort on the saddle that my cycling shorts with a built in chamois pad provide.

There were also three, 30 something cyclists at the hostel near the end of a north to south End-to-End ride. They had maintained an impressive 120 km daily average so far and planned to do the same the next day in this terrain! Despite an evening at the pub in Lynton, they got away the next morning at 7.30. We older chaps cheered them on envying their energy but speaking for myself, glad to be travelling at a more leisurely pace.

Later, at breakfast I attempted to learn something about my heavily clothed cycling roommate and another man. It was like pulling teeth. Neither of them was pleased with their regular lives. The cyclist, whom I thought well beyond retirement, was actually still working and probably no older than myself. Grudgingly, he told us that he worked as a quality control inspector at a firm that made work uniforms. The impression he gave was that the work was boring and unimportant. The other man repeatedly said that he wished he could cycle but it hurt his shoulders and neck; he was equally dismissive of his work. It was dispiriting and we parted company immediately after breakfast.

Forda Farm

A steep lane down from the hostel led to nearby Lynton where I searched for an Internet facility that I had been told about. Someone finally told me that it wasn't a stand-alone operation but was accessed through the library. Once located, I found a notice apologizing for being closed on one of the two days a week they were meant to be open.

Frustrated that the day was eroding without accomplishment, I went to the TIC to see about finding a B&B in the Holsworthy area. As Holsworthy was outside Lynton's catchment area, this TIC had to contact another TIC to find something. After about twenty minutes, they found a farmhouse some 10 kilometres north of Holsworthy with a convenient nearby pub for my evening meal. The landlady even offered to drive me to the pub and pick me up later. The price was higher than I wanted to pay but I did not want to spend anymore time looking. The distance was nearly 75 km and it was already 10.30. The TIC attendant wrote down directions for finding the farm and provided a very focused detail map from the Internet.

The nice lady at the TIC told me that the first 40% of my journey (to Barnstaple) was all-downhill. She obviously was not a cyclist. On average, the road may have lost altitude between Lynton and Barnstaple but there were a number of significant up hills inside that average producing a most un-downhill like cycling experience.

At Barnstaple, I decided to join the Tarka Trail (a converted railway bed) that I felt certain would be flat. This had been written up in my guidebook but without the crucial information that it was accessed from the car park of the railway station. Although there was no city signage to help out, the Trail was very heavily used.

I found the Trail pleasant and reasonably fast, but just a bit boring. Hills are definitely unwelcome when they have to be climbed but they provide variety and generally there is a bit of a reward on the down slope. However, the trail had some attractive watering holes. The first, a former station stop turned café, had long queues so I carried on to the next one. This was a railway car converted to a café. A chatty grandmotherly type sold me a lemon mayonnaise chicken sandwich and a ginger beer that I enjoyed with my book at one of the picnic tables arranged on the old station's platform. Grandmother lost most of her charm in my opinion as she regularly came out on the platform for a smoke.

The Trail and I parted company at this point, as I rejoined the main road towards Holsworthy. My pace was better than expected, providing time to take tea at a country club along the road whose cafe was open for non-members.

Cream teas are de rigueur in Devon so teacakes were unavailable. But the day was warm and their beer garden was inviting so I agreed to forgo my favoured teacakes and have the scones, strawberry jam and clotted cream that comprise a cream tea.

The TIC Internet map showed that I should now be fairly close to the Holsworthy Beacon that was indicated as the landmark for a turn to the east for the farm B&B. But my detailed road map was so dissimilar to the Internet map that they could have been for different countries. The waitress, a local girl, could not make them out either.

Relying on the detailed road map, I turned east at the next intersection. Conveniently, it was signposted to the small community where the B&B was located. But I should have known that there are often many lanes that approach rural villages even though maps don't show them all. Of course, this was the wrong lane, making all the subsequent directions provided by the TIC also wrong.

My stop at a farm for directions created considerable interest. The farmer interrupted his tea to come out to the road to speak to me and was soon joined by his wife and son. None of them knew Forda Farm but she rang her uncle and got specific directions for me. They were cheerful and interested.

Nevertheless, their rural-style directions ('follow that ridge where you can see the white farmhouse') were still a little vague for someone more comfortable with 'take the first left after passing Barclay's Bank '). So later I had to flag down a passing vehicle to confirm my directions and then stopped at a farm implement repair shop to ask again.

By this time, I was so close that the directions were a seemingly unambiguous 'down the hill, at the dip'. Nevertheless, once at the dip, it would still have been easy to completely miss the farm. There was no B&B sign, the Forda Farm sign was small, very faded and faced away from me. I was going slowly because the road surface was rough and just happened to look over my shoulder right at the dip.

My friendly, chubby and barefoot hostess Val turned out to be the Chair of the Devon Farm B&B's. She made me a welcoming cup of tea with assorted biscuits and joined me in the lounge for a chat. This was a nice gesture but I got the impression that her girth was at least partially a product of these chats that were as welcome to her as to her guests.

My en-suite room was very well appointed and comfortable. Val provided a jug of bottled water because the farm's large herd of dairy cattle could have contaminated their well.

After my shower, as promised, Val drove me to Woody's, the local pub/restaurant that she recommended. She offered to pick me up after dinner but as it was only about a ten-minute walk I borrowed a torch from her to be able to walk back.

The pork roasted in cider with mashed potatoes and peas that I chose was massive but very plain. I sat alone, reading for about half the meal until another single man came in and sat at an adjacent table facing me and ordered the identical meal. I was drawn, somewhat reluctantly away from my book, into conversation but, as is usually the case, found that it was interesting.

He had just retired and moved to this area from London. Apparently, he had been visiting North Devon for years finally deciding to buy his retirement home here. I suggested that he must have found property values in Devon much more affordable than London. This was obviously a sore spot. He claimed that commercial property prices in London had plummeted following the Twin Towers disaster in New York on the risk that a similar terrorist attack might hit London. He believes he lost £100,000 as a result.

My next faux pas was to praise Ken Livingstone, London's Mayor, for the stiff parking charge levied in Central London that so significantly reduced traffic and grid lock in that section of the city. According to my dinner companion, its other effect was to severely reduce trade for many businesses in Central London, including his.

Relying on the closing minutes of twilight, I successfully negotiated my way back to Forda Farm and met Val's husband, Richard. He was just finishing off a huge bowl of strawberry shortcake and reading a very scholarly, most un-farmer like, history of the WW II Normandy invasion. This year is, of course, the 60th anniversary of the invasion and celebrations are only a few days away.

Our conversation led to my accommodation for the next night that was unbooked at the moment. Val immediately undertook to find me a place with her contacts. After about an hour she located a vacancy at another farm near Padstow and got detailed directions for me.

Next morning Val arrived at my bedroom door with a promised cup of coffee and still barefoot. Later, as I worked on the huge farmhouse breakfast, we talked about her university work towards a degree in agriculture that she never completed partly because at the time she could not drive (a medical condition) a tractor. The degree required a period working on a farm and she could not find a farmer willing to take on a non-driver. She wasn't unhappy about it all as she felt very satisfied with what she had accomplished with her B&B business and being chosen as Chair of the Devon Farmhouse group.

Heavy morning mist spoilt Richard's plans for harvesting silage today and certainly dampened my spirits for the day's run. As I left, Richard was hosing off the tractor with the help of one of the two Hong

Kong schoolboys that are spending the long summer holiday at the B&B instead of returning to Hong Kong.

Cycling Museum

Braving the mist, I made my way along the lanes to Holsworthy Beacon, which turned out to be a village rather than the landmark hill and tower I had expected yesterday. Turning south to re--join the A39, I encountered severely limited visibility. I could see perhaps no more than 50 metres ahead. Following the guidebook again, I turned west towards Bude on the A3072 at Holsworthy.

Today's guidebook distance looked to be close to 100 km and I was thoroughly tired of climbing hills. I also wanted to have time to see the cycle museum near Camelford. My guidebook route took me there via coastal lanes and side roads that would no doubt have been lovely and peaceful but might take too much time to allow a stop at the museum. Careful study of the map suggested that I could cut perhaps 15 km off the trip by using a different route was so encouraged by this time-saving discovery that I stopped for lunch at a roadside café that looked as if it catered to lorry drivers but it was unexpectedly very clean, pleasant and reasonably priced.

The turn-off to the museum appeared a little while after lunch and surprise, surprise, it was actually signposted. In a few minutes, I found the museum, housed in an old railway building, surrounded by odd metal sculptures and looking somewhat desolate. The parking lot was empty and the door to the building was locked. I had just about decided that the museum was closed when a voice called out 'hello'.

The woman curator had just taken advantage of a lull in visitors to walk across the small parking lot to her home for a cup of tea. We entered the museum; she delivered her opening spiel, collected my entrance fee and left me to it. The place was chock a block with memorabilia: old advertisements, product boxes, posters, parts and accessories, books, magazines and of course cycles. The cycles were arranged in pretty much chronological order of cycle development starting with the mid to late 19th century. Most of the exhibits were of British origin but both France and the US were represented also. Accompanying this display was a constantly repeating four-part set of period cycling songs of the *Bicycle Built for Two* ilk. Initially, the songs set an appropriate, nostalgic mood but the set took only about ten minutes before immediately starting over. By the end of my 45-minute stay, I could take no more.

There were samples of military use, of postman cycles, of exotic developments such as the 'Zero'; a chainless cycle recently marketed in Britain but with late 19th century French origins. Various styles of tables and chairs made from cycle chain wheels and painted bright colours were for sale at reduced prices. The husband produced these in an adjacent workshop and was probably also responsible for the sculptures outside.

Although the displays were poorly lit and provided no history other than a date, it was an interesting stop that showed the progression of cycle design from the huge front-wheel, tiny rear wheel 'ordinary' to the equal sized wheel 'safety' that modern cycles resemble so closely. The museum represents this couple's collection over about two decades.

So much more could be done. The cycle had a powerful effect on mobility for all social classes and on gender equality. Exhibits illustrating this and the history of cycling dress would have been interesting. Technical exhibits dealing with the effects of frame and wheel weight, with gearing and a comparison of the relative energy efficiency of the cycle with other forms of transport would have been fascinating. (See appendix for details).

But the couple's resources don't run to that. Entrance fees are obviously barely adequate to keep the museum open. Manufacturers have been unwilling to do more than provide a single sample of their products, sometimes not even that.

Back on the road, I returned to the A39 headed for the long bridge into Wadebridge where Val's directions told me to go. Feeling the need for some connection with the wider world, I stopped in at a Wadebridge newsagent to buy a paper and to confirm my directions.

As it turned out the long bridge Val referred to was a totally different and new bridge. I had come into Wadebridge down a lovely slope without needing to. Correcting this, of course, required a climb – of over three kilometres. After that the directions were roughly accurate but imprecise. I have become paranoid about going the wrong way and stopped to ask about three more times to be sure.

I had been told to go to 'Greenfields' a bungalow at a particular intersection. It was there but no one else was. The bungalow was obviously part of a farm that catered to caravans and campers so I cycled down the farm road to the main farmhouse and spoke to the matriarch of the family. She pleasantly passed me on to Richard, her

Panniers, Pedals, and Pubs

son, who was in the barn working on his tractor.

Richard, a good-looking young man in rude good health, welcomed me. 'My girlfriend Kelly is returning to the bungalow in a few minutes and she will show you the room'. As, I went back up the lane, she arrived, a large friendly blonde but not nearly attractive enough for a man like Richard.

Kelly got me settled and advised me that there was a great pub, The Cornish Arms just a half mile away for dinner. My room had a television and tea making facilities as well as being adjacent to an almost private lounge but the washroom was nearly at the other side of the house and was shared with all the other guests and well as Richard and Kelly. I passed their room enroute for a shower and as their door was slightly ajar could see that the tidy housekeeping ended inside that door.

The distance to the pub was only double Kelly's estimate. I arrived by 7.30 but seating was already very limited and I wound up in the billiards room, tucked in a corner just out of harm's way from protruding cue sticks, elbows and bums. Access to the ladies' loo was just off to my left so I was treated to a constant stream of round-trip female traffic. All ages and shapes were represented; with most of the middle-aged ones squeezed into something meant to make them look younger. It was Friday night. The men playing billiards had obviously not bothered to change or clean up but come straight from work. They were noisy, smoking, drinking and taunting each other. It was interesting to watch but not conducive to a peaceful meal with my book. The meal was acceptable but did not live up to the pub's billing. Although come to think of it, I had interpreted Kelly's 'great' to relate to the food. More likely, she meant the happy atmosphere.

On the way back to the B&B, I stopped at a small house with some massive sculptures where I had noticed people taking pictures earlier. The sculptures were varied and interesting but the walls of the house were more so. The entire front and one side were covered in rectangular plaques, each one referring to some famous person in the history of the world with a very concise statement about that person such as Bertrand Russell, 'philosopher' along with their dates. The range was wide, covering celebrities in music and film as well as scientists and politicians. Several of the plaques on the sidewall were blank awaiting their person.

On my return to the bungalow, Richard kindly offered me the

use of their washing machine for my laundry, thereby saving me both time and money. (Later during this trip I had to pay £3 to use a hostel's washing machine.) I read the *Telegraph* in my 'private lounge' while the machine was working and later hung the laundry on a rack suspended from the kitchen ceiling over the Aga cooker. The rack was raised and lowered by a rope pulley. Agas burn continuously generating perfect drying conditions. Next morning, the clothes were totally dry and pleasantly warm just as if they had been taken from a tumble dryer.

How Far Is It – Really?
The night in between was not at all pleasant. Somehow, I picked up a bug, was coughing up phlegm and had to find my way across the dark house to the toilet several times throughout the night. Despite the lack of sleep, I climbed out finally at 6.45 to make a cup of coffee and work on my notes. At least the coffee kept my throat lubricated. When Kelly appeared at 8 with my breakfast, she took pity on me and gave me a box of throat lozenges that helped a lot. But for the first time ever, I could not finish my breakfast—the fat, bursting sausage looked particularly loathsome. I was not feeling well and rationalised the waste by thinking that this heavy, fat laden meal was not healthy anyway.

Padstow, an old Cornish fishing town, was my next port of call. Like many similar towns, the main road circled the harbour and was itself ringed with commercial buildings and homes. Other streets that ran in spoke like fashion from the ring road hub were full of shops touting postcards and other tourist oriented items. This was pretty standard stuff but the narrowness of the streets and the quaint architecture produced a picture postcard ambiance.

Padstow is on the Camel Trail, another cycling and hiking track made from a disused railway line. I cycled back towards Wadebridge on the Trail for a while enjoying the lovely riverside scenery, the narrow cuttings through steep rocks, and the colour and scent of wildflowers. The Camel Trail was popular with walkers and busy enough to support two cycle hire shops.

Attractive as it is, Padstow is dedicated to tourists and didn't feel like a normal village. It was not representative of regular British life --- so I became disenchanted and left at noon heading for Newquay on the B3276. On the way, I diverted to St. Mawgam, a village recommended by the AA, but did not find any reasons to justify the recommendation. This diversion added a hard six kilometres to my route but, according to the map, brought me back to the B3276 about three kilometres further south for a net increase of only three kilometres.

The road signs disagreed. Newquay was still as far away as when I made the diversion. Five minutes later, another sign indicated that based on the distance remaining, I was travelling at 38 kilometres an hour! Another five minutes more and yet another sign suggested negative speed! In fact, I averaged just 11 kilometres (positive) an hour today (excluding stops) despite Richard's belief that the road to Newquay was flat.

From Newquay to Perranporth, the road pretty much hugs the coastline, rising and dropping with regularity and passing a number of public beaches. These typically had cafes and shops selling beach gear. The day was very warm and sunny bringing lots of people and a buzz of activity. People were surfboarding and swimming. Some had come just for the sun and were reading newspapers facing away from the sea while protected by canvas windbreaks. I stopped at one such spot for lunch and found an amazing and stereotypically British range of choice at one café. It offered eggs and chips, sausage and chips, beans and chips, etc.; the only combination not listed was chips and chips! I chose another place.

Perranporth wasn't the small out of the way coastal village with little activity that I had assumed but a very busy beach town, renowned for its perfect surfing waves. The hostel sat high above the beach but by the time I arrived a thick mist had rolled in obscuring the view of the beach and quickly swallowed one barely visible surfer paddling out from shore.

The small lane leading to the hostel was barred with a lane wide farm gate with a people-sized swinging gate at one end. This gate was designed so that one had to move the swinging part forward, turn right and then swing it back and turn left to get on the other side. Only one fairly slender person could negotiate this at a time. Wearing a rucksack made one almost too thick to enter. Consequently, it was impossible to get a bike through the swinging gate. I had to unload the panniers, lift them over the gate to the other side and then hoist the cycle over the gate the same way.

Finding the hostel closed until 5 pm increased my irritation over this difficult access and frustration of yet another poorly signposted hostel. When I complained about the entrance to the warden, he said the lane and site were the property of the Electricity Board who requires this degree of control on access to the site.

This was a very small hostel, consisting of a common lounge with perimeter benches and long tables that served as a place for eating, conversation, games and reading. Most of the sleeping rooms opened on to this lounge. There was also a members' kitchen and outside storage for surfboards and cycles.

I was drawn to John, an English, fifty-ish, former dustman who described himself as having been in 'waste management'. John was hiking using local bus services to get between hostels and the hiking trails. He had sold his home to an investor, leasing it back at a market rate. This action freed up enough cash to make him feel independent so he quit his job and decided to travel until he got tired of it.

One of John's most important possessions was an MP3 player loaded with his favourite music. We met while he was hunting round the hostel for a place to recharge it. John claimed to do a lot for charity, taking part in various fund-raising marathons and giving to many others. He was constantly complaining about the inconvenience of the bus service schedule. John was an initially likeable, uncomplicated guy but his constant, repetitive chatter soon wore me out.

Next morning, over breakfast with John, I had my back to the sleeping room doors and did not notice an American woman enter the lounge and sit down behind us. I unfortunately chose that time to make a very audible negative comment about Americans in general and have felt bad about it ever since. I normally firmly disagree with others that generalise from stereotypes and I knew nothing negative about her. It was a rude, ignorant thing to do.

Breakfast consisted of two scotch eggs, steamed tomatoes, tea and orange juice purchased last night from the village convenience store. In the middle of my transaction, a middle-aged, bottle-blond 'surfer guy' with earrings breezed in for cigarettes and tried to persuade me to go elsewhere for the scotch eggs. This 'persuasion' was loud and directly in front of the shopkeeper. I think he was just full of himself, but it was a strange experience. On the way back to the hostel, I saw him outside a pub, successfully impressing some teen-aged girls.

Land's End

St. Just, a hostel location near Land's End, was my next overnight destination. I planned to travel the coastal roads to and around Land's End and then go on to St. Just. It was an undemanding schedule, allowing plenty of time for absorbing the scenery. The day started out with a heavy mist that cleared rapidly. In fact, it became so warm and humid that I abandoned the helmet for most of the day.

One spot, Hell's Mouth or Hell's Gate, was so especially dramatic that I stopped to climb to the cliff top and stayed several minutes simply soaking up the vista of waves crashing over rugged rock outcroppings. Later, I found a nice teashop in Redruth and enjoyed my meal outside in the warm sunshine. It felt idyllic. Apart from my morning faux pas, this was proving to be one of my best days.

The phone card (my first experience with one) that I had bought at the start of the trip promised a rate of 5 pence per minute for calls to Canada making my £10 card good for 200 minutes. So, it was a great surprise yesterday to be told there were only 22 minutes left after only two calls of about 30 minutes each. Since it was a post office card, I stopped in at the Mousehole post office to see if they could explain. Apparently, the problem was that I was using British Telecom (BT) phone boxes. BT makes a surcharge on competitive cards—based on my situation—the surcharge more than doubled the cost!

I also went down the lanes to Lamorna Cove. The last kilometre or so ran along a lovely, leafy lane bordered by a bubbling creek. Idyllic appearing cottages whose roofs were just at or slightly below the lane level amidst dense vegetation overlooked the creek. A sense of joyous contentment prevailed, produced by the lack of distance or time pressure and the sunny, warm day.

This gently sloping lane ended at the cove with a convenient café that I somehow managed to resist. I went out as close to the sea as possible and met a young Canadian woman from Vancouver who was hiking along the coastal path from Penzance to Land's End. She was supremely confident of her ability to manage the 11-kilometre trip and return. (Later that evening at the hostel, a New Zealand couple who had gone to Land's End to see the sunset told me of encountering a Canadian woman who was just arriving at Land's End after 10 pm. She had lost her way on alternative paths because directions on the main coastal path were not clear. Without wishing her any ill will, I could not help wondering if the experience had dented her confidence at all).

I left Lamorna and went on towards Land's End on an indirect route involving a side trip to the Minack Theatre. Considered one the world's most remarkable open-air theatres, it got its start in 1932 with a production of *The Tempest*. The 750-seat theatre and exhibition centre sit atop the cliffs. Performances are given most evenings through the season. There was a reasonably steady procession of visitors; many were there just for the photographic opportunities and I was pressed into service at least twice to take pictures of couples and family groups.

My trip notes say that I had lunch on the beach at St. Bunyan. Obviously, the heat and lack of a helmet distorted my senses. St. Bunyan is comfortably inland. I do know that I made it to Land's End and spent sometime just silently absorbing the ambiance of waves and rocks before checking out the 'attractions'. A group of Yorkshire tourists were posing in front of the famous Land's End signpost that shows the direction and distance to New York, Paris and other famous cities. For this group, a sign showing the details for Settle, Yorkshire had been added. The picture was to be posted on to them at home assuming there was even any film in the camera

Land's End is very popular with the British and foreign visitors. The site has been developed accordingly. There is a hotel, a variety of places to eat, film shows of sea rescues, beached fishing boats to explore and tacky souvenirs to buy. A line painted on the tarmac of the parking lot indicates the 'official' starting point for the End-to-End cycle ride. It must have been added since my ride in 1990. There was also a small brass plaque dedicated to a man that was killed in a road accident during his twelfth End-to-End ride.

I don't truly understand it but the End-to-End is the definitive indicator of serious British cycling. There are many other, more difficult rides but this is the one that seems to stand out. And while many try to finish in the shortest possible time, completion is the crucial factor--it doesn't seem to matter how long you take. Nevertheless, knowing that some manage in a week or less, I usually don't volunteer that my 1990 trip took 19 days.

By the time I had my fill of Land's End, it was about four so I set off towards St Just and the hostel, about 10 kilometres away. Enroute, I encountered a small aerodrome boasting a café and could not resist. Inside some grandparents were treating their grandson to the close-up views of arriving and departing small propeller planes.

Despite being in Cornwall, cream teas were not even on this café menu but teacakes were—good for me but a clear sign that this aerodrome was not high on the list of tourist spots. I did, however, make a faux pas in asking for black currant instead of the strawberry jam that is so ubiquitous in Devon and Cornwall. The waitress' response was

'Sorry, we don't have any; you are the first person that has asked me for something other than strawberry in thirteen years.' Must have made her day.

The café and waiting area were well stocked with United Kingdom Independence Party (UKIP) pamphlets. The party's signs, primarily concerned with the upcoming European Parliament elections, have been dotted around the roads in this part of the country. As best I can understand it, UKIP wants to undo Britain's membership in the EU and in particular to defeat the newly drafted EU constitution that would significantly weaken Britain's sovereignty. Member countries of the EU must hold referendums by 2006 on this constitution. (Voters in France and the Netherlands both rejected the constitution in 2005, which effectively kills it, as currently drafted).

A nice breeze flowed through the café cooling the 82 degree Fahrenheit temperature and creating a very pleasant retreat. But I was the only customer and the waitress started to fidget about 5 pm providing a not too subtle hint that she wanted to close the café, so I reluctantly left.

Again, the hostel was poorly signposted. I saw one sign indicating the distance, travelled further than that, arriving at a T-junction that required a left turn and another kilometre or so to get to St. Just. My speedometer clearly showed that I had already come too far. So, I retraced my route looking very carefully at all intersections. About two kilometres back, there was a right hand turn with a small, YHA sign stuck totally out of sight for anyone travelling in my direction and nearly invisible for those coming the opposite way.

This hostel was really out in the country but very active because of the proximity to Land's End. When I arrived, a couple from New Zealand was just checking in and I think the hostel was at least half full despite this being early in the season. Katie, the warden and cook, a very large lady, was hard pressed to squeeze into the very narrow reception area just off the kitchen. She is a very busy and committed woman who works seven days a week in the season from 7.30 in the morning to past 10 at night. She is training a young woman as an assistant to get some relief.

Later in my stay, Katie told me that, given her workday, all her shopping has to be done very early in the morning –as early as 4.30 am. Because of its location, Katie offers both breakfast and evening meal and clearly took pride in being adventurous with the menus. We talked about the national hostel organisation generally and its financial health as I was concerned about the number of closures I had experienced in planning this trip. She said that hostels were being trimmed where heavy maintenance is required, where the real estate values are particularly high or where performance is poor. Katie was very proud of her own performance –turning a profit close to target. New hostels are being opened in other locations.

John, my waste management guy from the Perranporth hostel, is here, still concerned about re-charging his MP3 player and the bus service. An Irish guy breezed in after dinner while I was reading in the lounge. As soon as he discovered I was Canadian, he declared, "I love Canadians" and disappeared. He reappeared a few minutes later wearing a CANADA t-shirt and headed off for the nearest pub. There may have been a back trail from the hostel to St. Just but even so it would have been a walk of at least three or four kilometres. He had hitchhiked here so I knew he had no transport.

Sometime, during the night, the Irish man and someone else came crashing into the sleeping room, turned on the light, paying no heed to the complaints. I was still suffering from the bad cough but was using lozenges to control it and muting the sound with my pillow when I had to cough. Another person had a cough even worse than mine but did not try to muffle it. I must have slept part of the night as I was tapped on the shoulder at one point and asked to stop snoring. Of course, the real snorer could have been the guy below me. All things considered, it was a bad night.

In the morning, I met Jim, an Englishman apparently in his mid-fifties, about to start his own End-to End trip. Officially, of course, he had to cycle down to Land's End to start. As mentioned earlier, he was using the same guidebook and had discovered a number of errors.

Saint Piran and St. Ives

Today's plan was fairly relaxed; go west to the coast and then north to St. Ives, back down to Penzance and then return to St. Just. Tomorrow morning, I need to get into Penzance for a train over to Plymouth to catch the afternoon ferry to Brittany. So, one of my objectives today is to determine the cycling time between St. Just to Penzance to judge when I need to leave the hostel tomorrow.

My first stop of the day was at the Geevor tin mine in Pendeen. As I arrived, a group of schoolchildren wearing construction helmets

Panniers, Pedals, and Pubs

was assembling with their teachers for a tour. The mine operations here ceased in 1990 so current activity is limited to these tours and a gift shop. I was tempted but the nearly C$16 charge and an hour wait for the next tour put me off. Instead I wandered round the shop, learning that the black cross flag I have seen so much of is St Piran's, the patron saint of Cornwall. It looks a lot like the St. Andrews flag of Scotland with a black, instead of blue, diagonal cross. According to legend, St Piran floated over to Cornwall from Ireland on a millstone. There are three St. Piran's churches in Perranporth.

I carried on to Zennor, a small village off the side of the road. There was a small stone basin along the road into Zennor in which, according to the sign, strangers were to put their money during the period of the plague. At that time, the basin contained a vinegar solution to cleanse the money before it was spent in the village. This basin was very close to a small museum of rural life with a gift shop offering refreshments. Making the second bad choice of the day, I enjoyed some shortbread and apple juice in the garden but did not visit the museum.

My vision of St. Ives was of an idyllic, unspoilt fishing village whose harbour was dotted with colourful artists wearing berets and smocks and garrulous, bearded fisherman hauling in nets bursting with fish. OK, that is a bit over the top. But St Ives did not come close.

The place was full of art galleries but I saw no one that looked remotely artistic or was even engaged in producing art. The village was a bit more upscale (due to the galleries) than other seaside resorts, the harbour was attractive and there was a lovely sweep of sandy beach off in the distance but there were no visibly active artists. St. Ives was very popular. Its narrow, single car width lanes were full of people and cars but again much of the activity was related to tourism.

I was very hungry but, despite exploring all the lanes, could find no place to leave the bike during lunch without blocking the narrow pedestrian passages. So I was effectively barred from any of the interesting pubs and cafes and had to settle for a Cornish pastie, an Eccles cake and a fruit drink sitting outside on a harbour side bench with the gulls and pigeons fighting over every crumb that dropped.

The weather became cool and overcast again, encouraging me to head for Penzance up the long climb up out of St. Ives. A sign at the top showed that Penzance was about ten kilometres. Two kilometres further on, the next sign showed no change in the distance, 25 metres further and the distance increased! This may be no big deal in a car but is very frustrating on a loaded bike.

Fortunately, this pattern ended, eventually bringing me to Penzance. I needed to time the Penzance to St Just distance and judge whether the return tomorrow morning would take more or less time than today's trip. I kept mental totals of the accumulating distance in two categories --up and down. This was an interesting exercise that made the time pass quickly so that before I knew it I was back at St. Just.

Rather than go directly to the hostel I went into the village to buy a newspaper and some things for breakfast since my departure would be too early for the hostel breakfast. Despite this side trip, I still had a good hour at the hostel before dinner and chose to spend it devouring the paper and a nice cuppa.

There always seem to be interesting stories about life in Britain. Today's paper was no exception. I read about the problems caused for small, beautiful villages by the influx of weekenders and second homebuyers that has pushed home prices above the ability of villagers to buy. This has forced many villagers to move to be able to afford a first home. These exits have reduced school enrolments forcing some closures. In addition, current British law offers a discount on property taxes ('council charge') for second homes, putting pressure on village finances.

Another story dealt with the huge gap in life expectancy between the classes that still exists despite eight years of government efforts to close the gap. The article referred to a recent book that attributes long life to the ability to control it. More moneyed classes are generally better educated and consequently have healthier life styles. As a result, they have a broader range of occupation choices offering jobs that are more interesting and flexible.

Then, paralleling the situation at home, an article reported that British bankers are strongly advocating the right to merge to become big enough to compete with the monster-sized US banks that have been created in recent years. The opposite argument in both countries is, of course the potential reduction in domestic competition.

Tonight, the hostel was full of Germans travelling and eating together. I shared the remaining dinner table with two vegetarian women that were camping on the hostel grounds. They were very standoffish; communicating in hushed tones between themselves and limited their interaction with me to 'pass the salt'. This exchange was too brief to determine their nationality and their own conversation was so quiet that it provided no clue either. So, I read my book.

Off to France

It was another bad night, partly due to my continuing cough but also because of the need to be up early. The upstairs dormitory room was still hot from the day and, unable to check the time in the dark room without disturbing others, my sleep was fitful. At 5.45, when enough light penetrated the room to see my watch, I finally gave up and started preparations for departure.

My first discovery was that last night's efficiency in packing for a quick getaway had resulted in my razor and blood pressure medication being buried in one of the panniers. These were loaded on the bike, now in the shed, and inaccessible until Katie went on duty at 7.30, my planned departure time.

So, I cleaned up as well as possible, dressing warmly in anticipation of rain and/or cold. I had a breakfast of pork pie, tomatoes and tea in the members' kitchen with my book. A new adventure was ahead of me –this feeling was intensified by the cool, misty stillness of the morning. The simple tasks of breakfast preparation and yesterday's timing run produced an empowering sense of control and self-sufficiency, no doubt increasing my life expectancy!

Katie was only five minutes late opening the bike shed so my parting was virtually on time. The run to Penzance was special at this cool, quiet time of day and faster than anticipated. In fact, I arrived at the railway station nearly an hour before train time, providing an opportunity to re-stock my supply of throat lozenges, supplement my breakfast at the station café and to shave.

The early arrival also ensured that I got one of the two cycle spaces on the train. The train was ten minutes late but quite empty. Despite the considerable number of seats available, I chose to sit opposite a well-formed young woman who complemented the external scenery.

This was an all stops milk run, to Plymouth. Unfortunately, my human scenery left the train about half way through the two-hour trip. By the time we reached Plymouth, it was nearly lunchtime, so I bought a sandwich, drink and a paper and enjoyed those while still in the station.

Ferry passengers were warned to arrive at least 45 minutes early or risk not being able to board, so not knowing how far away the terminal might be, I left the station. The route between the railway and the station was very well marked but involved heavy lunchtime traffic and a couple of major roundabouts. In each case, the required roundabout turn meant moving across two lanes of traffic on the approach. I made very obvious hand signals well before starting the move and the traffic was kind to me, making the trip smooth and efficient and left me feeling pleased at my skill.

My arrival at the terminal was an hour and three-quarters before sailing time; yet there were already queues in each of the several entrance lanes. I sat in one for a while wondering whether cyclists were considered vehicles or foot passengers since foot passengers boarded the ship at a different point. A light rain started to fall, adding a sense of urgency to finding out my classification, so I cycled up to the distant passenger lounge and ticket office and learnt that I was a vehicle.

Returning to a further back position in the queue, I and the other 'vehicles' fumed as the just now arriving officials seemed in no hurry to start processing us. Once they started, my particular queue was especially slow. This processing involved passport and ticket inspection; I later learned that the yellow van that was first in the queue was 'of interest' to the authorities.

After passing through this first stage each vehicle was assigned to a lane for boarding the vessel but still had to wait at a point just about 100 metres from the entry ramps. I was the first in my assigned lane and found myself alongside the suspect yellow van in the adjacent lane when I got there. Two Muslim appearing men were in the van and immediately started a conversation that sounded like a veiled apology for holding everyone else up. They were puzzled why the authorities asked them so many questions.

Shortly thereafter we were allowed to board and I was directed all the way to the bow directly in front of a huge lorry. A crewmember quickly lashed the bike to the side of the ship, leaving me to escape the exhaust fumes by scurrying between vehicles to a door in the centre of the ship leading to the upper decks. (If you do anything similar, it is important to take note of the deck you park on and the door you used to exit. This information is very useful to know at disembarkation time if you have any desire of finding your vehicle again. The companionways (stairs) are narrow and people traffic flows only in one direction on

Panniers, Pedals, and Pubs

arrival. So it is important to know the right deck, door and side of the ship.)

I was immediately impressed with the ship. It was very spacious and well maintained with a bar lounge and two or three restaurants catering to different budgets. The wait staff was dressed in crisp white shirts, ties and black trousers and did not wear the 'bored out of my mind' expressions that one often finds in tourist-oriented restaurants and cafes in Britain.

Given the damp conditions outside, I initially sat in the bar lounge reading but felt a little conspicuous without a drink. Reading was difficult as I was in earshot of three men in earnest conversation –two demonstrating excellent listening skills while the other totally dominated, providing them with endless detail outlining his superior experience and knowledge of the world.

This became increasingly hard to take, even at a distance, so I went outside onto the open deck. The weather was wet, cold and overcast. It was miserable. I was missing no scenery, as nothing was visible; so, I decided on an early evening meal. Eating generally cheers me up.

The cafeteria had a good selection of main courses, interesting looking desserts and wine by the carafe. Its prices were also more acceptable than the other restaurants. I chose pork and ginger with vegetables, a fruit tart and a carafe of red wine. The cutlery was good quality and the napkins, although paper, were heavy and did not fall apart with the first use. I enjoyed the meal immensely but it was over far too soon.

Next, I explored the souvenir shops, checked out the newspapers and magazines, a duty free shop and even some expensive clothing shops. This afternoon's crossing was not full so there was ample seating even for the window seats. In fact, I did not begin to look for the special rooms of reclining chairs until about the last two hours of the six-hour crossing.

Not realising how comfortable and ample the other seating would be, I had reserved one of these reclining chairs at the time of booking, thinking I might be able to get in a nap since our arrival was at 10 pm. I might as well not have bothered. The reclining chair room was overrun with French teenagers that had no interest in sleep or quiet. They kept coming in and going out, shrieking and generally being modern teenagers which is to say loud, superficial, silly and totally inconsiderate

To be honest, I don't know that I could have slept anyway. This was such a departure from my usual trips that I was energised by the change and concerned that I might not be able to find the hotel that had been booked for me in Roscoff. Would it still be open if I did find it?

Eventually, I abandoned the attempt to nap and returned to the lounge which was much more sedate. By this time, arrival was imminent. Once we were allowed to go down to the vehicle level, I headed straight down to the correct deck but chose a companionway on the wrong side of the ship. Correcting this meant climbing all the steps back, fighting the flow of traffic in the opposite direction, to get on the other side.

Once there, everything was all right, but I barely got the bike untied when I was waved off the ship—the very first one to exit! I emerged into a seemingly welcoming twilight, on French soil, free to go wherever with no customs officials or passport control to contend with. This was still the European Union and officially my journey was no more significant than leaving Ontario to drive into Quebec but it felt so different!

My French cycle and camping company had booked me into the Hotel d'Angleterre. I had no idea where this was but headed into the city feeling positive, confident and eager for this new experience. Roscoff was attractive, well maintained and foreign—the evening air was soft and the limited light enhanced the feeling of adventure. This was exciting! Deeper into the city, signs appeared for several other hotels but not for mine. I stopped a well to do and well turned out matron to ask for directions. Despite our mutual lack of each other's language, she very pleasantly managed to direct me with hand and arm movements. The Hotel d'Angleterre loomed up in the dusk like a small chateau, making me fear that I had been booked into an expensive hotel due to some miscommunication. The attractively decorated and antique filled lobby further intensified this fear.

A pleasant woman confirmed that I did have a reservation. She then showed me where to store the bike before taking me up to the room. The expensive ambiance disappeared as soon as we reached the staircase; the vibrant colours of the lobby were replaced by drab, dimly lit walls and worn carpets. My room was clean but just adequate with a washbasin but no toilet or shower.

After she left, I quickly got ready to take a shower—assuming that the hotel had such facilities. There had been light in the corridor when she showed me to the room but the corridor was dark when I re-opened the door. Then I discovered a button on the outside wall of my room. This proved to be the corridor light switch, allowing me to examine each door for signs of a bathroom. The search took me the full length of my corridor, around the corner and all the way back to the stairwell. At this point there was a door with no number that proved to be the single bath for this floor. I went in, assessed what I would need to bring from my room, and went back to the corridor---it was totally dark again! The switch was obviously timed to just give you enough time to find the stairway.

Back in the bath, I stripped off and eagerly jumped into the large shower only to discover that it did not work. I got out, suddenly noticing the large window looking across to the homes on the opposite side of the street. A flimsy lace partial side curtain provided the only privacy. Suddenly, an internal voice said, 'what the hell, this is France'. So I set about filling the high-sided narrow ancient tub, pretending to be unconcerned that I might be overlooked. A tub bath is not, of course, a new experience. But shampooing your hair and rinsing it without even a hand held spray requires an on-the-knees posture and a bobbing for apples action bound to amuse any observers.

This situation reminded me of my medical for an overseas assignment early in my career. The examining room door opened onto the full waiting room and for some inexplicable reason, that door was opened just as I, lying on my stomach with my feet facing the door, had been elevated into position for a proctoscopy, truly letting it all hang out!

As I came down for breakfast in the morning, a Chinese man greeted me at the door to the breakfast room. Assuming him to be another guest, I returned his greeting and continued into the room. Wrong. He was the breakfast attendant and escorted me to a table pre-laid with the standard French breakfast components. His only task was to determine and deliver my preference for coffee, tea or chocolate.

The breakfast room was big with a high ceiling and wide board, seemingly original wood floors, wrought iron chandeliers painted French blue, lots of country antiques and attractive tablecloths. There was only one other occupied table giving the room a feeling of being at peace.

The coffee was excellent and my pot, supplemented with milk, provided nearly three cups. Orange juice, a fresh croissant and some crusty bread comprised the rest of the meal with a large quantity of fresh butter replacing the fat content of a 'full English'. It was a very satisfying first petit d'jeuner of the trip continuing my excitement with the beginnings of my French adventure.

On the Road Again

A light rain was falling as I start loading the bike for today's trip to Huelgoat. Huelgoat is east of Roscoff, a little more than half way to the home site of Breton Bikes in Gouarec where the cycle/camping tour was to begin. Despite the rain, I prolonged the loading routine to watch a small man delivering coal from a large flatbed truck, bag by bag, on his back into the basement of the hotel. The only modern aspects of the scene were the blue nylon bags instead of burlap and the truck in place of a horse-drawn cart. Otherwise, the scene could have been from over a hundred years ago.

My next discovery was how difficult it can be to find your way on French roads, particularly if you are trying to find a numbered highway. Initially, I went round and round within Roscoff, making no progress and winding up outside my hotel again a half an hour later.

Breton Bikes had provided me with a suggested route that pretty well coincided with one that I had prepared for myself. The problem was finding the indicated road and once having found it making sure you stayed on it. The French use roundabouts to good effect, like the British. And for the most part, the French roundabouts were attractively landscaped. Negotiating them felt very strange, at first, because you go round them anti-clockwise (i.e. turning right on to them instead of left) instead of clockwise as in Britain. Often a turning off the roundabout would be signposted for several locations. I wasn't sure what the French convention was. Were the towns listed in the order that you reached them or the other way round. Sometimes, the town I wanted was not listed and often the route number was not shown. I was constantly getting out the map and trying to see if a particular town shown on the sign was somewhere on the same route as the town I wanted.

It was very frustrating and confusing, causing me, at one-point, to get on a stretch of dual carriage-way which was illegal as a couple of drivers pointed out to me as they passed shaking their fingers at my transgression. Fortunately, an acceptable exit appeared before I was crushed or apprehended. At the end of the exit ramp, there were signs to two different towns, neither of which was my destination. It was only very careful map review and asking directions that got me going toward the sign-posted town that led to my unnamed town destination.

This put me on the D769, a minor road that ran almost all the way to Huelgoat, putting an end to my route problems, I thought. The D769 did reduce my problems but it did not eliminate them. As long as the road was not interrupted with roundabouts, I was fine but stick in a roundabout, erect a signpost that fails to mention the route number and it was back to the map, trying to locate where I was and if the named towns were anywhere on the D769.

Fortunately, Morlaix appeared before another confusing roundabout did. Morlaix is an attractive and well-maintained river port city with lots of colourful boats in the harbour and pretty flowers on the streets. Arriving here proved actual progress and offered an opportunity for a lunch break.

I found a small, unpretentious café that had reasonable prices. The inside was very pleasant with blue-grey stained wainscoting, a seaside motif on the walls and bright yellow tablecloths—much nicer than the exterior suggested. I ordered a croque monsieur and café au lait grande in honour of this being my first lunch in France on the trip (any excuse for food will suffice). A small, excellent salad came with the sandwich and the coffee was superb—so good that I asked for a refill. I definitely enjoyed that lunch but from a budget standpoint it was a disaster. Unlike North America, coffee refills are not free and coffee is very expensive. Those two coffees cost a total of $8, more than the sandwich and salad!

After lunch, I continued in the same direction and on the same road that I entered Morlaix on, but there were no indicators that it was still the D769. Now I had to rely on town names. The road seemed to run harder after lunch but that could have been the combination of a full stomach and the heat. I stopped and stripped off the long sleeve shirt and cool weather long cycling pants and was immediately more comfortable. It was 3 pm but I had only done 48 km so far!

However shortly afterwards, I saw the first sign for Huelgoat—it was only 15 km further. The last bit of this was downhill, bringing a beautifully blue lake into view. On the other side of the road at the edge of the town was a wooded grotto of huge rocks beneath which a stream tumbled. The stream was fed by the lake, which spilled down under a bridge and through the rocks. Together these two features made Huelgoat a special memory.

Robert Adams

    The road running alongside the lake was populated with shops and cafes that offered waterside patios across the road at lakeside. My imaginatively named Hotel du Lac faced this lake. By 4.15, I was installed in my room, had cleaned up, changed and was on my way to explore the grotto on foot.

    The grotto hiking trails began at the edge of the bridge with the main access trail winding through trees whose roots battled the rocks, breaking the trail surface. The initially fairly narrow trail broadened as the huge rocks (more like boulders) gradually ran out robbing the trail of its drama. I took advantage of a park bench in a large open area to sit and absorb the scene while catching up on my notes.

    Carrying on revealed that the trails generally ended at a nearby campground so I returned to the lake to enjoy a waterside pression (beer) at a bar. Then after a shower and after a brief walk round the village to compare restaurant offerings, decided to have dinner on my hotel's piazza. During dinner I completed an Iris Murdoch novel and chatted briefly with a couple from Wiltshire. It was one of those conversations that don't get much beyond an exchange of generalities but it did demonstrate how little people really know about Canada. And often, what they do know is out of date. This man's knowledge of Canadian theatre seemed to be entirely based on reading some patronizing comments about Christopher Newton and the Stratford, Ontario Festival, in the 1950s. I set him straight on that, informed him about the annual six-month long Shaw Festival in Niagara on the Lake and that Toronto was the second largest theatre city in North America after New York. But I would bet that he retains the 1950s view rather than the update.

    So far, I am very impressed with Brittany. The cleanliness and friendliness, the quality of the food, how reasonable a carafe of wine can be, all contribute to this impression. Huelgoat is beautiful and I certainly like the luxury of a soft, clean bed. Two hotels in succession have dulled my anticipation of the camping experience.

    Next morning, I stretched my petit d'jeuner in the hotel bar out for almost an hour with my next book, Arthur Hailey's *Evening News*; packed up and paid my bill. It was a bit of a shock to learn that my dinner cost an extra 10% for the privilege of eating on the piazza.

    A light mist while loading the bike made me realise I had left my cycling gloves in the room. Since I had already checked out and surrendered my room key, this would be the first true test of my ability to communicate. I went into the bar and somehow the necessary three nouns came tumbling out without thinking, - 'vestment, chambre and clef' were enough even without verbs to convey my meaning. I was told to find the chambermaid for help. As it turned out, I had not locked the room and easily retrieved my gloves without having to challenge my communication skills further with the chambermaid who was on another floor.

I decided to navigate by just following the signposts to the major towns on my route and not worry about the route number or smaller towns in between. There were no dual carriageways along the way so this worked as far as Carhaix, where I stopped for an early lunch at a McDonald's on the outskirts to make up for yesterday's crimes against the budget.

Getting out of the Carhaix area was another story. None of the routes/towns on the map showed up on any of the signposts. Frustrated and somewhat desperate, I decided to go into the centre of the city from one of the roundabouts and then try to find my way out. Almost immediately, there was a sign pointing to exactly where I wanted to go and it was smooth sailing from that point.

The countryside is not as attractive or manicured looking as the UK but is still pleasant. It is very rural with lots of cattle but these French cattle are not responding to my greetings. Perhaps it is my pronunciation and accent—but 'moo' sounds pretty much the same in any language doesn't it?

I arrived in Gouarec just before four and went immediately to the post office to buy a French phone card. A several page instruction manual in French accompanied the card. This seemed to advise a different access code to the system for each country that you might be calling. I asked the very pleasant woman behind the counter to interpret for me. She was unfamiliar with the instructions and with English but after several minutes of broken English discussion and checking with her supervisor appeared to agree with my interpretation.

As I returned to my bike, a red Fiat convertible sports car driven by a grey bearded and tousle-haired chap pulled up, calling out 'Are you Bob?' It was Geoff Husband, owner of Breton Bikes and the leader of the tour I was about to take. We had never met, just corresponded by email but it was a good guess. After a hearty welcome and directions to the campground where 'home site' was located, he drove off on some errand.

I found the campground nestled between the Brest-Nantes canal and a river. The camp entrance had an office and storeroom in a block of buildings that also housed the washrooms and laundry facilities. There were a few caravans nearby, but otherwise the site seemed almost empty. However, as I cycled through the gate, a man and his daughter from Vancouver greeted me. They had just completed a trip with Breton Bikes and told me that home site was at the far end of the campground.

Having located the spot, I went back into the village for a late afternoon coffee in a bar and read my book for a while. Returning to the campground and home site brought me to a large white tent that was Breton Bikes' bike storage and maintenance area.

Geoff was there talking with another Canadian woman (also from Vancouver) that had just completed a week's solo trip using Breton's equipment. Her tent and foam-sleeping mat were transferred to me and Geoff showed me how to erect the tent, threatening good-naturedly that I had only this one opportunity to learn.

Then he showed me the bike that he had prepared for me based on my personal measurements. The bike was new and an appropriate French blue but had a weather-beaten Brooks saddle that sagged. This proved to be surprisingly comfortable. The handlebars were 'sit up and beg' style with thumb operated gear changers mounted next to the handgrips. The bike was equipped with very low gears suitable for climbing the Pyrenees. Geoff encouraged me to try this bike tomorrow before deciding whether to use my own or his on the tour.

I took it out immediately for a trial and to find a phone box to test my new phone card. Apart from needing to raise the seat, the bike was comfortable and worked well but I had no success with the phone card. Thinking that perhaps the phone box was faulty, I went back to the camp and tried their public phone, again with no success.

This minor disappointment triggered deterioration in my attitude that attached to this tour. My comfortable hotel rooms of the last two nights made the tent seem small and unappealing; the site was cool and damp being bordered by two bodies of water and none of my tour companions had arrived yet. Geoff had told me earlier that five of the intended group had cancelled at the last moment, leaving only five plus him.

I had understood Geoff to say that we would all get together for dinner tonight at the Brevet Hotel. In the space of about an hour, the situation had changed to an exclusive romantic dinner for Geoff and his wife Kate together with the site manager, Dave and his wife who had just arrived from England. I was on my own, usually my preference, not a concern, but now I felt abandoned.

Dave left his job as a teacher, came to Brittany a year or so ago and leased this campsite from the town. He now lives on site in a small caravan, but his wife Marianne remains working in Cornwall. They have been assessing where they want to live on a permanent basis but appear close to deciding for France.

The story is similar for Geoff and Kate. They have been here for twelve years, own an established successful business, have three fully bi-lingual children in French schools and are well integrated into the community. Geoff also was a former teacher.

For me, a long-time Anglophile, encountering two couples that have or are close to abandoning Britain for historical enemy France is intriguing. Both of them answered 'lifestyle' as the primary reason for their decisions. Over the course of the week, I learned that the reasons aren't financial in either case. Geoff discussed enough of the economics of his business for me to know that a British teaching salary would produce more income. Apart from housing costs, the French cost of living appears about equal to the British. Dave admitted that he was living on the financial brink currently.

But both men now have much greater control over their days. They have the flexibility to enjoy an unrushed conversation over a coffee break or to listen to a cricket test match while preparing cycles for next week's clients. Geoff's children can visit his workplace and see what he does for a living. However, these advantages reflect more of their chosen new occupations rather than differences between Britain and France.

One of the remaining tour participants, Rawdon O'Connor, arrived about six. He and Geoff are long-time friends and Rawdon had often participated in these tours as back-up leader. This time, he told me, he was definitely not taking any responsibility. Although it did not happen immediately, Rawdon and I became good friends on this trip. He is a very interesting guy as well as a dedicated and capable cyclist. I learned from him and enjoyed his company.

The French Way
After a few days in Brittany, I came to also appreciate some of

what Geoff and Dave must have meant by "lifestyle". The pace of life seemed more relaxed, more measured. People were regulars in the boulangeries and patiserries, in the bars and cafes. They were greeted as friends more than customers, with handshakes and sometimes kisses. There was a pleasant routine rhythm to life that was comforting and reduced stress.

Most of us are familiar with the apparent contradiction between the rich French diet and their relatively low incidence of heart disease. Red wine consumption is often suggested as the rationale but I think that their lifestyle might also be a positive factor.

Some of my observations may be due to Brittany being a relatively poor part of France where, by necessity, sincere interpersonal interaction takes precedence over conspicuous consumption. Newfoundland exhibits similar characteristics. Or, I may be drawing quick, unwarranted conclusions due to my being on holiday in an unfamiliar country. Anyway, I am now a Francophile also, at least in part.

I took my dinner that first night in Gouarec alone at Hotel Brevet, embarrassing myself with excruciatingly limited French that somehow made it also difficult to communicate intelligently in English when I encountered the two British couples in the bar. I think my sense of abandonment temporarily reduced my self-confidence.

Although this hotel was highly recommended, I was not overly impressed. Perhaps the prospect of spending the night in a cold damp tent spoilt my mood. Rawdon joined me for a drink as I was finishing and we walked back to the camp together.

Breton Bikes supplied a sleeping bag and I fashioned a makeshift pillow from a plastic bag and spare clothing but could not get comfortable. Despite staying fully clothed, I was cold and my cough was still with me. Sometime in the middle of the night, I needed the washroom. This meant finding the tent zipper, pivoting my legs out through the opening, searching for my shoes under the flap while assuming a tilted "Z" like shape, half in, half out, of the tent to put the shoes on without getting the interior of the tent dirty.

Bursting with need, I highly resented the seemingly interminable long walk to the washroom at the far side of the campground with only moonlight to guide me. Once there, the washroom was pitch black and I could find no light switches. I left the door open to allow moonlight in but this barely illuminated the urinal just inside the door. Suddenly, all the lights came on. Had I set off some alarm? Would an armed security guard burst in? No, I obviously read too many espionage novels. Some one else had arrived and knew that the light switch for both the male and female toilet block was on the outside of the female block. Dave told me the next day that this was a timed switch that allowed seven minutes to complete your activities. I trudged back to the tent, reversed my 'Z' exercises, popped a cough lozenge and tried to get some sleep

Next morning, Rawdon introduced me to the French breakfast routine. We walked into town to the patisserie for croissants, decadent fruit and chocolate pastries, and then proceeded to a bar for coffee or chocolate in his case. It could not have been later than 9.30 when we arrived but already there were men at the bar having a Saturday morning beer.

We sat at a small round table in a café like area diagonally across from the bar and gradually started sharing our personal lives with each other. Rawdon is a large man dressed almost entirely in black with about a two-week growth of beard, an initially intimidating appearance. There was no pretence or posturing on his part and neither of us gave the appearance of education, wealth, or savoir-faire. As the week wore on, it became increasingly clear that he is well educated, widely travelled, and very considerate.

He complained about the hike to the washroom, I agreed and revealed that I made the trek without a torch. So, he suggested that we go to the supermarket after breakfast to buy one and anything else that might make the camping experience more pleasant. This was only a few minutes walk away and as our day was totally free, I agreed.

Later, he introduced me to the bargain that lunchtime can be in France. A large number of French workers receive lunch vouchers as part of their compensation. In 2004, the value of these averaged around eight to nine Euros daily. Consequently, there is tremendous demand for lunches at that price and the competition is fierce.

We went to a café in Gouarec that went out of its way to attract customers. For 8.50 euros, they provided a cold buffet of sausage and salads as an appetizer, followed by a choice of main course, a dessert, cheese and wine. The small rich coffee was another euro. At the end of the week, a group of eight of us had lunch at this same cafe and were given six bottles of wine between us. They kept bringing more as we ran out—with no extra charge! In the evening, the story is different; an equivalent amount of food is much more expensive and each and every glass of wine is extra. I found that red wine is an excellent cycling lubricant so the lesson was fill up at lunch!

These lunch arrangements are a powerful example of France's different life style. For much of my career, apart from an infrequent business lunch, lunchtime was either a quick sandwich at my desk or a brief fast food offering consumed in the food court of a nearby mall. The three-martini lunch and company cafeterias with three-course, quality meals were largely history. Drinking at lunchtime was largely limited to expense account lunches when one was entertaining and even then a single glass of wine generally sufficed.   Here in France, employers and employees consider a leisurely lunch, at a restaurant, with 'adequate' quantities of wine to be natural and normal. Vive le difference!

The personal revelations continued during lunch in between discussions of French life as seen by Rawdon. I asked his opinion of the French work ethic. Half-jokingly he replied, 'Would that there were some'. He went on to tell me how difficult it can be to find a professional or service when you need it. Some professionals take Mondays off by tradition; most schools are closed on Wednesdays, requiring parents to make special arrangements or close down their shops or businesses. Sundays, particularly in Brittany, all the shops and bars are closed by midday at the latest. Tuesdays, Thursdays and Fridays are the only reliable days to get business done.

We talked about the move by France to a 35-hour workweek. Apparently, the government's objective was to create more jobs, oblivious to the fact that business would try to extract greater productivity during the shorter workweek to maintain profit levels. In France, having a job is crucial to one's social status. However, performing well in that job seems to be a far lower order concern. In fact, shortly after I returned from this trip, I read a review of a French book that advocates employees do whatever they can to frustrate their employers----Dilbert with a French twist!

Rawdon told me some of his history in the British army in the Middle East and Northern Ireland. He had to speak fairly generally as the work was essentially espionage. Rawdon also worked with the British Foreign Office as their expert on Aden. Now he is a free-lance translator living in France. I found him a very interesting and comfortable companion and later was surprised to realise how similar Rawdon is to Ron, another cycling friend. Ron and Rawdon are both fit, large men; both have a military background and Ron was a retired professor of linguistics while Rawdon deals in language as a translator.

The Group Assembles

When we returned to the campsite after lunch, an older couple from New Zealand were packing up to return home after a solo Breton Bikes experience. The rest of our group had arrived and were in various stages of putting up tents and loading their gear in panniers. We introduced ourselves to Yassmin from England, a married thirty something woman but alone on this trip, and Murray and Cara, a sixties couple also from New Zealand. Yassmin lives on a houseboat in Kent, works as a secretary in the legal department of a hospital and is studying towards a degree in Archaeology. Murray is a plumbing and drainage inspector for the county in Oamaru, on the east coast of the South Island.

Geoff has issued what can only be considered command invitations to a 'pig roast' at his children's school this evening but there are a few hours before that it is to start. So, I went off to try my phone card again.

This time, I enlisted the help of Dave, the site manager. First he explained that the campsite phone did not work so it was not a good indicator. We hopped on a couple of campsite cycles parked outside his office and went off to a nearby phone box that I had missed yesterday. Dave's interpretation of the instructions got me into the system but I could not access my Canadian number. We tried several times with no more success.

Now embarrassed at this imposition on Dave's time, I suggested he go back to the camp while I carried on. Something caused me to look at the board inside the phone box where the international calling instructions were posted. There was the answer; the country code for Canada that applied in Britain was different in France. As I recall it now, instead of just plain 01, it was 001. That extra nought was all that was required; I made my weekly call to Mari—a day early but almost precisely at our pre-agreed time!

There was still time before the pig roast for some practice on the Breton bike, so I transferred my rattrap pedals to Geoff's bike and went out on a road running parallel to the canal for about twenty kilometres.

Geoff had convinced/coerced each of us to attend the pig roast but at ten euros each, we weren't likely to find a more economical dinner. We all walked to the school, about 15 minutes away. Tonight's event was the culmination of a full day's activities. They were announcing prizes from a drawing when we arrived. People were milling about, patronizing the cash bar, waiting for the pig and chatting. A few children and adults made fairly feeble attempts to dress in the traditional black and white Breton fashion.

There was ample home-prepared food to accompany the pig. Geoff demonstrated his generous nature that was so evident during our tour by buying wine for our group. As a former internal auditor, I observed how the internal controls established to ensure people proved they had paid for the meal broke down in the general good nature of this community event. People were supposed to buy a ticket and surrender it when they received their meal. There were different stations for the roasted pig and vegetables, for the salad and the desserts. Sometimes you were asked for your ticket, sometimes you weren't. Second helpings were allowed. I saw no one refused anything for lack of a ticket.

Having planned this trip as a Celtic excursion to witness similar traditions, I should not have been surprised that a young Breton bagpiper provided the entertainment, but his entry from behind me was initially jarring. A young British couple and their eight-year-old daughter joined our table. The daughter's shirt was covered in blood, as was the back of her head from a fall earlier in the day. This generated some comments but no particular concern. I knew that such injuries often look far more serious than they actually are. Our son, Cameron fell at age four, cut the back of his head and spouted blood all over. Mari was very alarmed, rushed him to hospital and summoned me from the office but there was no serious effect. Everyone here was very informal and relaxed.

We returned to the campsite as a group and gradually retired to our respective tents, as twilight became darkness. It was still cold and damp; my cough continued making this night as uncomfortable as the night before although I could now walk to the washroom with the aid of a torch and knew where to turn on the lights. I had also learned that one of the four stalls contained a modern toilet instead of the 'hole in the floor- squat and leave it' older style that so dismayed me on the first day. Apart from the unaccustomed posture required to use these, one needs to be very quick and nimble to avoid the flood of the flush.

Next morning, our group gathered at a local bar for breakfast with Geoff, Kate, their children and Dave and Marianne. This was one of the best (i.e. ample) breakfasts of the tour. The bartender greeted all the males individually with a handshake and the women in the double-kiss French fashion. He then poured our coffees in bowls considerably larger than even the café grande size. Each of us had a croissant, a couple of baguette rounds and access to a plate stacked with crepes. The fresh butter and jams were almost unlimited and refills of the coffee were automatic. All of this was provided for €5.50 each.

Boules

This ample, leisurely breakfast made a nice, friendly communal start to the day. By the time we returned to the campsite for final preparations, three American women—a mother and her two teenage daughters-- had arrived. They were travelling the same route as the rest of us but staying at hotels rather than camping.

By about eleven, everyone's panniers were packed and their saddle heights adjusted. We set off east along the canal towards a large open-air Sunday market. The market backed along a pasture on one side and faced a bar with a nice outdoor terrace that soon claimed several of our number. Apart from providing local colour, the objective of our stop was to buy food for a picnic. There were stalls for bread, for cheese, for meats, for preserves. Some also sold wine or cider.

As Mari will attest, I am not generally overly concerned with hygiene standards in my own home but can become quite squeamish when strangers are involved. So this market was a bit of a cultural shock coming so early in the tour. It was somewhat like jumping in icy water all at once rather than easing in gradually. The bread was unwrapped until purchased; no one wore surgical gloves or hairnets. The same people that took your money handled the food. There was no refrigeration for the meat. If anyone of the sales assistants wanted to wash their hands, it would have been necessary to go over to the bar; I would be surprised if any did.

Everyone else seemed ecstatic with the market ambiance and its 'exotic' wares. There was nary a murmur of discontent about the lack of hygiene. I held my tongue. Laden with our lunches, we cycled off and climbed partially up a forested hill before abandoning the cycles to walk further up to the picnic site----a large group of rocks adjacent to an ancient tomb. The weather was warm but we had not yet warmed up enough to each other for more than awkward and stilted conversation.

This awkwardness broke down considerably that evening when after our campsite meal, we walked from the campsite over to the nearby hotel where the American women were staying. We ordered beers and played boules outside the hotel as they enjoyed their dinner in the hotel. Soon, they were beckoning us to the window to pass food out for us to eat. It was a five-course meal and the appetizer alone would have been adequate.

The 70+ proprietress of this small, un-rated hotel was a lovely warm grandmotherly type, and also the cook. She took great pride in treating her guests well. The Americans did not want to offend her by not eating everything

Boules is played in a long rectangular space; ours was slightly more than a metre wide and enclosed by wooden walls like a long sandbox. Someone throws out a small ball towards the far end. Different coloured larger balls identify the separate teams. Each team member attempts to roll these larger balls from the near end as close to the small ball as possible, sometimes intentionally knocking the other team's balls away. Only the team with the most balls closest to the small ball wins any points.

We split into two teams of three with Geoff and Rawdon as captains because they were the only ones that had ever played before. The hotel proprietor kibitzed our game, pointing out the lay of the pitch and suggesting how the ball should be thrown. We listened politely but ignored the advice as we had quickly realised that it was worthless. Lubricated with beer, playing this game was reasonably diverting for me despite being on the losing side. Fortunately, the skill required was minimal and I managed enough close balls to allow our team to get on the scoreboard and preserve some self-respect

The Americans finished dinner and came to watch. They had never played boules either but were persuaded to play the winners of our competition. Rawdon, as a bachelor, appeared to particularly enjoy providing up close coaching for the mother.

As the light faded, Geoff was showing signs of wanting to end play. We soon discovered that he was agitated about not hearing or seeing the World Cup football (soccer) match between France and England that had started at eight. Before long, he disappeared into the small hotel's kitchen where he could watch the game on television. Some minutes later, remembering his duties as group leader, he came back out to invite us to join him for the last ten minutes of the game. I did, unconsciously justifying him staying until the bitter end.

The promised ten minutes became at least twenty but the game was closing on a England win, pleasing both Geoff and myself when France scored twice in the last two minutes to turn the tables. It was indeed a bitter end!

We walked back to the campsite, deflated by the loss and mainly silent except for Geoff's periodic muttering 'I don't even like football! How could they lose the game like that?

Around the Campfire

Next morning we went back to the hotel for breakfast to find the Americans just returning from a run. I silently chastised myself for thinking them soft to stay in hotels rather than camp out. They were still moaning about the size of the dinner they had consumed last night but managed to devour a good sized breakfast. Rawdon continued his solicitous counsel of these attractive women –this time about the pleasures of hot chocolate as a breakfast beverage.

There really was nothing out of place in Rawdon's actions. He is a kind and considerate person. It is just amusing to witness how much more considerate and interested a man becomes in the presence of attractive women. (Some women have a special magnetism or force of personality that can completely overcome a man, making her seem irresistible. Later, on sober reflection and objective observation, or perhaps rejection, the same woman can appear ordinary, even plain.)

We separated permanently from the Americans shortly after breakfast as their hotel-based route ended the day at Rohan where we were to be by lunchtime. Initially, our route was down hill but then ran flat through very pastoral scenery on quiet roads spotted with some beautiful Breton homes and cattle.

Although the cattle were still not responding to my 'moos', I was definitely in a better mood during than the last few days. A decent night's sleep away from the cold damp of the Gouarec campsite was obviously a major factor and the warm sunshine with light breezes off the canal added to the sense of contentment. I even concluded that I enjoyed cycling in France more than Britain. That is close to heresy for me!

We lunched heavily at the Rohan Hotel, starting with an aperitif, followed by the full luncheon voucher special of appetiser, main course, dessert, wine and coffee. The total price was 11.50 euros or C$18.40.

With that much food, it was fortunate that the rest of the day's route was along the canal path and required little exertion. All the lock stations and operators' homes along the way were different but each was very attractive, with flowers in every imaginable place showing the operator's considerable pride in its appearance.

Towards four, we arrived in Josselin, the first of our two chateau city stops. While the others stopped for a cooling beer, I searched for a phone box to ring my daughter. I thought she might think it special to have a birthday call from France. Unfortunately my greetings had to be delivered via the answer phone. Disappointed, I also attempted a call to my mother with the same result.

I rejoined the group for a trip to the market to buy tonight's dinner. The others were looking forward to cooking but after the failed telephone calls; I had no interest in any choice that required cooking. Truth be known, I'll avoid cooking whenever possible.

Geoff conducted a prolonged search over the campsite for the location that offered the best combination of proximity to the facilities, to the rising sun (for drying the tents and any laundry) and reasonably flat surfaces. Most of the sites were OK but Rawdon quietly advised us that site selection was a special concern for Geoff, so just let him do his thing.

We gathered for a very relaxed dinner. Some of the others had bought wine and cider that they shared along with some pre-dinner nibbles. We sat and talked while the individual methanol-fired camp stoves boiled pasta or fried sausages. Everyone but me had bought far more than they could eat, so my somewhat meagre dinner became amplified. Although I never asked to share, this pattern tended to repeat itself over the week, giving me a reputation as a scrounge. Toward the end of the week, I bought things for the group to share to restore some portion of my now tarnished image.

Around the campfire that evening, the group began to open up and share personal information starting with our respective ages. Murray claimed to be 64, relieving me of the responsibility of being the senior member. It was only at the end of the week that he added the detail, 'next birthday in December', making me oldest by a month! Cara, his wife, did not reveal her age.

During this evening of revelations, we discovered some of those astounding coincidences that so often occur in group settings. Yassmin, the product of an unusual combination, a Yemeni father and a Welsh mother, speaks Arabic, as does Rawdon. Murray and Cara's daughter, a nurse, had married an American and moved recently to

Albuquerque, New Mexico, where my daughter had just moved. Their daughter had earned her US qualifications working in the same hospital in Little Rock, Arkansas where a cousin of mine is a pharmacologist.

We discussed a full range of subjects from music, to books, Ireland and Palestine. Yassmin admitted that she had been a masseuse and was persuaded to try to ease Rawdon's lumbago. He removed his shirt and lay face down on the grass at the edge of our campfire circle while she administered the massage kneeling beside him. Geoff quickly whipped out his camera to get pictures for the Breton Bike's website as evidence of the wide range of services provided. We had a good time, the conversation was both serious and humorous and carried on to nearly 11 when we could barely see to get ready for bed

Bistromatics

The tour continued much along this placid, pleasant pattern for the balance of the week interlaced with some interesting experiences. Geoff's role in selecting the routes, finding restaurants and booking campsites was crucial, leaving us only personal responsibilities. But I was disappointed that he did not make more of an effort to acquaint us with the history and culture of the area. Although our tour's name was Two Chateaus and the Blavet, we did not visit either chateau. The little that I learned about Brittany came from observation, asking questions and our experiences.

For example, when the regular Wednesday closing of the patisserie threatened breakfast we bought out the grocery store's entire supply of croissants. We learned not to wake the devil by walking round a church anti-clockwise and that many church ground graves had been moved to centralised large cemeteries away from churches presumably due to the extreme separation of church and state in France.

At the lovely, canal-side village of St. Nicolas des Eaux, an elderly English woman, her tongue significantly loosened with beer, joined us at an outdoor table where we stopped for a beer after dinner. She claimed to have lived in the village for the past two years after her husband abruptly abandoned her. She was starved for an audience but we quickly became satiated and parted company as soon as we could do so without giving offence.

Our dinner that evening had been at a round table in the corner of a creperie. This was our second dinner at a creperie making us feel experienced and relaxed. In an attempt to dispel my growing scrounge reputation, I ordered a bottle of Muscatel as a table aperitif while we waited on our meals.

Yassmin introduced a French word that intrigued Murray, initiating a series of attempts by him to pronounce it correctly. Murray had great difficulty with the language to the point that he continually referred to the French currency as 'dollars'. His successive attempts at this word during the evening progressively mangled it beyond recognition. His failures were comic, fuelling our good mood and generating more humour. We gradually evolved into a state where every comment, no matter how mundane or inane, was witty and hilarious.

Then came time for 'Bistromatics', a term developed years ago by Geoff and Rawdon to describe the mathematics of working out each person's share of the total bistro bill. This involved identifying the various charges on the bill with the appropriate individual and recording the amounts in separate columns on a table napkin. At our previous creperie meal, the individual amounts did not equal the bill's total, even though the exercise was made easier because sales taxes and gratuities are built into menu prices.

This evening, I volunteered to do the math and was successful in matching the totals. Our good mood continued and we had a lot of fun in the process as I gathered money from each and made change at the table. The proprietress, hovered, looking a little agitated, concerned perhaps that our meal would be under funded. I enjoyed the exercise so much that the green calculation napkin came home with me as a souvenir!

Bicycle Physics

Our route left the canal towpaths on the way back to Gouarec, becoming hilly and providing opportunities for coasting at speed around downhill curves. Rawdon explained the physics of doing so and helped improve my technique. He also taught me how to determine the proper tyre pressure. This is so dead simple that I could not believe I had not realised it myself. It is just a question of the weight of the rider divided by two (half for each tyre) and adjusted for the width of the tyre. This determines the required PSI (pressure per square inch) since the fore to aft portion of the tyre supporting the cycle at any moment is about one inch. Tyres narrower or wider than one inch require proportionally more or less pressure. Geoff believed that one had to modify this approach to accommodate the weight of the cycle and the gear but Rawdon thought that was unnecessary. I am inclined to agree with Geoff on this one. (For those of you who may be oriented this way, the following shows how this approach applies to my situation: my weight of 160 lbs produces a weight of 80 pounds per wheel. This weight rests on about a one-inch length of the tyre at any point in time. But since my tyres are 700 X 38 mm, the width is roughly 1.5 inches; so that the inch of fore-aft tread provides 1.5 square inches of total tread. Thus the necessary inflation pressure is 80 lbs. divided by 1.5 or 53.33 lbs. per square inch. Adding a total of 60 lbs of gear brings the required pressure up to 73.33 lbs per square inch for each tyre). This is the minimum rather than the optimum pressure as most tyres can hold higher pressures that will reduce rolling resistance.

After a near week of almost perfect cycling conditions, warm sunshine and cooling breezes, the weather became cool and threatened rain on Friday, our last day. Geoff needed to be back in Gouarec early to prepare for a community concert that evening for which Kate had committed him as a performer. So we arrived about 3.30 after a huge, late lunch.

The others left to buy food for the evening but I stayed to get my tent up before the threatening rain became a reality. I still had a few leftovers and did not feel particularly hungry anyway. We all chose to camp much closer to the facilities this time, giving us access to some covered picnic tables and eliminating the long trek to the toilets in the dark.

It was also a good opportunity for me to launder my week's accumulation of dirty clothes. Dave's wife, Marianne, sold me the necessary token for the machine and provided the soap. The €3 cost (C$4.80) for one load, although high by North American standards, seemed reasonable compared to the three pounds (C$ 7.35) I had paid in England.

Despite the good times we had together as a group, this brief respite of doing things on my own, including a few uninterrupted moments with my book, were very welcome. I looked forward to the next week of solo cycling along the coast.

The group returned with more than enough food for everyone. I was again invited to share and did so having recovered some appetite but this time I made a financial contribution to each of them to cover my consumption. We ate at the picnic tables, somewhat subdued by the realisation that our week together was over. Conversation turned to what each of us was to do next. Yassmin and Rawdon were headed home, back to work. Murray and Cara were going off by themselves for another week of cycling with Geoff's equipment and I was destined for the Emerald Coast enroute to St. Malo and the ferry back to Britain.

Final Parting

We breakfasted and lunched together as a group on Saturday. Yassmin and a British couple, that had just completed a solo week, left afterward for the St. Brieux railway station by minibus. Geoff had arranged for the minibus to collect their cases from the campsite and them from the restaurant. In a clear demonstration of the Breton pace of life, the minibus driver sat patiently for fifteen minutes while his passengers finished their meals and goodbyes.

After lunch I returned Geoff's bike, removing my pedals. Geoff gave my own bike a quick check over and lubricated the chain. I went out for a short 15 km unladen ride and was invited to coffee with Dave and Marianne on return. The remainder of our group was somewhat adrift. We were all going our separate ways tomorrow and feeling somewhat distant already. Rawdon came to the rescue, suggesting that we go in his car to a Rostrenan creperie he knew, called Kumquat. Although Murray and Cara had already had an early meal, they readily agreed. It was a short run of perhaps twenty minutes, so we were soon in the cobbled square that housed the restaurant. Being a busy Saturday night, however, we could not be seated inside. The outside patio was chilly but all of us, including Murray, who protested that he wasn't hungry, enjoyed a full meal.

After a particularly chilly Saturday night (5 degrees Celsius), we repeated our initial joint breakfast at the generous local bar with all of Geoff's family, Dave and Marianne from the campsite, Murray and Cara and Bill and Melissa, an American father and daughter from St. Louis. This last couple had arrived late on Saturday and chose to do the same self-guided route that Murray and Cara were going on.

It was a cool, overcast day, consistent with the night before. My route initially ran in the same direction as the others, so the five of us rode together for about 40 minutes until our routes deviated. My mood immediately lifted. Despite having enjoyed the week together, there was an immediate sensation of release from the constraints of being in a group situation and of empowerment to now be in control of and responsible for all the decisions.

The bike was running well, chewing up the countryside at a pace that exceeded the group's best full day. My lunch stop was in Quintin where I found a lovely park with picnic benches alongside a pretty river. Facilities, sorely needed after three hours on the bike, were also available. Geoff had trained us well enough about the unavailability of food after noon on Sundays that I had picked up some lunch items before leaving Gouarec. These I enjoyed while reading my latest book—a John le Carre that Geoff gave me. Pleasant as this was, I was still envious of the happy people wining and dining on the patios of three cafes that overlooked the river.

A light rain began to fall at about five and quickly turned heavy. I took refuge in an open, empty residential garage that appeared just in time. As usual, just getting out my book was a sure way to end the rain; so, within ten minutes, I was back on the road.

Val Andre, a coastal town and my objective for the day, showed up just before six. I went in search of a reasonably priced hotel. French hotels post their number of stars on their signs providing a helpful guide to quality and price. Based on my hotel experiences getting between Roscoff and Gouarec, I knew that two stars were good enough for me. So, I ignored three star and better hotels. Hotels also post their rates outside for each level of room offered. After a bit of looking round, I found the imaginatively named, two star Hotel de la Mer and booked their cheapest room at €39. My cycle had to be housed inside in a narrow corridor that was adjacent to the kitchen and home to the lobster tank.

Despite this inauspicious beginning, I decided to have dinner here. The hotel claimed to have a gourmet restaurant and I had some budget surplus. After a shower and attired in my dark blue sweatshirt and khaki cargo trouser 'out on the town' outfit, I entered their bright and colourful restaurant. The budget surplus would only accommodate the cheapest selection but that turned out to be excellent as was the service. I managed a whole half carafe of wine myself and finished off with the crisp sweetness of my favourite blackcurrant sorbet.

All in all, it was a successful day, good distance, pleasant scenery, excellent meal, a stroll along the adjacent seafront after dinner, and after eight days, a real bed!

Liquid Fertilizer

Monday began and continued cool, overcast and drizzly. I went back a few kilometres to the picturesque port at Dahonet, which I had passed through yesterday, to watch the harbour activities. There were sailboats and motor launches as well as a class of students boarding a small boat for some instruction. A monument stood on a small bluff at the mouth of the harbour and a walking trek provided access to the surrounding cliffs. I took a short walk and some cliff pictures but was eager to be on my way.

My guidebook to Brittany had recommended the medieval city of Dinan that was a relatively easy 60 kilometres away. Dinan was also a similar distance from Cap Frehel where I am booked in at the hostel tomorrow. After losing some time trying to find the right road, I set off to the east for Dinan,

Today's lunch was also in a park, and along a river at Plancoet. This park was equipped with a pond and ducks but no toilet facilities. Fortunately, it was deserted as I found it vital to apply some liquid fertilizer to some of their ornamental bushes. Plancoet had been on the Tour de France route in some year past and commemorated the honour with a floral display in the park. It seemed an appropriate place to have stopped.

Dinan

From this point, the direct route to Dinan was on a major highway, so I diverted to the minor roads that are shown in white on the map and commonly referred to as the 'white roads' This added about 10 kilometres to the distance and some confusion as there were several T junctions and a few had no directional signs at all at the intersection.

Appearing on my right as I rode into the city was the Hotel de Marmite. I just had to stay there as my Australian brother-in-law enjoys vegemite, marmite's close cousin, for breakfast every morning. Fortunately, the hotel was in my price bracket, in fact, it was the best price yet, and had a vacancy. I was given a key for a storage garage across the street to secure my cycle. My room was well equipped with en-suite facilities and good lighting. Something must be wrong with the place though as I seem to be the only guest.

I walked into the town, dodging under awnings to avoid a heavy rain shower and took refuge in a bar to get a coffee to accompany a just acquired Far Breton and an apple Danish pastry. The pastries were enjoyable but not special and the coffee was expensive. It is still hard to get used to paying for each refill. But it was a pleasant break and served to wait out the rain.

Dinan is a wonderful old medieval town with delightful old houses and streets, surrounded by 13th-to 15th century ramparts and guarded by a castle. All this is in a spectacularly attractive setting 75 metres above a charming stretch of the lovely Rance River with a nice little port. The port side streets featured interesting looking shops and restaurants overlooking a variety of colourful river craft. I found this area at the end of a steep, cobbled stone street that began at an impressive stone archway and meandered down to the water between ancient buildings.

As it was late on a Monday afternoon, many of the shops were closed and the number of tourists was slight. Although, the architecture was very different and it was a river at the bottom rather than the sea, I was reminded of the village of Clovelly in Devon.

At about seven, I rang my mother, thinking that it would be exciting for her to receive a call from her eldest son from France. At first she did not recognise who I was and then she thought I was already back home. It would have been just after lunch for her and she may have been napping as the conversation was heavy going and largely one-sided.

That experience and the continuing threat of rain must have dampened my hunger as the few restaurants that were open seemed unsavoury and uninteresting. So I returned to the hotel to shower and decided to patronise their dining room rather than risking rain. Initially, I was the first guest but then the only person in the bar came in. This was an inauspicious beginning but I did not need to worry. I spent about twice what I had intended but still managed to stay on budget for the day in aggregate. The food was very good.

Cap Frehel

After an enjoyable breakfast with lots of orange juice and good, fresh bread, I set out enroute to Cap Frehel on the northern coast of Brittany. The Cap or cape is sort of a national reserve or park that is on the 'must' list of many Brittany guidebooks. The day started cool and the weather forecast suggested rain so I wore my cool weather long tights. The ride through Dinan's centre was fun, judging traffic and the lights, negotiating roundabouts and feeling in control again after a week of group activity. Yesterday's scouting of the best route out of the city was a big help. First objective was Ploubalay that was an easy run at an average speed of just over 19 km an hour.

Ploubalay offered a comfort stop that was sorely needed after all the juice and coffee at breakfast. This facility was in a public parking lot and proved to be unisex with the urinals in full view of anyone walking in the door. I thought I had adopted the French indifference to such situations but still caught myself being grateful to be finished and leaving when a woman walked in.

I carried on to Matignon, arriving about noon and was surprised to find a shop selling international newspapers in the small town centre. I bought a *Daily Telegraph* and delayed lunch by at least half an hour while I sat on a bench, eagerly absorbing my first real news in over ten days. As usual, I found most everything in the paper to be interesting from criticism of the heavy volumes of reports required from primary school teachers to the new European constitution and its devastating effects on British autonomy, if adopted, to the discovery (from tooth enamel) that the builders of Stonehenge were from West Wales as were the Bluestones that they used.

After a long internal budget debate with myself, the budget lost and I adjourned to an adjoining creperie for a warm chevre salad with melted chevre on toast. This, together with a quarter carafe of red wine, and John le Carre's *Call of Dead* improved an already good day.

Cap Frehel was an easy hour and a half further on. It proved to be a popular spot with lots of cars and buses going past the tollbooth. The site is covered primarily with low-level gorse through which numerous paths crisscross. Many people chose to park outside the tollbooth and simply walk in on the paths, avoiding the charge. Cyclists weren't charged, so I rode right in. The cliffs weren't nearly as dramatic as I had hoped but it met my need for coastal scenery nevertheless. I sat on the cliff edge with my eyes closed, absorbing today's first sunshine, appreciating a gentle breeze and the hum of bees in the nearby gorse. Then I moved to another spot to sit some more but it was so relaxing that I was afraid of dozing off and falling over the edge. After a few minutes, this pleasant reverie was interrupted by a strong wind and mist together with disappearance of the sun.

Cliffside, Cap Frehel, Brittany

I cycled back into the nearby village of Plevenon to find something for tonight's meal at the hostel. Fortunately, the grocery was open, but being a Monday, the patisserie was not, so my plan for a coffee and delectable pastry was foiled.

Disappointed, I set off for the hostel. Its access road was about half way back towards Cap Frehel. The turn was marked with the French equivalent of YHA, Auberges de Juennese Francaises. I was somewhat apprehensive about French hostels due to a dimly recalled bad memory of my first experience at a French hostel that I visited with my younger brother, Byron, in 1957. As I remember, that was our introduction to the squat style toilet.

This building was unexpectedly reminiscent of the Bates motel in Hitchcock's *Psycho*. Three picnic type tables sat outside together with some stuffed furniture that would have been more at home in a rubbish tip. No one was around as I was early for opening time.

Half an hour later, the warden emerged from her living quarters. She had a record of my reservation but no record of my payment by MasterCard. Her English was somewhat better than my French but we still had quite a struggle communicating. Consequently, I misunderstood the purpose of the long narrow tube-like sheet that she gave me. I assumed it was the French equivalent of the sheet sleeping bag provided by British hostels and protested to her that I was too big to fit inside it. I need not have worried. What she had given me was intended for use as a pillowcase!

She took me upstairs to my room, grabbing what I now assumed was the fresh sheet bag from a closet. The room was outfitted with two beds, a washbasin and a small open wardrobe. Stacked on top of the wardrobe were two grubby blankets and two sausage shaped bags of cut up foam rubber. These, I reasoned finally, were the pillows to be stuffed into the five-foot long pillowcase.

The supposed sheet bag was just a single sheet, not a bag at all. Improvising, I folded it lengthwise with the open side away from the wall, thus creating an upper and lower sheet to separate me from the blanket and bare mattress. This worked very well. The hostel was virtually empty so I had the room to myself.

The members' kitchen had a fair amount of left behind food, including a large bottle of wine but given the other conditions in the hostel, I wasn't tempted even though my purchases at the grocery store proved to be inadequate for my appetite.

I was the only person at breakfast the next morning and was surprised to find a place laid with a stack of small crisp toasts, orange juice, jam and muesli. After a minute or two, a young woman arrived with a full pot of coffee and abject apologies for the lack of baguettes and croissants. The bakery was not open today and so no fresh bread was available. I could not complain, the quantity of food was far greater than most French breakfasts and I would have paid much more just for the coffee elsewhere than the €3 the hostel charged for the entire breakfast.

My plan for today was to explore as much of the Cap Frehel peninsula as possible with no destination other than nearby Fort la Latte and return to the hostel in the evening. So I was free to go wherever the fancy took me.

My French skills were sufficiently adequate to cope with the fort signs claiming that it was an important historical spot but they would not have been up to the detailed history inside the fortress. So, I instead chose to explore the views and walks around it, looking across to Cap Frehel, then set out along the coast road southeast of the cape.

The day was overcast and cool (That has a familiar ring about it!). There was a strong wind off the sea, so strong that I had to fight all the way, leaning heavily to my right, to avoid being blown into the path of the overtaking cars. The wind produced magnificent surf crashing into the lovely, long sweeps of almost deserted white sand beaches. A few stalwart surfboarders in wet suits were taking advantage of the conditions but I couldn't enjoy the view properly for concentrating so hard on staying out of the traffic. Eventually, this road led me to Sables d' Or, a newish looking beachside community with a very wide street lined with restaurants and tourist shops but of little interest for me.

After a disappointing repeat of yesterday's Matignon lunch there, I suddenly realised that if the bakery wasn't operating today, perhaps the grocery store would not either, raising the prospect of famine tonight. I headed back to Plevenon and found that indeed the grocery store was closed. Although fuelling my stomach is a major pleasure and preoccupation, I suddenly turned stoical and headed back to the coast.

This foray brought me to a small village called St. Giran. There, a steep road led down to a small parking lot/park overlooking the sea dotted with colourful fishing and sailboats. There was a convenient park bench facing the sea that I claimed for my own. The sun decided to make an appearance, so I took the opportunity to sunbathe a while, enjoying the quiet peace and beauty of this spot. Others arrived and departed, mainly English tourists including one nursing mother with huge dispensers. These tourists stayed only briefly but one visitor was a local fisherman dressed stereotypically in beret and loose corduroy jacket. He provided some interesting action as he took a small boat from the beach, rowed out to a larger boat anchored in the bay and set off in the larger boat for some evening fishing.

Walking back up the steep road, I encountered a walking couple that asked me a question in French. This was the perfect time to use a phrase I had been rehearsing for a day or two: 'Je parlais Anglais seulement'. Their response, after a slight delay to digest my comment, was 'So do we'. It wasn't clear whether their delay reflected my poor pronunciation, the phrase or both. Fortunately, I had just passed a sign leading to the hiking path they were looking for and could help.

Continuing with my aimless cycling, I came across a very picturesque looking creperie called La Clepsydre in Pleherel-Plage that claimed to be open tonight from 7 pm. Since it was only a few kilometres from the hostel there was time to go back for a shower, return to the creperie for dinner and still possibly have time to see a sunset at Cap Frehel.

A family of three Canadian cyclists from Montreal had just arrived at the hostel. They were spending most of their summer in France and perhaps some time in Vietnam. All their cooking and camping gear was carried on a specially built trailer that the father pulls. He is a university professor in computer sciences but is considering early retirement in a few years to set up a cycle touring company that would concentrate on France. He was already acquainted (by email) with Geoff Husband of Breton Bikes. I did not learn much about the mother as her English, although better than my French by far, was not adequate for real conversation Their son, now eleven, has been making these trips with his parents for the past three years.

La Clepsydre was an excellent choice, boasting a fireplace, red-painted wooden ceiling beams, a black and white tile floor and red checked tablecloths. The pleasant and attractive waitress complemented her husband, a cheerful and competent chef. I enjoyed a Montangarde gallette, citron crepe, vin rouge and café.

An hour and a half later, I emerged, at peace with the world, to a still bright sunshiny evening for my sunset quest ride to Cap Frehel. Traffic was light, enhancing the very pleasant five-kilometre ride. The coast was cooler and windy but being nearly at the end of my trip made me want to savour every moment and wait for the sunset. However, it was getting colder by the minute. I realised that there could be an hour's wait, that I had no cycle lights to negotiate in the dark after sunset and regretfully decided to return to the hostel at about 9.30.

St. Malo

Next morning, I breakfasted early and alone on the remainder of my orange juice and plain crepes. Today's trip to St. Malo promises to be long and may be difficult as most of the bridges over the Rance River are major highways, not open to cycles.

Much of my earlier route from Dinan to Cap Frehel had to be re-traced to find a suitable river crossing. This navigational challenge added to the day's enjoyment. It required careful map reading to find the right combination of white roads to get across the Rance. After crossing the river, I arrived at Chateauneuf just before noon, starving, as my breakfast had been early and inadequate.

Rural Home with Straw Donkey, Northern Brittany

The day was alternately cool and overcast and sunny but still in a savouring every experience mood, I wanted to take my chances and have lunch outside in a park. Conveniently, one appeared above the main street just opposite a patisserie. By the time my purchases were made the weather reverted to cool and overcast but I stuck to the plan although I did not dawdle.

While eating, I took the time to work out a cycle friendly route into St. Malo. Once there, the first port of call was to find the embarkation point for tomorrow's early morning ferry back to England. I had heard that the hostel here was extremely large, noisy and busy so decided to cancel my booking and find a hotel close to the port instead.

My hotel search began adjacent to the port in the fortress-like walled city known as Intra Muros. The city was left in utter ruins in July 1944 when the Americans fought to dislodge the Germans and free it. The French rebuilt much of the city as it had been, re-creating history for future generations. Prominently posted at the formidable entry gate was a red and white sign listing dozens of hotels. Inside, the cobbled streets and 15th century architecture contrasted dramatically with the broad boulevards, busy traffic and port activity outside the gates.

Intra Muros attracts thousands of tourists with its myriad cafes, restaurants, hotels and high-end international brand shops. I immediately wanted to explore and was frustrated with the need to first find lodging.

Signs were conveniently posted at relevant intersections pointing the direction to various hotels and helpfully showed the hotel's rating using the star system. I looked for two stars on the assumption that the price would be in the €40 range that I had paid elsewhere. The first two stars' cheapest room was €50, the next one was slightly cheaper but full as was the third. Mild panic was beginning to set in as I had passed a three star charging a minimum of €90—would I have to pay that much to get a room?

Then out of the corner of my eye, I saw Auberge des Chiens du Guet, a colourful and picturesque inn with its own outdoor café tucked into a corner of the wall at a sea-facing gate, Port St. Pierre. Les Guets were fierce mastiff dogs that for five hundred years were let out at nightfall to discourage any Englishmen from sneaking up and taking the town by stealth. The dogs were recalled at dawn by a trumpet blast. (3)

The Auberge had no rating but it did have a vacancy and the manageress told me I could have a room for €34. Success! As she escorted me to the room, she made some remark about a shower being on the ground floor. I took little notice of what she said but later after returning from dinner, I wanted to take a shower but could not find any on my floor. Remembering her comment, I came downstairs prepared with towel, shampoo, etc. and went into the public washroom on the ground floor. There was no evidence of a shower. An entrance to the kitchen was adjacent to the washroom and the cook just happened to be standing in the doorway, taking a break. With my vast knowledge of French and in as sophisticated a manner as I could manage, I blurted out 'Douche?', trying not to think of the word's common English meaning.

The cook took me back into the washroom and pointed to an internal locked door. Drawing again on my considerable vocabulary, I managed 'Clef?' He conveyed that I would have to see the manageress. I found her dealing with her customers in the restaurant and this time put both words together 'Clef de Douche?' Surprisingly, she understood (perhaps the towel, shampoo and soap did the communicating). She came out into the hall, marched over to the kitchen and retrieved a large ball attached to a key from the top of the refrigerator. Voila! It felt a little strange, showering in the facilities used by restaurant patrons but there was no other shower in the entire inn.

Next morning I happened to see the hotel's posted tariff which showed that a room for one person was €30 not the €34 that she had told me. So, I decided to challenge the situation with the manageress. Despite our mutual inabilities with each other's language, after some several minutes we managed to communicate effectively. For me, effectively meant that she reduced the price. In the process, I finally understood that because the room could accommodate more than one person she had originally quoted a price based on its capacity not its actual occupancy.

All of this was accomplished in time for me to cycle to the ferry terminal by the appointed hour. The day was beautiful, by far the best of the trip so far and I immediately made for the upper deck to stake out a chair in the sunshine. Apart from two meals, most of the crossing was spent there devouring yesterday's *Daily Telegraph* and soaking up the sun. The mid-day main meal had to be savoured with a carafe of vin rouge but for my late afternoon snack I had my first cup of tea since landing in France a fortnight ago. I can't remember a more enjoyable cuppa!

Portsmouth, Windsor, Eton and Home

The good weather lasted all the way to the Portsmouth terminal. For me, disembarkation meant quite a delay as this time the bike was moored at the stern and all the cars got off first. While waiting in the increasing fog of carbon monoxide, I discovered that I had misplaced my favourite souvenir, a black and white Breton cycling cap. Trying to find it would have meant fighting my way up the companionways through other passengers on the way down to their cars and possibly being late to get off. So, I reluctantly wrote it off. (Geoff Husband, who operates Breton Bikes, very kindly bought and sent me a replacement—as a gift!)

Portsmouth is a naval city; one of the sights is the historic naval dockyard, which houses several vessels, including H.M.S. *Victory*, the flagship of Admiral Horatio Nelson at the Battle of Trafalgar against the French in 1805. The vessel has a special place in British heroics because Nelson won the decisive engagement but was killed just as victory was his. (A newly published book, *Nelson's Purse,* deals with the recent discovery of the still full purse that Nelson carried at the time of his death). Also housed at Portsmouth is a less fortunate vessel, the ill-fated 16th century *Mary Rose*, which sank soon after its launch. Portsmouth docks had their origins in the 12th century, and the world's first dry dock was built here as early as 1495. (4)

The Portsmouth hostel, some distance from the harbour, was reached through some poor and depressing residential areas heavy with early evening traffic. The 'one size/style fits all' council houses looked as if they had been built in the early socialist fervour in Britain. Lack of ambition appeared ubiquitous. The contrast with what I had seen of Brittany was unfavourable to Britain. The hostel building itself was interesting being a 16th century manor house but was poorly maintained and managed

I loaded up the hostel washing machine with my week's worth of accumulated laundry and went into the member's kitchen to scrounge a cup of tea. The only other occupant, a man in his sixties, was sitting quietly eating a meat pie that had been wrapped in wax paper. He was very neat and tidy in his dress and eating habits but did not look at all out of place in the hostel. I formed the immediate impression that he was trying to live very frugally as a matter of necessity.

Imagine my surprise then when during a long conversation, he told me that he spoke eight languages, had lived in New York, Chicago and Montreal and had visited 150 different countries. He told stories of having met both Sadam Hussein and Omar Gadaffi; living in Denmark with his former Danish wife; and travelling all over the world in a technical sales job. His entire story was in sharp contrast to his apparent current circumstances—perhaps I am too gullible—but it all had the ring of truth.

A younger Briton of an entirely different stripe joined us later. This man was grossly overweight and a whiner. He complained bitterly about Britain as a place to live, the monarchy, taxes, etc. On learning that I was a Canadian, he claimed to want to know all about Canada, but never got around to asking any questions.

Both these men were in my dormitory room. The fat one complained that he 'was chesty and not too good on his pins' despite being considerably younger than either of us. He had brought both a small television and a heater to the hostel and negotiated a swap of beds in order to have access to an electric point to use both appliances. Sometime during the night he disappeared and we never saw him again.

Celebrating my return to England, the heavens bestowed a light drizzle and gloomy atmosphere next morning tempting me not to cycle. My plan had been to do one of the day trips featured in the Ordnance Survey (OS) Cycle Tours series, return to Portsmouth and then take a train to Windsor this evening.

The rain moderated somewhat so I convinced myself to carry on with the original plan. Now that I was back in England, it was time to resume the tea and teacakes routine and those treats had to be earned. About half past ten, I promised myself to make my ritual stop in Hambleton, the village that I was approaching. Miraculously, at a bend in the road that marked the edge of the village was a teashop attached to a small grocery. The tearoom window displayed a closed sign but as there was a couple already inside, I ignored the sign and went in.

While there, I studied the map carefully and decided to not return to Portsmouth but carry on northwards, cycling all the way to Windsor. This would be a better accomplishment than the original plan and save the train fare as well, perhaps financing a special dinner tonight.

The more I thought about it the more this plan deteriorated. It could have been done but would have meant a late arrival at Windsor. Packing up the cycle and cleaning up afterwards could mean that my hopes for a great dinner would have to be forfeited. So, I compromised and cycled as far as Basingstoke and took trains from there. Amazingly, this saved only about two pounds on the train fare compared with coming all the way from Portsmouth. It may have been the time of day or the fact that it required changing trains at Slough and Reading.

I am happy to report that I did dine well, treating myself to a scotch and ginger, lamb dopiaza, sweet nan and a lager, completing this journey with the same meal, in the same restaurant where it began just a month ago.

After a hearty breakfast next morning, I had a couple of hours before having to leave for the airport so set off on a walk to Windsor Castle to see the Changing of the Guards. This did not particularly intrigue me so I was not especially disappointed that the ceremony was not to be performed today. The Queen was in residence and attending chapel and the noise of the ceremony would disrupt the service.

This gave me time to walk some of the river, watch the boats, people, swans and ducks and to visit the village of Eton. Eton is just across the river and feels a part of Windsor itself. The famous school sits several blocks along the road over the bridge. Unfortunately, there was no public access into the quadrangle of the school but there was a fair amount of activity in the archway leading in. Several boys were crowded round a notice board that perhaps announced examination results. A few of them came out together apparently on their way to church. Even without their pinstriped trousers and tailed Edwardian style jackets they would have been obviously a cut above. One, sporting a handsome golden brown mane, sharply aquiline face and erect posture looked right through me with total self assurance of his superiority. The timing of my arrival was perfect as soon the street was teeming with similarly dressed boys moving towards the church. Tomorrow's future leaders and don't they know it!

King Henry VI established Eton as a religious foundation in 1440. Initially it was to include an almshouse, a chantry and a men's choir. Henry expected to generate revenue by attracting pilgrims to see two dubious relics—fragments of the True Cross and of the Crown of Thorns. Henry also funded a school and provided scholarships for 70 poor scholars. Today, Eton College is known as 'the chief nurse of England's statesmen.' Eighteen former Prime Ministers have been Etonians. (5)

All that remained was to return to the B&B, taxi out to Heathrow and start thinking about the next trip. But there was one little bonus yet to come. My taxi driver had noticed a traffic accident on the motorway as he came to collect me so he took a back road route to the airport. Along the way he pointed out the Windsor Castle gate through the Great Park where Queen Elizabeth exits if she wishes to avoid the crowds and he showed me the home of Jackie Collins the author. According to the driver she is not liked but her sister, Joan, the actress, is very popular.

Despite the longer route and having to use an estate car this driver charged less for the trip to Heathrow than his colleague had on my arrival. Check-in was straightforward until I was advised that instead of the two cases limit that applied for my Canadian departure there was a weight limit per case as well. Fortunately, the loaded cycle case's weight of 26 kilos was within the limit and I avoided an extra charge.

This brought my most recent tour and the last one of this book to a close.

GETTING UNDERWAY

Training
Fully-loaded cycle touring is a totally different experience from van-assisted touring. Ideally, one should train for several weeks with full panniers to build the extra muscles needed to shift the weight of all that gear and develop the ability to cope with the change in cycle dynamics that it produces. Apart from minimising the aches and pains, training also will help reduce the initial disappointment and discouragement of slower speeds, tougher hills and sluggish responsiveness.

This, you will recognise, is the wisdom of hindsight. Even now, with five fully loaded solo tours under my belt, I was only able to train properly for the last one. On my first trip, the consequences of not training were severe. By the end of the second day my ankles were so swollen that I could barely climb the stairs to my bed or descend to the breakfast room. I did not seek medical attention for fear that the doctor might advise ending the tour, which I definitely did not want to do. So, I loosened the strings on my cycle shoes to improve circulation and carried on. Within a few days, the ankles returned to normal.

A bigger problem is learning how to control the cycle with a heavy load. A loaded cycle requires more distance to stop, cannot take sharp turns at the same speed or angle, and is more difficult to keep upright if you start to fall. And, if you fall in the UK, Australia, New Zealand or Japan, be sure you know to and will instinctively fall to the left. This is something you have to think about hard for the first few days until it becomes second nature. On the first day of my Circle Tour, the loaded cycle dynamics and a rough road surface caused me to fall to the right directly into oncoming traffic. Obviously, the experience was not fatal but definitely was not a highlight.

Roads and Maps
The infrastructure of early roads in Britain provides a rich network for exploration—it just requires work with ordinance survey maps to find a route that combines tranquillity with beauty and convenience. Most of the A roads should be avoided for the speed and volume of the traffic. The B roads offer the best combination of safety, access to teashops and facilities and lovely countryside. The unmarked roads and lanes are more peaceful but are often too isolated to provide the mix of interesting experiences I crave. And, being unmarked, can easily

frustrate following a pre-determined route.

I am indebted to Bicycle Books of San Francisco for the following extract from *Cycling Great Britain* by Tim Hughes and Joanna Cleary.

'The original classification of the principal A-roads in the 1930s was based on a clockwise radial pattern from London. The A1 headed north for York and Edinburgh, the A2 headed southeast to Dover, the A3 southwest to Portsmouth and so on round to the A6, which headed northwest to Carlisle on the Scottish border. The system was completed by the A7 from Carlisle to Edinburgh, A8 from Edinburgh to Glasgow, and A9 from Edinburgh to the northeast tip of Scotland, John O' Groats.

The next tier of roads in the hierarchy was numbered as they diverged from these single-number roads: for example, the A10, A11, A12, and so on lie in the sector between the A1 and A2 and the A20, A21, A22, lie between the A2 and A3. Further subdivisions down to three-and four-figure A-numbers filled in the network. ...Some important A roads are designated "trunk" roads and have special green signing; these are likely to be busy...

With B roads we begin to come to more comfortable cycling, although B-roads within about 60 km of London and close to some other big cities can be busy. B-roads usually have a four-figure number and fit generally though less precisely into the same numbering system.'

This wealth of roads creates a sometimes-dense network, making an accurate map essential. Outside the cities, a 1:250,000 scale (1 cm = 2.5 km) produced by the Ordnance Survey (OS) and others is probably the best available compromise between bulk and usefulness. The available OS Landranger 1:50,000 scale is detailed enough to show virtually every road and track, together with details of villages, towns, churches, lakes and rivers and other landmarks. Unfortunately, unless your tour is highly concentrated within a fairly small area, you may need several of these maps for a tour of more than a few days. An in between scale such as the Michelin 1:100,000 French maps would be ideal but these are not available for Britain. I have heard of a recently introduced new series, called Goldeneye, that is designed specifically for cyclists with a scale of 1:126,720 and are plasticised. Their range is limited to the more popular areas.

Hostelling

As a homeowner I find paying for a place to sleep a particularly annoying expense. Accommodation can be the biggest single cost of these trips and despite delightful experiences in lovely B&B's and interesting conversations with both guests and hosts; there are less expensive alternatives. So, after my first trip, I became a member of Hostelling International, formerly known as Youth Hostels. The pure accommodation cost varies with location but currently is the range of £11-12. Breakfast and evening meals, when available, run about £4 each.

Hostelling is popular among cyclists, walkers, school groups on field trips and others who don't mind sharing rooms with strangers or perhaps like me are just trying to save some money. The movement, at least in Britain, seems to be under financial pressure as some of the less frequented hostels have been closed.

Hostels come in all shapes and sizes. I have stayed in what had been a 16th century stone mill with capacity for perhaps only 30 people; in a wooden former scout hut and in a large, modern but very basic hotel style building. All of them have member kitchens and dining areas. Some offer breakfast and dinner cafeteria style. The smaller hostels often close shortly after breakfast and do not re-open until about 5 pm while the larger ones may be open all day and have television and reading lounges. Staff in the smaller hostels probably live in and earn very little beyond their room and board.

This range of hostels provides variety to offset the constant of bunk beds (a minimum of four and more often eight to a room together), communal shower and toilet facilities. Gender differences are respected both in the sleeping and bathroom areas, at least in Britain. On arrival, one is issued with a freshly laundered sheet bag complete with integral pillow cover. The beds come equipped with a lightweight duvet and pillow. Most times, it is a matter of first come, first served whether you get an upper or lower bunk. This is an important choice, particularly if you regularly need to get up in the night. Doing so from the top bunk without turning on any light or disturbing the person beneath you can be quite a feat, particularly if no ladder has been provided. Occasionally, you are assigned a specific bed. Operating on the experience of two previous tours, I did not realise this was the practice at the Cambridge hostel in my Circle tour in 1999, I was rudely awakened at about 1 am by a Chinese member, demanding that I vacate 'his' bed. The adjacent obviously empty bunk was not acceptable.

You are unlikely to contemplate a tour like those described in this book unless you already love cycling. But, fortunately, if you are not yet fully persuaded, there are guided, van assisted, inn-to-inn type tours of five to ten days that offer an intermediate alternative that can be very pleasant in their own right and might pique your interest in my sort of tour. Van-assisted, inn-to-inn touring, while more expensive, is also more comfortable and avoids the need to cycle fully loaded. Yet another alternative, available in some parts of Britain, is a 'sherpa' service that will move luggage between hostels for hikers and cyclists.

The inn-to-inn type tours often give you the option of using one of their bikes or bringing your own. Either way, you should be familiar with the aspects of cycle construction and set up that are important for your safety and enjoyment.

The Bike

Any visit to a well-stocked cycle shop presents a potentially bewildering degree of choice between racing, hybrid, commuter, mountain and perhaps even touring bikes. These differ in their wheelbase and geometry (the size of the angles formed by the various tubes), the materials used in their construction (steel, aluminium, carbon fibre, titanium), the width and smoothness of their tyres and the style of handlebars (dropped and curved backwards or straight, 'sit up and beg' bars).

These differences reflect the various purposes for which bikes are used. A touring bike needs to be strong enough to carry the extra weight of the panniers, tents, etc. Ideally, it also will have a longer wheelbase to better cushion bumps and thus be more comfortable on long rides. This comfort comes at the price of a less responsive ride and poorer acceleration. The longer wheelbase makes the transmission of pedal power less efficient.

A properly equipped tourer will also have stronger (more spokes) wheels and strategically placed screw holes (braze-ons) to hold pannier racks and water bottles. European touring bikes that often double as commuter bikes typically come with wheel driven generators to power lights. I have no experience with these but would do without them personally in favour of something lighter (no pun intended). There are lots of alternatives if you expect to be riding at night or in other low visibility conditions.

Bike Size

Bike size is important for comfort. The height of the handlebars and the reach from the saddle to the handlebars determines the weight your hands have to support while riding and the angle of your neck and back. And, should you fall forward off the saddle you'll be grateful if your tender, sensitive bits don't smash onto the top tube.

The 'right' size is partly a function of your pubic bone height. This is a measurement taken in socks or bare feet with the feet about 25 cm apart. Measure from the pubic bone down to the floor. The result is the appropriate saddle height for you. Saddle height is measured from the top of the saddle down to the centre of the pedal along the plane of the seat tube with the crank in the same plane.

The length of the seat tube generally is the basis for stated frame sizes. (Not all manufacturers are uniform in the actual end points for this measure). Consequently the frame size should be less than the saddle height by the combined length of the exposed seat post and the crank. Together these will typically total about 25 cm. So a pubic bone height of 85 cm would indicate a frame size of 60 cm. One of my references quotes a 1967 study at Loughborough University, England that found the optimum saddle height to be 109% of pubic bone height. This finding reflects the fact that muscles have ranges of optimum stretch and that leg muscles exert more power as they approach the fully extended position. The 109% is considered to provide the best combination of maximum muscle stretch and maximum pedalling fluidity.[1] In my opinion, this 'optimum' is more suited for racing than touring.

These guidelines will probably produce a larger frame size than most bike shops will recommend. Their concerns may be driven primarily by the stand over clearance issue that, while important, is hardly as big an issue as riding comfort. If your frame is too small, the amount of exposed seat post will have to be greater to provide the right saddle height and the top tube length may be too short to permit comfortable handlebar height and optimum riding posture (roughly a 45 degree angle in the back and a pronounced bend in the elbows). Complicating matters further, at least one manufacturer (Giant) now offers only three frame sizes, requiring the amount of exposed seat post to take up the slack. Some top tubes are now angled down to the seat tube, allowing adequate stand-over height on larger frame sizes. So, the old rules of thumb don't still always apply. You need to choose on the basis of comfort and the type of riding that you generally do.

Women have to be particularly careful because most cycles are still built in accordance with typical male measurements. Since a larger proportion of a woman's height is in the legs than most men, a bike with the right seat tube height will probably have too long a top tube for a woman. Riding on such a bike would force more of the woman's weight on to her palms and wrists causing numbness. Fortunately, now a number of manufacturers offer women specific cycles with shorter top tubes, more upright seating, narrower handlebars and shorter gaps between the bar and the brake levers.

Assuming that your bike 'fits', the remaining points deal with improving its comfort and efficiency.

Saddle Position

Too low saddle position is the most common problem I see for adult recreational cyclists. These people look as if they have borrowed a child's cycle for a quick ride and given how uncomfortable they look may never do so again. A too low saddle reduces pedalling effectiveness by making it impossible to get the full benefit of your legs' power.

The most often used guide to proper seat height is to have the seat high enough that your leg is almost straight in the down position of the pedal. You should be wearing your cycling shoes when making this adjustment and the pedal crank should be aligned with the seat tube. It is wise to have someone hold the cycle while you sort this out or you can balance yourself against a wall. When you have fixed the height, pedal backwards. If you are sliding from side to side on the seat, you need to lower the seat a bit. If not, keep raising the seat until you just start to slide.

The saddle is attached to a seat post that fits inside the seat tube and is held tightly in position by an adjustable bolt at the top of the tube. It is very important that enough of the post remains inside the tube (at least 8 cm) to provide a secure grip. If you need to raise the seat a lot, it may be necessary to buy a longer post.

The fore/aft position of the saddle is also important. It affects the amount of reach required to hold the handlebars and also determines where your knee is in relation to the pedal. This latter aspect affects the amount of power you can deliver to the pedals and where you will feel pain in your leg after a long day's ride.

Your knee is the pivot of power. Ideally it should be directly above the ball of your foot on the down stroke. The length of your foot, angle of your seat post and the fore/aft position of the saddle all affect where your knee actually will be. A quick rule is to position the saddle so that when you are on the bike, the centre of the axle on a pedal in the forward position is directly below the bit of bone just under your kneecap. This can be tested with a plumb bob.

Generally, saddles should be absolutely level with the ground to take most of the weight off your arms and back. Some competition cyclists do tilt the saddle slightly forward and it may be necessary for some body types.

Handlebars

The style of handlebars is perhaps the main area where personal preference can dictate without significant loss of function. A good choice is the upright style, common on hybrid and commuter bikes. It is comfortable and allows one to watch the scenery in a more natural posture. This is particularly true if your daily distances are likely to be moderate (up to about 50 km). These handlebars are also easier on the neck and shoulders. The dropped handlebar style has advantages for longer rides and for increasing your speed. These advantages come from the greater variety of hand positions, the nature of those positions and the ability to lower the body, stretching the back and reducing wind resistance. This variety of available hand positions on dropped bars helps minimize the numbness in the wrist and hands that many experience when riding in the upright position with the hands straightforward.

Handlebars are held in place by a post called a stem that fits inside the head tube and has a fitting at its top for the handlebars. These stems are sometimes shaped like right angles with the handlebar holding bit jutting forward. This style extends the handlebars forward increasing the reach and having a similar effect to moving the saddle backwards. Stems of different lengths are available as are adjustable stems that can be used to raise the handlebars or extend the reach without moving the stem in the head tube. As with the seat post, it is important to have at least 8-10 cm of stem inside the head tube.

Advice for the best handlebar height varies. Most common is that handlebars should be at the same level as the saddle. Some advise positioning the top of the handlebar 25 mm lower than the saddle and others believe they should never be more than 75 mm lower. No doubt these lower positions would be more aerodynamic but if you are more concerned with comfort, I would keep the handlebars level with the saddle, perhaps even slightly higher.

Foot Position on the Pedals

The ball of your foot should be over the centre of the pedal axle for comfort and the best transfer of power. Toe clips ('rat traps') limit the forward movement of your foot to ensure that you maintain this position while pedalling. The clips also allow you to pull on the up portion of the pedal circle, which increases pedalling power. Pedalling without clips limit the cyclist to simply riding the momentum of the up part of the stroke.

Most cycling shoes available today are designed for use with special clip less pedals. These shoes have a built in cleat that locks onto the pedal, holding the foot in the right position. Cyclists who regularly use this arrangement are convinced that their pedalling is more efficient.

But, it can be difficult getting used to clip less pedals. Disengaging the foot from the pedal requires a lateral movement that feels odd after years of riding with the rat trap strapped pedals. Combining the force necessary with the strange movement can be literally upsetting as I have discovered several times.

My family, at my request, made me a Christmas present of clip less pedals and shoes a few years ago. The following spring, on my first ride of the season, I set off, dressed in cold weather black stretch tights and my yellow jacket and yellow helmet. Perhaps fifteen minutes later, having temporarily forgotten my new gear, I had to stop at an intersection and could not disengage my feet. The only option was to fall over. Even in this stationary state, I could not get my feet off the pedals and must have looked like a huge bumblebee in the throes of death. Motorists even stopped to offer help!

I had to unlace the shoes and pull my feet out to be able to stand and get out of the traffic. Reading the instructions later, I learned that it is necessary to adjust the tightness of the connection between shoes and pedal so the amount of lateral force necessary to get out is an easy move. It would also be a good idea to balance against a wall and practice the movement because it is not a natural, reflexive move. After a number of other falls, I moved the pedals to my 'other bike'.

Loading the Bike for Touring

This section will only be relevant if you plan on a tour without 'sag wagon' assist. Without such assistance, you will have to transport clothing, cycle spares and tools and possibly camping gear if you intend on being totally self-sufficient.

Touring cycles carry such gear in special bags, called panniers, that are carried on both sides of the bike on luggage racks at the front and rear of the bike. For the best handling, it is important to divide your overall load between front and rear. The two sides of fore and aft panniers should be as equal in weight as possible and carry the heaviest part of their load at the bottom of the pannier.

Even though panniers can be made of waterproof material, torrential rain will find its way through the seams of the very best bag. So it is wise to wrap your gear in sturdy plastic bags with tight closures before packing them into the panniers. When doing this try to organise in such a way that you can readily find what you need without unpacking everything.

Labelling each plastic bag with its contents helps with this organisation as does keeping all your bike spares and tools in a single pannier. As front panniers are smaller, one of them would be a good candidate for the tools. All your cooking equipment could be put in one of the rear panniers and your clothing in the other as long as you maintain balance on both sides of the bike. Tents and sleeping bags should be wrapped in plastic bags or dry bags and placed lengthwise on the rear luggage rack, securing them well with bungee cords.

As already noted, riding with full panniers changes the bike's handling behaviour. For best handling, the weight should be distributed roughly 60% to the rear, 35% to the front and only 5% in a handlebar bag. Weight loaded high in the panniers creates instability; so do heavy handlebar bags and large items strapped atop a front or rear rack. It's best to keep heavy gear packed low and close to the frame. The extra weight increases the bike's tendency to head for the outside shoulder and makes it roll a lot faster on a descent. You will need to brake sooner and harder going downhill than with an unloaded bike.

The trick to mounting, dismounting, and walking a loaded touring bike is to keep it vertical so its weight stays centred over the wheels. Otherwise, it'll take lots of strength to keep it from tumbling over. (2)

Abandon any thoughts of a wearing a loaded rucksack to safeguard your valuables. This creates instability and is thus dangerous as well as tiring. A handlebar bag that snaps into position, making it easy to remove, is the best place for valuables. Thus when you stop to shop/use the washroom/what have you, the bag can be quickly unsnapped and go in with you. Camera, maps, book, passport and money can be accommodated in most of the available bags. It is also very desirable to have a transparent plastic envelope on the top of these bags to hold the route and map for the day.

I plan my routes extensively prior to leaving and type out each day's route plan showing road numbers, turning instructions, places worth visiting, etc. in large bold face type. These can be printed on acetate using a photocopier and then cut to fit the plastic envelope. Most recently, I printed these on regular paper then glued each day's plan on appropriately sized pieces of leftover plasticised washroom wallpaper! These were durable and stiff enough to slide easily into the plastic envelope.

I find this approach much more efficient than stopping periodically to check a guidebook. If you have a cycle computer, you can make these daily plans even more helpful by showing the distance from the day's start for each turn. Then you are aware ahead of time that you need to take some action at kilometre 34.7, etc. Doing all of this is a lot of work but I find considerable enjoyment in the task, consulting maps and guidebooks and making my own decisions about where to go and what to see.

Tools/Spares Needed

Punctures are the most likely problem, so have a couple of spare inner tubes in the right size for your tyres. If you run a common size tyre, you can probably get by with only one spare as they should be easily replaceable at most cycle shops. Using Kevlar or similar reinforced tyres will significantly reduce the probability of a puncture.

If you are touring loaded, it is best to have the stronger set of wheels mentioned earlier. Even so, rough roads and bumps can break spokes, so it is worthwhile having a couple extra of these even if you are uncertain how to mend a broken spoke. This task requires skill and experience, as the wheel must be 'tuned' after replacing a spoke to produce equal tension across the full circumference of the wheel and allowing it to run 'true'. A single broken spoke may not require immediate attention if you have a 36 spoke wheel as the others can take the additional strain. More than one broken spoke may well cause the wheel to run out of true and possibly rub against the fork or chain stays. This needs attention right away. If you are carrying spare spokes, it is much more likely that you can find someone to do the repair ASAP.

You should have some cycle lubricant and enough tools to deal with virtually any repair of which you are capable. One must is a rivet extractor for repairing the chain. It's almost impossible to improvise when you don't have one, and it is small, light, and inexpensive. A spare chain link is also advisable but I don't recommend a spare chain due to the weight.

One could go on and on but it is time to get out and cycle!

APPENDIX

ENGLAND AND TEA

'The first recorded English request for a pot of tea is in a letter dated 27 June 1615 from Mr. R. Wickham, agent of the East India Company on the Japanese island of Hirado, to his colleague Mr Eaton at Macao, asking him to send on only 'the best sort of chaw'. However, it was not until 1658 that the first advertisement appeared in England for what was to become the national drink. It was published in the officially subsidised weekly, *Mercurius Politicus*, for the week ending 30 September and offered: 'That Excellent, and by all Physicians approved, *China* Drink, called by the *Chineans, Tcha*, by other Nations *Tay alias Tee*...sold at the *Sultaness-head*, 2 *Copheehous* in *Sweetings* rents by the Royal Exchange, *London*'. At around the same time, the coffee house owner Thomas Garraway published a broadsheet entitled 'An exact Description of the Growth, Quality and Vertues of the Leaf TEA', in which he claimed that it could cure 'Headache, Stone, Gravel, Dropsy, Liptitude Distillations, Scurvy, Sleepiness, Loss of Memory, Looseness or Griping of the guts, Heavy Dreams and Collick proceeding from Wind'. 'Taken with Virgin's Honey instead of Sugar', he assured potential consumers, 'tea cleanses the Kidneys and Ureters, & with Milk and water it prevents Consumption. If you are of corpulent body it ensures good appetite, & if you have a surfeit it is just the thing to give you a gentle Vomit'. For whatever reason, Charles II's Portuguese Queen was also a tea-drinker: Edmund Waller's poem dedicated to her on her birthday praised 'The Muses's friend, tea (which) does our fancy aid, /repress those vapours, which the head invade, /and keep the palace of the soul serene'. On 25 September 1660 Samuel Pepys drank his first 'cup of tee (a China drink)'.

However, it was only in the early eighteenth century that tea began to be imported in sufficient quantities—and at sufficiently low prices—to create a mass market. In 1703, the Kent arrived in London with a cargo of 65,000 lbs. of tea, not far off the entire annual importation in previous years. The real breakthrough came in 1745, when the figure for tea 'retained for home consumption' leapt from an average of under 800,000 lbs in the early 1740s to over 2.5 million lbs. between 1746 and 1750. By 1756 the habit was far enough spread to prompt a denunciation in Hanway's Essay on Tea: ' The very chambermaids have lost their bloom by drinking tea'.

..........By the 1770s... almost 94 per cent of imported coffee was re-exported, mainly to northern Europe. This was partly a reflection of differential tariffs: heavy import duties restricted domestic coffee consumption to the benefit of the burgeoning tea industry. Like so many national characteristics, the English preference for tea over coffee had its origins in the realm of fiscal policy." (1)

TEACAKES

Teacakes have been prime ingredients of my British tours. Since these aren't cakes in the North American sense, it is only fitting then to provide instructions on producing the type to which I am referring. The recipe below was taken from Mrs. Beeton's Cookery and Household Management, 1970 edition that was a Christmas present from my oldest daughter Susan, then seven, to her mother.

1 lb. Plain Flour	1 oz. Sugar
½ teaspoon salt	½ pint warm milk
2 oz. Lard and margarine	2-3 oz. Currants
½ oz. Yeast	

Sift warm flour and salt and rub in the fat. Cream the yeast with the sugar, add the warm milk to it and mix with the flour and fruit to a light elastic dough. Put to rise to double its size. Divide risen dough into 4-6 pieces, knead each into a round and roll out to the size of a tea plate. Place on greased baking sheets, prick the top neatly, and allow to prove for 15 minutes. Bake in a hot oven (425 degrees F., Gas 7) for 20 –25 minutes.

If liked the cakes may be brushed with egg and water before baking or rubbed over with margarine after baking.

INTERESTING AND WORTHWHILE TEASHOPS

England and Wales

Tintern Railway Shops and Tearoom, near Tintern Abbey, Wales

Nanwich Tearooms, Cheshire

Mulberry Tree, Kirkby Stephen, Cumbria

Wig & Mitre Pub, Lincoln

Crown & Anchor Hotel, Grantham, Lincolnshire

The Bull Hotel, Wrotham

Turner Hill Farm, near Crawley, Sussex

Police Station Café, Helmsley, Yorkshire

Sinners Coffee House, Berwick upon Tweed, Northumberland

Brief Encounter, on Keswick to Settle Rail line between Cumbria and Yorkshire

Newcastle Hotel, Rothbury, Northumberland

Wordsworth Hours, Cockermouth, Cumbria

Grange, Derwentwater, Cumbria, near Seatoller

Crown Inn, Kirksowald, Cumbria

Bush House, Selborne, Hampshire

National Trust Tearoom, Selworthy, Devon

Scotland

Crown Inn, Kirksowald, Ayrshire

Machrie Bay Tearooms, Isle of Arran

Kilmartin House Café, Kilmartin, on A816 near Loch Awe, Argylll

Coffee Pot, Salen, Mull

Armadale Castle Café, Skye

Fig Tree, Broadford, Skye

Off the Rails, Plockton, Wester Ross

Robert Adams

CYCLE CALORIE CONSUMPTION

Calorie consumption while cycling depends on body size, type of bike, terrain, and wind conditions. Speed, however, is also important and can dramatically affect the energy used in cycling because of its effect on wind resistance.

The chart below shows calorie consumption estimates for different weights and speeds. These numbers were developed for *Bicycling* magazine by physiologist James Hagberg, Ph.D. To use the chart, just select the speed that you cycle at and multiply the coefficient at that speed by your body weight to get the calories you will burn per minute. The chart shows this calculation for a 150 lb./68kg cyclist.

The chart assumes flat terrain. Going uphill increases energy consumption. Cavid Swain, Ph.D., a member of Bicycling's Fitness Advisory Board considers that it takes an extra 22 calories to climb 100 feet (30 metres). This is an average value for a cyclist and cycle weighing a total 176 pounds (80 kg.) coasting downhill should save calories from the chart figures but not enough to offset the consumption of first going up the hill.

Average Speed (Miles Per Hour)	Km Equivalent	Coefficient Calories Per Pound Per Minute	Calorie Consumption Per Minute for a 150lb/68 kg Cyclist
8	12.9	0.030	4.4
10	16.1	0.036	5.3
12	19.3	0.043	6.4
14	22.5	0.051	7.7
15	24.2	0.056	8.4
16	25.8	0.062	9.2
17	27.4	0.068	10.1
18	29.0	0.074	11.1
19	30.6	0.081	12.2
20	32.3	0.089	13.4
21	33.8	0.098	14.6
23	37.0	0.117	17.6
25	40.3	0.141	21.2

Adapted from Bicycling Mileage Guide and Training Log published in 2002 by Rodale, Inc. Emmaus, PA 18098

Panniers, Pedals, and Pubs

COST OF TRANSPORT
COMPARATIVE ENERGY CONSUMPTION

"Our patients, the long-suffering and generally under-exercised British public, continue to show such massive unawareness of the many advantages of the bicycle that it becomes a therapeutic duty to contrast for them this clean, quick, quiet and civilized machine with that oxygen-eating, air-defiling dissipator of energy—my faithful motor car. I say faithful because anything less would be churlish, and it is with reluctance that I expose to public gaze the imperfections of a family friend. But already the clouds are gathering round the internal combustion engine as we have used it, and we are being forced to consider less wasteful ways of getting ourselves about. For a car uses only 20% of the combustible energy of its fuel in moving forward: 4% goes to essentials such as transmission, dynamo, fan and water pump, but over 75% is lost as heat—40% through the exhaust and most of the remaining 35% by conduction and convection through something misleadingly called a radiator (the only thing it does hardly at all). The cyclist is altogether more temperate. Indeed from the standpoint of physics he is not a heat engine at all, but a constant-temperature energy converter more analogous to a fuel cell; and his contribution to the increasing entropy of our solar system is commendably small. His expenditure of energy in terms of his car's use of petrol is equivalent of 1,500 miles to the gallon (536km/l), and, which puts him even more on the side of the angels, he leaves the air cleaner than he finds it, thanks to the trapping of inspired particulate debris by mucous sheet covering his bronchial and branchiolar epithelium."[1]

(Note: This was written shortly after the first oil price shock in 1973. Many improvements have been made since in fuel efficiency, emissions and alternative technology. Nevertheless worldwide consumption, air pollution, and oil prices continue to increase, so the argument in favour of cycling is as strong as ever-see following page).

---

[1] R.E. Williams, "De Motu Urbanorum", British Medical Journal, 4 October 1975 as quoted in The Penguin Book of the Bicycle, Roderick Watson & Martin Gray, pages 80-81, 1978

Robert Adams

COST OF TRANSPORT
Rank on basis of Calories per gram of weight per kilometre

Ranked from most to least:
1. Mouse
2. Fly
3. Humming Bird
4. Rabbit
5. Mouse
6. Fly
7. Humming Bird
8. Rabbit
9. Helicopter
10. Dog
11. Pigeon
12. Car
13. Man
14. Horse/Jumbo Jet
15. Salmon
16. Cyclist

Note: The mouse consumes 400 times the energy(relative to body weight) of the cyclist to travel the same distance.

Note: This ranking is based on a graph by V.A. Tucker of Duke University, North Carolina, quoted in *The Penguin Book of the Bicycle,* referred on the previous page.

PANNIERS, PEDALS AND PUBS
DAILY COSTS IN POUNDS

TOUR	TEA & CAKES	HOSTELS & B&BS	FOOD	RAIL & FERRIES	OTHER	TOTAL
END TO END (1990)	0.32	10.33	4.88	3.71	3.71	22.95
PEAKS, LAKES & DALES (1995)	0.95	13.21	8.80	1.97	4.41	29.34
CIRCLE (1999)	1.20	17.48	9.54	0.91	4.78	33.91
NORTHERN ENGLAND & SCOTLAND (2002)	1.71	14.42	11.17	4.13	3.63	35.06
CELTIC (2004)	0.88	15.50	11.95	3.49	7.24	39.06

Robert Adams

GLOSSARY

BRITISH	NORTH AMERICAN
Aerodrome	A small airport or airfield. Becoming obsolete.
Aga Cooker	A type of heavy heat-retaining cooking stove or range burning solid fuel or powered by gas, oil or electricity, and intended for continuous heating.
Anti-Clockwise	Counter clockwise
Barley Water	A drink made from water and a boiled barley mixture.
Bloody- minded	Pig headed: stubborn
Biscuits	Either cookies or crackers. Sweet biscuits are cookies.
Bob's Your Uncle	There you are! You're done.
Breeze Block	Cinder block (building material)
Brewer's Dray	A low cart without sides for beer barrels
Caravan	House trailer
Cattle Grid	A grid covering a ditch, allowing vehicles to pass over but not cattle, sheep, etc.
Ceidleh	An informal gathering for conversation, music, dancing, songs and stories (usually Scottish or Irish).
Chips	French fries

Chock a Block	Crammed together, full
Clock Off	End work
Cobble	Run up; put together roughly
Compere	Master of ceremonies
Coverlet	A bedspread
Cow	Roughly Dog (when used in a derogatory sense in relation to a female). In Britain, the sense is more a coarse and unpleasant woman rather than an ugly one.
Council	Literally, a local administrative body of a village, town, borough, city or county but is used in the same manner as North Americans use "town".
Cream Tea	Afternoon tea with Devonshire cream, which is rich, sweet, delicious, and thicker than North American whipped cream. The cream is layered over the jam.
Crisps	Potato chips
Crown Land	Crown land in Canada (Government land in the US).
Dale	Valley (a northern British term).
Dog's Breakfast	Unholy mess
Driver	Engineer (railway)

Eccles Cake	A flat round cake made of pastry filled with currants (somewhat like a mince pie).
En Suite	Usually used in connection with a bedroom to indicate that a bathroom is attached.
Estate Agent	Real estate agent
Estate Car	Station wagon
Fell	A hill (a northern English term).
Film	Movie
Flying Scotsman	Famous historic railway engine on the King's Cross-to Edinburgh line.
Flyover	Overpass
Full English	Traditional English breakfast. Components may vary but will almost certainly include eggs, toast, tomato, baked beans, bacon and sausage.
Gents	Men's toilet in a public place
Goods Van	Railway term—freight car
Grammar School	A selective state secondary school with a mainly academic curriculum. Increasingly rare since the late 1960s when comprehensive schools became national policy under the Labour government.
Green Grocer	Fruit and vegetable shop

Higgledy- piggledy	A state of disordered confusion
Hoardings	Billboard
ITV	Independent Television. A television network that unlike the BBC permits commercials.
Left Luggage	Check room at a railway station or airport
Lemon Cheese/Curd	A conserve of lemons, butter, eggs, and sugar, with the consistency of cream cheese.
Loo	Washroom, restroom, toilet.
Lounge	Living room
Marks & Sparks	Slang for Marks & Spencer, one of Britain's oldest and most famous retail stores. Specialises in clothing and food products.
Midges	Gnats
Milk Run	A routine expedition or service journey. In a railway context indicates a train that stops frequently.
Mini	Legendary small car designed by Alec Issigonnis for Austin-Morris (later British Leyland). Featured a number of technical innovations.

Mushy Peas	No real equivalent. This is a style of serving what could have been decent green peas that renders them a mushy overcooked mess.
Non-Conformist	Member of a Protestant denomination other than Church of England (synonymous with dissenter).
Off Licence	Liquor, bottle or package store, licensed to sell alcohol for consumption off the premises.
On Offer	Available, as in "what's on offer"?
Open University	University courses offered over the television and radio. Open to the general public regardless of prior academic achievement. Satisfactory completion involves coursework submitted by post.
Pasty	A pastry case with a usually savoury filling, baked without a dish to shape it. The most famous is the Cornish pasty.
Pavement	Sidewalk
Pebble-dash	Mortar with pebbles in it used as a coating for external walls
Point	Electric socket (or railway switch). Often used with an appropriate adjective, such as power or razor.
Prawn	Small shrimp. Shrimps the sizes that North Americans are familiar with are called scampi.

Pub	Bar. In Britain, pub is short for public houses that are more than bars. Public houses often serve meals and function as community the social centres,
Pudding	Dessert. In Britain, the term specifies a cooked sweet such as plum pudding.
Puncture	Flat tyre
Queue	Line of people or vehicles waiting for something such as a bus or traffic light
Rates	Property taxes. The British are gradually adopting the term "council charge" in place of rates.
Ring	Call (as in telephone). The British use both terms.
Roundabout	Traffic circle that allows vehicles to enter when clear and exit on any of several spokes located round the circle.
Rucksack	Backpack
Sit up and Beg	Flat, upright cycle handlebars like those used on commuter, hybrid and mountain bikes.
Smalls	Undies
Sultana	Same in Canada. White raisin in US. In the US, Sultana is a trademark for a particular brand of seedless raisin whether dark or white.

Summer Pudding A dessert made of crust less bread and mushed summer fruits. Served cold after the mass has soaked and congealed.

Surgery Doctor's office. Often a separate part of Doctor's residence.

Tea Tea, the drink. Can also indicate afternoon tea that is taken about four pm with biscuits, teacakes or scones. But primarily the term working class and children use to mean an evening meal or light supper. This use is short for high tea.

The High Street The main shopping street in a town, often actually named High Street.

Tin Airtight metal can for foodstuffs, etc.

Toff Slang for a distinguished person, a swell; indicative of a way of life more than of wealth.

Torch Flashlight

Verge Grass shoulder at edge of road

END NOTES
Countryside
1. AA Illustrated Guide to Britain' (Drive Publications Ltd., 1971) pp 488-490
2. AA Illustrated Guide to Britain, pp 450-452
3. AA Illustrated Guide to Britain, pp 406-408
4. AA Illustrated Guide to Britain, pp 374-376
5. AA Illustrated Guide to Britain, pp 336-338
6. AA Illustrated Guide to Britain, pp 262-264
7. AA Illustrated Guide to Britain, pp 188-190
8. AA Illustrated Guide to Britain, pp 104-106
9. AA Illustrated Guide to Britain, pp 66-68
10. AA Illustrated Guide to Britain, pp 20-22
11. Arthur Eperon, *Brittany*, (Pan Books, 1990), p. 3-4

Peaks, Lakes and Dales
1. Hunter Davies, *A Walk Around the Lakes*, (J. M. Dent, London, 1993) p.91
2. Tim Hughes and Joanna Cleary, *Cycling Great Britain*, (Bicycle Books, 1996), p. 160
3. Tim Hughes and Joanna Cleary, *Cycling Great Britain*, p. 119

Circle
1. Leon Fitts, *Stone Circles*, (British Heritage, March 1997), pp. 36-7
2. Tim Hughes and Joanna Cleary, *Cycling Great Britain*, p. 86.
3. Leon Fitts, *Stone Circles*, p. 35
4. Tim Hughes and Joanna Cleary, *Cycling Great Britain*, p. 94
5. Tim Hughes and Joanna Cleary, *Cycling Great Britain*, p. 95
6. Tim Hughes and Joanna Cleary, *Cycling Great Britain*, p. 96
7. *AA Illustrated Guide to Britain*, 1971 p. 410
8. Tim Hughes and Joanna Cleary, *Cycling Great Britain*, p. 39

Northern England and Scotland
1. *AA Illustrated Guide to Britain*, p 445
2. Tim Hughes and Joanna Cleary, *Cycling Great Britain*, p. 130

Celtic Cycle
1. Tim Hughes and Joanna Cleary, *Cycling Great Britain*, p. 78

2. Norman Davies, *The Isles, a History,*
 (Oxford University Press, 1999), pp. 352-3
3. Arthur Eperon, *Brittany*, p. 30
4. Tim Hughes and Joanna Cleary, *Cycling Great Britain*, p. 77
5. Jean Paschke, *The Prince's Alma Mater,*
 (British Heritage, Dec. 2001/Jan. 2002) pp. 45-49

Getting Underway
1. Eugene A. Sloan, *The All-New Complete Book of Cycling,*
 (A Fireside Book, 1980) pp 85-87
2. *250 Best Cycling Tips,* (Rodale Press, 1997), p. 45

Appendices
1. *'250 Best Cycling Tips',* (Rodale Press, 1997), p. 45

2720405

Made in the USA